Randall B. Ripley is chairman of the department of political science at The Ohio State University. A graduate of DePauw University, he received his M.A. and Ph.D. at Harvard University where his dissertation was awarded the Sumner Prize.

Professor Ripley has served as an intern in the U.S. House of Representatives and has been a member of the research staff at the Brookings Institution. He has held Woodrow Wilson, Danforth, and Brookings research fellowships.

Among his previous publications are *Party Leaders in the House of Representatives, Power in the Senate,* and *American National Government and Public Policy.*

CONGRESS
Process and Policy

CONGRESS

Process and Policy

BY

RANDALL B. RIPLEY

THE OHIO STATE UNIVERSITY

W · W · NORTON & COMPANY · INC ·
New York

Copyright © 1975 by W. W. Norton & Company, Inc.
First Edition

Library of Congress Cataloging in Publication Data

Ripley, Randall B
    Congress.
    Bibliography: p.
    Includes index.
    1. United States. Congress. I. Title.
JK1061.R55   328.73   74–26863
ISBN 0–393–09250–X

Published simultaneously in Canada by
George J. McLeod Limited, Toronto

This book was designed by Jacques Chazaud
The type is Times Roman and Helvetica
Set by Fuller Typesetting of Lancaster

Printed in the United States of America

2 3 4 5 6 7 8 9 0

To J. C. and D. L., for good ideas

TABLE OF CONTENTS

LIST OF TABLES

LIST OF FIGURES

PREFACE

As a basic text on the Congress of the United States, this volume portrays the institution and its principal activities. An effort has been made to take the reader beyond description to an analysis of the way in which Congress makes public policy. The concern with policy has given the volume its particular dimensions. Thus chapters are included on congressional elections and congressional relations with interest groups and constituents, the president and presidency, and the bureaucracy. Congressional relations with the federal courts are not examined, however, because that interaction is sporadic and not at the heart of the policy process.

A reader of this volume should come away with a good sense of Congress as an institution, of congressional relations with key portions of its environment, and of the importance of Congress as a policy-maker. Above all, he or she should come away with a sense that the members of Congress are not caught up in some ritual with inevitable endings but instead that they have a number of options open to them in relation both to personal behavior and the collective behavior of the institution. Congress is neither immutable nor is it moribund. Like many institutions, it appears conservative much of the time. But it is also important and influential as a policy-maker even in its most conservative mood and can enlarge that influence in periods of aggressiveness.

Although the author has worked in Congress and continues to be fascinated by some of the trivia of its workings, there is no aspiration to present this book as an "insider's" look at the daily routine of Congress. Gossipy details that do not have much utility beyond whatever intrinsic interest they possess are omitted. Nor is there a lengthy guide to parliamentary procedure as used in Congress or technical discussion of "how a bill becomes law."

In general, writing on Congress has been of two types. The first type is the scholarly study that focuses on the details of some rather minute portion of Congress (for example, the whip organizations, single committees, the behavior of new congressmen in one year) but that usually fails to pose broader questions about the meaning of the scrap of behavior investigated. The second type consists of attacks or defenses that betray rather great ignorance about the details of the institution. This book has an empirical focus rather than a normative one, although questions of "should" and "ought" are not ignored. The empirical treatment in this volume is essential to posing important normative questions; it is even more important in answering those questions.

The data for this study of Congress come from many sources. An attempt has been made to summarize the major relevant data-based literature on Congress. Not everything in the literature was found useful, however, and less useful items have been excluded as there seemed to be no obligation to summarize everything just for its own sake (some of these omissions are referred to in the footnotes). In addition to published studies, some original empirical work is presented for the first time. Where summaries of empirical studies do appear, they are presented in a non-technical manner that should make them accessible to all readers.

It is good form to state an author's overriding bias before the reader plunges into a book: I have long taken Congress seriously as a maker of public policy and continue to do so. Long before Watergate highlighted the dangers of allowing all important decisions to be made in the White House I was anxious for Congress to contribute vigorously to the solution of the most important public problems.

I also harbor the prejudice that before meaningful discussion of "reform" can occur, the discussants must have a thorough knowledge of how Congress works, and this can come only from serious study. The literature of reform is too often marked by a great deal of emotion and not enough attention to empirically based details. I believe systematic analysis must precede prescriptions for change. This prejudice does not mean that I am an apologist for all that Congress is and does. There is much in congressional practice and performance that distresses me as a citizen and as a political scientist, but that makes me even more eager to analyze it as objectively as possible as a necessary prelude to making sound normative judgments.

The organization of the book is straightforward. In part I Congress is presented in broad strokes. Chapter 1 paints a general picture of Congress in its environment and discusses the position of Congress in relation to policy-making. Chapter 2 summarizes the development of Congress. Chapter 3 presents an overview of how members of Congress are socialized into certain patterns of making decisions and how those decisions get made.

Part II investigates in some detail the impact of the principal components of Congress. Chapter 4 focuses on committees; chapter 5 focuses on the party leadership; and chapter 6 deals with a variety of other groups (such as state delegations) and both personal and committee staffs.

Part III focuses on the external relations of Congress that are critical to determining both the nature and the scope of its policy impact. Chapter 7 deals with the elections that provide the membership of the House and Senate. Chapter 8 explores congressional relations with interest groups and constituents. Chapter 9 discusses congressional relations with the president and the institutional presidency. And chapter 10 examines congressional relations with the bureaucracy.

Part IV, which contains chapter 11, offers a summary assessment of the impact of Congress on public policy.

The debts I have incurred in completing this book are numerous. Theodore J. Lowi provided one of his typically brilliant critiques of an early draft and I have tried to catch the spirit of his vision in the final version. My colleague Herbert B. Asher was extremely helpful in the preparation of chapter 3. Another colleague, William B. Moreland, assisted me in the data presentation in chapters 4 and 5. In this both he and I were aided by the cooperative staff of the Polimetrics Laboratory in the Department of Political Science at Ohio State and by the University's Instruction and Research Computer Center.

Above all, I am grateful to Grace A. Franklin for her patient and insightful assistance in both research for and editing of the entire manuscript.

J.C. and D.L. didn't have anything to do with this book in a direct sense but for their general guidance they deserve the dedication they have received.

PART I

Congress
in the
American
Political
System

1

THE NATURE
OF CONGRESS

ON 8 AUGUST 1974, RICHARD NIXON ANNOUNCED HIS RESIGNATION
as president of the United States to the American people. That
unique event in American history helps put the power of Congress in
perspective in two ways. In an immediate sense individuals and committees in Congress helped build the case against Nixon and his subordinates that led to resignation as an alternative preferable to impeachment
by the House of Representatives and conviction by the Senate. The work
of the Senate Watergate Committee and the House Judiciary Committee,
when combined with the activities of the special prosecutor, the federal
judiciary, and the press helped create the public sentiment that Nixon's
misdeeds were so unprecedented as to warrant an unprecedented ouster
of a president. Also, three leaders of Congress of the president's own
party—Senators Barry Goldwater (the Republican presidential nominee
in 1964) and Hugh Scott (the Republican floor leader in the Senate)
and Congressman John Rhodes (the Republican floor leader in the
House)—joined with the White House staff chief Alexander Haig and
Secretary of State Henry Kissinger in advising the president that there
was no way he could remain in office and that the national interest
demanded that he resign.*

---

* For the fascinating story of how these five individuals broached the subject of
resignation with Nixon see the column by Rowland Evans and Robert Novak
in the *Washington Post*, August 10, 1974: A-23; and the comments by Senator
Scott as reported in the same newspaper, August 12, 1974: A-1.

The political demise of Richard Nixon also affords a broader perspective on the place of Congress in contemporary American society. In many ways the twentieth century has been a century of presidential domination of the national government. Congress has been consistently more important than is generally recognized—this volume will document that point in later chapters—but it is true that on the greatest issues facing the American people the role of Congress has seemed to pale in comparison to that of the president. However, with the growing unpopularity of the Vietnam War in the late 1960s and early 1970s and the revelations of presidential abuse of power under Nixon the will in Congress to be more assertive seems to have been strengthened. A war powers act passed in 1973 and a budget reform act passed in 1974 were designed to give Congress more power on the major issues of war and peace and governmental impact on the economy. Watergate and its aftermath do not spell an automatic and dramatic reversal in the state of congressional power in relation to the executive branch in the mid-1970s but those events both afford an opportunity for Congress to assert itself vigorously on major policy questions and may well help prolong the will to make such assertions evidenced by the war powers and budget acts.

Congress, unlike most other national legislatures in the twentieth century, is at the heart of public policy-making.* Although certain details of its structure and practices have evolved since its creation in 1789 it has always played a vital part in determining the scope and character of American governmental activity. It shares its policy-making powers principally with the executive branch—both the president and the vast bureaucracy that has developed—and the interaction between Congress and the executive, often with spokesmen for private interests also involved, is responsible for most of the detailed decisions about specific policies and programs.

Congress can be observed from many perspectives. In this volume, the focus is on two related aspects—1) The characteristics and per-

---

* Other societies, of course, have very different traditions. Some legislatures are principally window dressing (as in the Soviet Union) with power lodged in a combination of party and administrative bodies. Some societies operate without national representative assemblies at all. This was true of Czarist Russia and Nazi Germany. It is also true of a number of nations in the contemporary world. For example, in early 1974 just in Latin America alone Cuba, Peru, Chile, Ecuador, and Bolivia had no national representative assemblies that actually met (some of them had constitutions providing for legislatures but the constitutions were all in a state of suspension). In modern Great Britain, Parliament is largely subservient to the policies announced by the executive part of the government. In other Western European nations a similar situation exists.

formance of Congress as an institution, and 2) the disparate and often fragmented membership of Congress, whose individual behavior and characteristics together determine a great deal about how the institution performs and is perceived. The interrelationship of the individual members and various subsets of members within the institution will be given considerable attention throughout this entire book.

This chapter sketches the place of Congress in the American political system by outlining the nature of the relationship between the individual member and the institution, discussing the principal functions performed by Congress that have a societal impact, and by beginning to explore the relations between Congress and the executive branch (a subject that will be treated in greater detail in chapters 9 and 10).

THE MEMBERS AND THE INSTITUTION: AN OVERVIEW OF THE RELATIONSHIP

The Impact of the Institution on the Members

Any institution has an identity that helps shape the behavior of each of its members. Congress, like most institutions, has developed norms specifying broad limits beyond which individual behavior is considered unacceptable or, to put it another way, broad limits within which members must pursue their interests. These norms are unwritten and can change but nevertheless channel much individual behavior. The phenomenon of norms and their content will be examined in detail in chapter 3 but the existence of norms and the fact that they do constrain behavior needs to be noted here.

A central feature of the congressional institution is the fact that its members are popularly elected from specific states and districts. The consequences of this for both the individual members and for the institution are enormous. Of necessity members are concerned much of the time with the locally-oriented interests of their constituents. This necessity in turn helps shape the general policy orientation of Congress. Because members attend to the needs of 435 districts and 50 states there are only rare incentives or opportunities to assert congressional primacy in large national policy areas. The constituency focus has a centrifugal effect that makes presidential-bureaucratic primacy easier to achieve than congressional primacy.

Also, given the diversity of interests in the various districts and states, natural impetus is given to a bargaining and compromising style of decision-making by the members of Congress. Many major bills are aggregates of specific provisions designed to benefit specific constituency interests. Bills are thus constructed inductively rather than deductively on the basis of national goals and standards.

Another result of constituency focus is that the diversity of interests to be satisfied prevents any single voice emerging as "the" congressional spokesman except very rarely. The internal organization of Congress reflects this fact.

The Impact of the Members on the Institution

Congress, like all institutions, has changed in character since it was established. Generally, the attention that is given these changes is directed toward those imposed on Congress by such outside influences as depressions, wars, and strong presidents. While the external environment is significant as a source of change, and one that will be examined throughout this volume, another important source exists within Congress itself. Its members make self-conscious choices that have consequences for the shape of change in the institution. The choices made by the members are wide-ranging—for example, specific policy stands, whether to support the party position and the party leaders on an issue, and how much attention to give to constituent interests—but two general areas have the most relevance to institutional change: 1) the choices individual members make about how vigorously to assert substantive policy preferences, and 2) the choices members make about whether to support stability (that is, the status quo) in Congress or whether to advocate and pursue institutional change. These choices are separate, but can be closely related to each other.

In many ways the easiest choice for individual members to make is to adopt a rather passive stance in terms of pushing for specific policy preferences and a conservative role in terms of supporting the institutional status quo. Members making such choices do not renounce all impact on public policy—rather they opt for highly specific, marginal impact most of the time. Such an option is attractive in general terms because it is immediately workable within the highly complex process by which legislation makes its way through Congress. It also allows many members to maximize their interests in such things as re-election, projects and services for their constituencies, and amicable relations with the bureaucracy.

Members who opt for a more aggressive stance with regard to their personal impact and the collective congressional impact on the substance of policy and for a more change-oriented position toward the institutions of Congress take a difficult route. They are likely to run head-on into frustrations generated by the slowness and complexity of the legislative process and may also jeopardize amicable relations with the bureaucracy and interest groups and thereby lessen their ability to produce projects and services for their constituencies.

Three factors influence the individual member's decision on the level of policy advocacy and on the stance as an institutional "conservative" or "reformer" that he or she deems appropriate: 1) a legislative process that is elaborate, time-consuming, and often frustrating; 2) the costs and benefits associated with either passive or aggressive policy advocacy; and 3) the two-way impact of institutional stability on the potential policy impact of the institution.

The Legislative Process. Through the years the congressional workload has increased enormously in size and complexity. This has had a number of results such as reinforcing a highly developed specialization of labor for individual members in committees and subcommittees and making necessary the increasing use of staff, both for individual members and for committees, to help with the heavy workload.

The increasing workload has also contributed to the development of elaborate rules that facilitate the processing of a large amount of business in reasonably good order. The rules are not impartial. They facilitate the legislative process but can also be used to substantive advantage by one side or the other. They also allow for relative invisibility in handling issues if visibility is not demanded by a sizeable group of members. And the rules in no way promote stronger or more disciplined political parties in Congress that might tamper with the freedom of individual members to follow their own policy preferences.

In general, the rules protect the status of the committee system by making it difficult for members outside committees or dissidents within committees to challenge successfully the legislative products of those committees. The rules ensure that any piece of legislation must go through several committee and floor processes in both houses. This means that the opportunities for defeating or amending proposals are numerous. Typically, a given bill will be considered by two subcommittees (one in each house), two full committees (one in each house), the House Rules Committee, a conference committee to iron out differences between the versions passed in the two houses, and a meeting of both houses (perhaps two—once for initial passage and once to consider the handiwork of the conference committee). Given this complexity and the protection offered committee and subcommittee decisions and members, the necessity of bargaining and compromise between members representing differing points of view and perhaps competing interests is underscored. (All of these points will be developed more fully in chapter 3.)

The Costs and Benefits of Passiveness and Aggressiveness. A passive member of Congress tends to be principally interested only in the work of his or her committee and of a few subcommittees. Within that province the member usually supports the policies advocated by the bureaucrats and the leading interest groups appearing before the committee or subcommittee and will suggest only small changes from those proposals. His focus is narrow and his manner is accommodating.

An aggressive member of Congress tends to have interests beyond the jurisdiction of his or her particular committee and subcommittee assignments. He is more willing to question the judgments of the bureaucrats and interest group representatives with whom he comes in contact. He will work for the adoption of wide changes from existing statutes when he thinks them necessary and useful. He is not willing to compromise on those issues about which he feels strongly.

A relatively passive congressional stance offers numerous benefits to members. It maximizes committee autonomy and thus the influence of committee members. The nature of most issues before Congress is likely to be non-controversial, which enhances members' perceptions of electoral safety. Proceedings can be relatively invisible, especially if the agenda contains few controversial items. Available time for members to spend on constituency-oriented business, including frequent trips to the state or district, is maximized by a passive congressional stance. Likewise, good relations with the bureaucracy, which facilitate servicing constituency interests, are more likely. Good relations with the president are valuable, at least for members of the president's party, because White House good will can influence the allocation of tangible benefits to members' states or districts, and good relations with the president are more likely to occur with a Congress that is relatively passive. Finally, members benefit from a low-profile, passive congressional stance because, given the fact of weak congressional parties, they are free to take policy stances of their own different from the majority of their party without fear of meaningful sanctions.

The costs of passivity are that Congress as an institution has little unified impact on national policy. Members who envision broad national policy goals have little opportunity to see their goals realized in a passive Congress. And consequently there is not likely to be any feeling of pride among members toward the institution they serve. But perhaps the most costly disadvantage of congressional passivity is that Congress leaves itself open to domination by the executive branch, a development that not only further weakens Congress but that may make passivity an entrenched characteristic, difficult to overcome.

Relative aggressiveness, on the other hand, presents a mirror image of the costs and benefits of relative passivity. The major benefits are that members increase their potential for seeing the adoption and implementation of national policy important to them and that they can take pride in the institution as an important participant in policy-making. By exercising its power, an aggressive Congress is much more likely to resist domination by the executive branch.

If a large number of members pursue policy aggressiveness, the possibility of diminished committee and subcommittee autonomy exists because members will rather freely cross jurisdictional lines in terms of their interests and proposals. Such a situation also enhances the possibility that more controversial issues will come before Congress in a more visible way because of the lessened importance of usually quiet and unreported committee meetings. This may pose a threat to perceived electoral safety on the part of a number of members.

If members increase the scope of their legislative interests and their willingness to pursue ends different from those proposed by bureaucrats and interest group representatives they may also reduce the time they have available to spend on constituency matters or in the constituency. They may antagonize parts of the bureaucracy, thereby reducing the desire of the bureaucrats to respond favorably to constituency-oriented requests. They run an increased risk of antagonizing the president, thereby reducing the desire of the White House to cooperate in providing a variety of tangible benefits for specific states, districts, and constituents.

Finally, if the desire to be aggressive about policy preferences spreads to the party leaders in Congress, they may begin to work to strengthen party mechanisms that will allow the imposition of greater "discipline" on members, thereby reducing the freedom of those members to take whatever policy positions they choose without much regard for a party position.

It is clear that the average member of Congress is likely to find passivity more attractive than aggressiveness. However, this is not an inevitable and unchangeable situation. At given points in the past Congress has, for a variety of reasons, opted for an aggressive stance. This option is still very much alive. Thus, although there is considerable pressure to be relatively passive, conditions emerge that produce quite a different response. One central argument in this book is that Congress is free to choose various courses of action. Pressures will be described that push more strongly in one direction than in another, but the ability of the men and women who constitute Congress to do something in the face of these prevailing pressures is specifically and vigorously affirmed.

The Impact of Institutional Stability. Members of the House and Senate are faced with a choice that involves their desire to support institutional stability in Congress or to strive for institutional change. This differs from the choice of change or stability in the substance of specific governmental policies. Yet there are ties between degree of institutional stability, degree of policy stability, and relative impact of Congress on the substance of policy. Unfortunately for the members, however, increased institutional stability can both strengthen and weaken the ability of Congress to have important substantive effects.

Thus, members of Congress interested in maximizing the policy impact of the institution face a dilemma. On the one hand, the institutional stability and organization possible under relatively stable conditions are likely to be necessary if Congress is to have major policy input of its own rather than depending on the executive branch for all direction and details. But on the other hand, stability also breeds substantive policy conservatism and tends to stifle innovation. Thus, in theory, a stable organization may be the most likely to have a large policy impact but in fact may become moribund, allowing competing organizations such as the Executive Office of the President or various parts of the bureaucracy to acquire policy initiative by default. Despite the claim that "reform" can cure congressional ineffectiveness, there is no pat answer to this dilemma. Both change and stability may promote either congressional potency or impotence. The advantages and disadvantages of either course have to be weighed again and again in specific situations.

CONGRESSIONAL FUNCTIONS AND SOCIETAL IMPACT

Congress performs a variety of functions, but one can be viewed as overarching: it helps, or at least tries to help, resolve differences of opinion about public policy between different individuals and groups in society. These differences of opinion can be narrowly divided or they can be poles apart. They can be pursued peacefully through argument or they can be pursued in a more physical manner through such measures as strikes, lockouts, demonstrations, and violence—both planned and unplanned.

If Congress is largely successful in the performance of this function and if the other institutions of society are also largely successful in performing the same function, then society is likely to be relatively stable.

If Congress and the other institutions of government are unsuccessful in resolving conflict, then societal instability may develop. Failure is, of course, possible; the Civil War is a classic example of what happens when the most fundamental societal conflict cannot be resolved through normal institutional channels.

Despite the ultimate importance of this overarching function, it does not have much analytical utility. Four more specific categories of the policy-relevant functions of Congress include lawmaking, oversight of administration, education of the public, and representation. These categories do not include every function of Congress, but they do include those central to congressional impact on public policy.

Congressional performance of these functions is not fixed—it varies as the environment varies and as the membership of Congress varies. Although environmental factors can have an important influence on the way Congress performs its functions, Congress nonetheless has a great deal of latitude in choosing its direction. The wishes and preferences of the collection of individuals happening to serve in it at any particular time are a principal internal variable that influences the performance of basic congressional functions.

Congress and Lawmaking

Prior to the Civil War, congressional lawmaking activity in the domestic sphere was basically limited to promoting the development of the nation by subsidizing a large number of private activities (for example, turnpikes and canals). This sort of interest has persisted to the present day and Congress is still heavily involved in the subsidy of a wide range of state, local, and private development activities, in such fields as agriculture, education, health, airport construction, and the merchant marine.

Once the Civil War had demonstrated that the federal government was also a national government, new problems, largely associated with the rapid industrialization of the nation, began to arise that involved public discussion of what the government should do. Corporate wealth, which rapidly made the Republican party its political handmaiden, began to alter the dimensions of American opportunity. The end of the homesteading era and the massive waves of immigration from Eastern and Southern Europe compounded the new problems.

The political system took about twenty years to frame even the beginnings of a coherent response. The response came in the form of involving the government—including Congress—in regulation. In the late nineteenth century Congress began the long development of regulation of railroads and corporations with the passage of the Interstate

Commerce Act in 1887 and the Sherman Antitrust Act in 1890. In the first fifteen years of the twentieth century other regulatory laws, such as the Hepburn Act of 1906, the Clayton Act of 1914, and the Federal Trade Commission Act of 1914, were enacted. Since then congressional concern with regulation has expanded greatly to include such matters as unfair business practices, all modes of transportation, power, radio and television, food and drugs, labor relations, and the securities market.

It took the catastrophe of an economic depression seemingly irreversible by normal means to legitimize the activity of conscious and planned redistribution of economic and social benefits in society on the part of Congress and the government as a whole. The economic disaster of the 1930s revealed the corresponding social disaster that had been developing for a number of decades. Congress made some attempts to redraw more equitably the social and economic lines that the mythical "free market" had produced. In the last four decades the congressional agenda has included a great number of topics involving debates over equality or inequality and degree and direction of redistribution; wages and hours, social security, medical care for the aged, national health insurance, aid to depressed geographic areas, public housing, aid to inner city public education, and job training serve as examples.

In the period after the Second World War—and in large part as a result of social forces unleashed by the domestic impact of the War—the congressional agenda of redistributive questions was expanded to include questions about racial discrimination.

Congress occasionally surrenders willingly some of its lawmaking activities in the domestic realm. For example, the adoption of the Reciprocal Trade Agreements Act in 1934 diminished the congressional role in the making of tariffs and increased the role of the executive branch, especially the president. Congress can also be aggressive in seeking out new areas of endeavor—congressional initiatives were responsible for the development of water and air pollution policy in the 1950s and 1960s, for example. Congress can also deliberately seek simply to maintain the existing situation in terms of the range of activities in which it is engaged.

Congressional performance of the lawmaking function in the realm of foreign affairs has varied from relatively passive to relatively aggressive. Congress can never absolutely control foreign policy—it is constitutionally prevented from doing so, given the powers specifically allocated to the president. It can put itself in a genuinely subservient role, however, as it did at the time of the passage of the 1964 Gulf of Tonkin Resolution, which gave the president a virtual carte blanche to proceed in Vietnam as he saw fit. In that resolution Congress responded to President Johnson's report on North Vietnamese attacks on two U.S. ships and the retaliatory air strike he ordered against North Vietnamese Naval bases by declaring their support for the President's "determination . . . to take all necessary measures to repel any armed attack against the forces of the United States and to prevent further aggression." * Only two senators and no representatives voted against this broad grant of authority that President Johnson used to justify rapid and massive escalation of the Vietnam War. Congress repealed the resolution in 1970, although the repeal was more important symbolically than in terms of any real impact on American involvement in Vietnam.

If Congress is relatively aggressive it can work jointly with the president and bureaucracy in a number of foreign policy areas to develop policy. This has been true in recent years in the consideration of some treaties and in the treatment accorded some aspects of foreign aid and immigration. In the making of war Congress has in the last few years become concerned about reasserting its constitutionally-granted powers. In November 1973 Congress passed a war powers bill over a veto. This provided that the president must report commitments of American troops to foreign combat within forty-eight hours. He must order the cessation of such combat after sixty days unless Congress has given its approval (although he can extend that period by thirty more days if he determines that American troops are endangered). There is no evidence yet, however, that presidential influence has been effectively curtailed in this area.

In short, when aggressive, Congress can be quite important in what might be called secondary areas of foreign policy-making and can have at least some importance in the primary areas. When passive, Congress gives up almost all influence in the primary areas and relegates itself to a small supporting role even in the secondary areas. It can never dominate foreign policy but its influence can never disappear altogether either.

Congress and Oversight of Administration

Congress has the responsibility of determining if its programs are being executed as it has intended and if the money it has appropriated is being spent on the purposes for which it was authorized. Oversight is the method of supervising both the programs Congress has created and the bureaucrats who administer them.

---

* For the full text of this important resolution see *Congressional Quarterly's Guide to the Congress of the United States* (Washington, D.C.: Congressional Quarterly, 1971): 221.

The General Accounting Office (GAO), the official watchdog arm of Congress, is vital in the oversight function, but its activities are necessarily limited by a sheer size problem—it has a limited number of personnel and cannot possibly oversee all of the programs run by the bureaucracy. Congress supplements the reports and information coming from the GAO with the oversight activities of its committees. In effect, almost all appropriations and authorization hearings become forums for Congress to oversee the activities of the bureaucracy as they administer programs.

An important feature of oversight, which is also tied to the lawmaking function, is the inclusion of standards for administration of programs and for program performance in original authorizing legislation. When standards are specified, Congress has a tool to use later in oversight hearings to assess how well a program is being administered.

Some programs have very specific standards included—the Social Security Act of 1935 contained remarkably clear standards to guide subsequent administration of the law. Other programs have poorly defined standards—the phrase "maximum feasible participation" (of the poor) contained in the Economic Opportunity Act of 1964 (an act designed to combat poverty in a variety of ways) proved to be confusing to most persons who came in contact with the law—federal administrators, city officials, and actual or potential beneficiaries. Some thought it meant only token formal participation of the poor. Others thought it meant genuine program control by a majority of the poor. Many took a middle position somewhere between the extremes. Congress never provided an authoritative interpretation.

The inherent nature of a program affects the kind of evaluation criteria, if any, that can be specified in authorizing legislation. In general, it is more difficult to devise measures of success for programs in human resource fields such as education, health, and rehabilitation, which attempt to improve the quality of individual lives. Evaluation criteria in other areas, for example, defense, seem to be more easily devised because the area deals with quantifiable items rather than with qualitative changes in education, health care, career opportunities, racial equality and similar aspects of human lives.

Congress can pursue its oversight activities in a variety of moods. It can be intent on very narrow questions, for example, "What did you do with the $10,000 for new downspouts at Fort Sill?"; or pursue very broad questions, for example, "What should the role of the federal government be in relation to the development of the nation's urban areas?" Much oversight approaches the "Fort Sill" end of the spectrum —in fact, some members of Congress seem intent on becoming day-to-day managers of specific programs. But a good deal of the other kind of oversight also takes place. In recent years hearings on the federal government and the cities chaired by Senator Abraham Ribicoff (D-Conn.), hearings on manpower chaired by Senator Joseph Clark (D-Pa.), hearings on national security organization chaired by Senator Henry Jackson (D-Wash.), and hearings on hunger chaired by Senator George McGovern (D-S.Dak.) all exemplify oversight of administration of the broadest kind—concerned not just with administrative details but with the scope and direction of policy in large and important areas. The Ribicoff hearings, for example, were conducted for thirty-three days scattered between August 1966 and June 1967. They dealt with all aspects of the federal government's relation to urban problems including, centrally, the problems of black citizens, the economic consequences of suburban development, and the enormous costs of education. These hearings helped focus governmental attention on a range of problems and helped stimulate discussion of possible solutions.

Congress and Education of the Public

Perhaps inevitably, Congress as an institution has never devised an appropriate mode of communicating its views about public policy to the public. As a multi-headed institution of members with differing party affiliations and policy views it is hard to imagine "the Congress" ever appearing as a single entity to the public. There is no one spokesman for Congress, even on relatively noncontroversial issues, and especially not on controversial ones. When members of Congress have locked horns with the president over some issue, the natural advantage lies with the president. He can state his position clearly in public with immediate and thorough coverage by the mass media. The leaders of the congressional majority on an issue can try to counteract it, but the congressional posture is almost always muddied because there will always be a vocal minority in Congress supporting the presidential position.

Individual members of Congress, however, can and do engage in educating the public. Indeed, most of the time that they spend in contact with the public, particularly constituents, is an attempt to educate (and usually to influence votes, but the two are not incompatible). Speeches, appearances, and newsletters to home states and districts are all opportunities for congressmen to convey informed views on issues important to the nation or some part of it.

Members take different stances with respect to education, and their stance is usually tied to their individual conception of representation. Some can play it safe by trying to take only positions they gauge to be popular. By following "the voice of the people" they try to maximize their chances for continued electoral success. In large part, of course, the "voice" they hear may be an echo of what they themselves have said and want to believe that "the people" support. Others, perhaps more courageous, may try to lead the public, taking positions they know may be unpopular.

Congress and Representation

The nature of representation is both a practical and philosophical question of great importance to those who write about government and to those practitioners who contemplate the deeper meaning of what they do. Numerous conceptions of representation have been advanced for the last several thousand years.* At root Congress can be called representative because it is an elected body and because a system of periodic free elections can remove from office any member judged by his constituents to be totally unrepresentative. It cannot be labelled representative in a variety of precise senses, however. For example, the characteristics of the members are different from the characteristics of the population as a whole. Members of Congress are better educated, wealthier, and more likely to be lawyers, white, and males than the general population. So in the traits by which we classify the population Congress is decidedly unrepresentative—or, to put it a different way, overrepresentative of certain characteristics. Nor can Congress be said to be representative in terms of exactly reproducing "public opinion" on a variety of issues. Senators and representatives clearly have and use freedom of judgment in acting on issues without, in most instances, specific instructions from the people they represent. Nor can Congress be said to represent all interests in society simultaneously. On some issues some individuals and classes of individuals are "losers" and, in a sense, their losses provide the benefits that are redistributed to other individuals and classes of individuals (the "winners").

But the fact of free elections coupled with the fact that most citizens acquiesce or consent to the legitimacy of Congress by accepting the results of those elections seem sufficient to establish a case for Congress as a valid representative institution. Even more important, it is evident that members of the House and the Senate think of themselves as representatives and worry about their behavior in that light. They are

---

* For recent useful discussions of representation see Hanna Pitkin, *The Concept of Representation* (Berkeley: University of California Press, 1967); and Charles E. Gilbert, "Operative Doctrines of Representation," *American Political Science Review* 57 (1963): 604–618.

very conscious of being representatives of their districts or states. They are aware that conflict may exist between the presumed demands of the district and the demands of party. They almost uniformly cite constituency (and conscience) as legitimate reasons for deserting party stands.* They use this language in explaining defection to the party leaders who usually accept the explanation. Conversely, they occasionally cite the demands of party or the unaminity of their fellow party members from their state or region in explaining votes to questioning constituents.

Members of Congress are genuinely concerned with what they think their constituency's attitude is. But their perceptions may be incorrect, in part because they may take their cues from a very small and biased sample.† Some may conduct polls to determine sentiment (a few of these polls are professionally constructed and thus produce accurate results); most probably rely on a combination of intuition and discussion with individual constituents whose views they trust and respect or at least those with enough political influence to make consultation prudent. Members who come from highly competitive districts or states are probably more likely to worry about representing with some precision the views of their district.° They may, however, badly misinterpret real feelings in their district.

A well-established fact—recognized by some members much more clearly than others—is that most constituents have no clear opinions on most issues with which senators and representatives must deal.‡ This means that an aggressive and self-confident member has a wide latitude within which to operate. It also means that when a member claims to be representing the opinion of his district he is, on most issues, representing the opinion of only a minority of his constituents, because most don't know or care about the issue at hand, and at any rate don't communicate any attitude to him at all.

Individual members of the House and Senate undertake a number of different kinds of activities that can be considered representative. First, they support the interests of individuals in a variety of "casework"

---

* Randall B. Ripley, *Party Leaders in the House of Representatives* (Washington, D.C.: Brookings, 1967): 140–141.
† Warren E. Miller and Donald E. Stokes, "Constituency Influence in Congress," *American Political Science Review* 57 (1963): 45–56; and George R. Boynton, Samuel C. Patterson, and Ronald D. Hedlund, "The Missing Links in Legislative Politics: Attentive Constituents," *Journal of Politics* 31 (1969): 700–721.
° See John C. Wahlke, Heinz Eulau, William Buchanan, and Leroy Ferguson, *The Legislative System* (New York: Wiley, 1962); and Heinz Eulau, John C. Wahlke, William Buchanan, and Leroy C. Ferguson, "The Role of the Representative," *American Political Science Review* 53 (1959): 742–756, for evidence at the level of the state legislature.
‡ John C. Wahlke, "Policy Demands and System Support: The Role of the Represented," *British Journal of Political Science* 1 (1971): 271–290.

activities. These cases typically involve deportation and immigration, selective service, social security, and tax matters. Casework activities may involve so-called "private legislation"—for example a bill to exempt named individuals from immigration quotas. They may also involve non-legislative congressional inquiries into various bureaucratic proceedings—for example, pursuing the question of the eligibility of a specific individual for social security or medicare benefits.

Members of the House and Senate also pursue casework for corporate entities. Typically, these cases involve enforcement and interpretation of the tax code or exemptions from various regulatory provisions. For example, when strict enforcement of federal safety standards threatened the last steamboat on the Ohio River with extinction, interested members of Congress from the region were successful in getting different standards applied to this particular boat. Defense contractors involved in cost overrun disputes with the government can regularly count on some congressional intervention on their behalf.

Members are also concerned with intervening in the division of federal largesse. Here they pursue not only such tangible and visible items as new post offices and dams for given localities and contracts for certain companies but also assist local units of government in seeking federal funds for such things as education, health, pollution control, job training, and housing.

Senators and representatives can also seek to represent broad classes or races. For example, some black members consider themselves representatives of the interests of all blacks; some conservative white southerners consider themselves representatives of the interests of all southern whites and perhaps all whites. Some members consider themselves spokesmen for all the poor or for some segment of the poor—perhaps urban, Appalachian, Indian, or Mexican-American.

Finally, senators and representatives can seek to represent "the national good." This applies to most members at least some of the time. In this vein some members are even led to take stands that are unpopular and endanger their seats. The early opposition of Senators Wayne Morse (D-Oreg.) and Ernest Gruening (D-Alaska) to the war in Vietnam provides a case in point. Their position on this issue—and their visibility in pushing it—contributed to subsequent defeats at the polls.

Most members of Congress pursue a mixture of these representative activities, although different members weight the activities differently. Thus it was not at all unusual to see the same Senator Morse who opposed Vietnam on grounds of national interest extremely vigorous in support of high tariffs to protect Oregon cherries. Nor was it unusual to see Senator J. William Fulbright (D-Ark.) simultaneously pursuing "national interest" concerns as chairman of the Foreign Relations Committee and promoting the welfare of Arkansas chicken and rice farmers.

RELATIONS WITH THE EXECUTIVE BRANCH: A BROAD PERSPECTIVE

Regardless of whether Congress appears to be pursuing a more aggressive or a more passive course, it must choose a direction of interaction regarding the executive branch—the president, the institutional presidency (that is, those offices that exist primarily to serve the president in an immediate sense), and the bureaucracy. This interaction is at the center of national policy-making.

Both the executive branch and Congress can be conceptualized as three-level institutions. The executive branch has the president, the institutional presidency, and the vast bureaucracy (peopled mostly by civil servants). Congress has party leaders, a committee structure, and rank-and-file senators and representatives. There are fifteen possible two-way relationships between these six institutional participants, but eight are especially critical and are summarized in Figure 1–1.

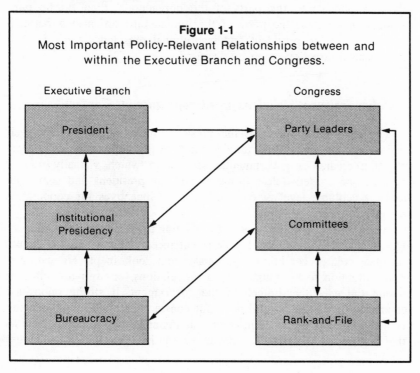

Figure 1-1
Most Important Policy-Relevant Relationships between and within the Executive Branch and Congress.

Within the executive branch, relationships are relatively hierarchical in that the direct relationship between the president and the bureaucracy is not very strong. Instead, the institutional presidency—particularly the White House office, the Office of Management and Budget, and cabinet and sub-cabinet officials appointed by the president—plays a critical mediating role between the president and his policy preferences and the various parts of the bureaucracy. Within Congress all of the possible relationships are consistently important in determining the legislative results emerging from the institution as a whole.

The relationship between the two branches has two levels. The president and institutional presidency relate mostly to the party leaders of the president's party. They rely on the leaders to relay their preferences both to committees and to rank-and-file members. Conversely, members of the House and Senate look to the leaders to carry information and preferences back to the president and presidency. Individual organizations within the bureaucracy, however, primarily relate directly to the committees and subcommittees responsible for substantive decisions involving them. The reason that central direction of policy is so difficult to achieve is the weakness of the link between the party leaders and the committees. The committees tend to be much more responsive to the parts of the bureaucracy than to the party leaders. Given that the parts of the bureaucracy are also imperfectly responsive to the president and institutional presidency there is often little central direction to policy decisions.

Policy-Relevant Relationships: Cooperation or Conflict?

The relationship between the president and Congress is relatively visible and its visibility is fully justified by its importance. The Constitution created a governmental scheme in which virtually nothing new can be started unless Congress and the president find some mutually acceptable level of cooperation. The incentives for cooperation are great.

A president has many reasons for wanting to get along with Congress. His image as a masterful leader is enhanced if no senator or house member creates conditions that make him look inept. He can give more attention to his public and press relations, or even his influence within the executive branch of the government, if strong opposition emanating from the Capitol does not constantly threaten him. He can comfortably leave the country for diplomatic ventures if he knows that a group of "barons" a mile or so southeast of the White House will not seize the occasion to aggrandize themselves at the expense of the sojourning "chief."

None of these reasons for wanting amicable relations with Congress is ignoble, but one eminently practical motive is more important, if not necessarily more noble. As the Constitution makes explicit, the laws of the land—including, critically, the essential functions of raising and disbursing revenue—require the approval of Congress. Thus, simply to keep the government functioning at a minimum level a president must be concerned with at least some congressional legislative activity—taxation and appropriations. Since every president also has grander programmatic ambitions, he must be concerned about and involved in a large part of congressional activity.

Members of the House and Senate also have many reasons for wanting to get along with a president, although their reasons are probably not as great as his. Nevertheless, members with broad programmatic aspirations stand a greater chance of realizing some of those aspirations if the president can be induced to support or initiate some of their ideas. Thus, for example, Congressional initiators of anti-air pollution legislation in the late 1950s and early 1960s made a major stride forward only when they finally induced President John Kennedy to support their views. Even members with few legislative ambitions will find White House support useful as they seek new post offices, dams, and defense contracts for their districts.

There are also conditions that promote conflict between president and Congress, however. These include: genuine disagreement over policy goals (disagreement that may be magnified for partisan reasons); the almost inevitable jealousies of individuals each responsible to their own constituencies; and the natural desire of potential competitors to maintain some information not available to the other party (this helps explain the continuing debate over "executive privilege" with regard to the sharing of information). Disagreement over policy goals is the most important source of conflict. Examples include the basically hostile reaction by Congress to President Nixon's initiatives in welfare and housing in the early 1970s and to much of President Kennedy's New Frontier program in the early 1960s.

The relationship between Congress and the bureaucracy is less visible to the public because of the relative lack of media coverage when compared to the attention given the relationship between Congress and the president, but it too is vital in determining the shape of national policy. The policies that emerge from this relationship are not as dramatically new as some emerging from the presidential-congressional relationship, but they are collectively important. And, equally important although less glamorous, the nexus between bureaus and committees determines many of the details of how ongoing programs will be administered. These seemingly routine and dull decisions can shape programs in ways very different from what the proponents in the White House and in Congress originally envision. These decisions also impact most directly on the citizens of the nation.

In much of the writing on the relations between Congress and the bureaucracy (and, surprisingly, the literature on this subject is scarce) the element of conflict is stressed. Not only is conflict depicted as a central and normal condition, but the discussions of these relations are usually cast in polemical terms. Typically, bureaucrats are portrayed as either trying to administer programs in the public interest despite the limitations imposed by parochial-minded congressmen, or else as trying to avoid the attentive eyes of public-spirited congressional watchdogs who insist on economy and efficiency instead of the normal "bureaucratic" (that is, wasteful) methods of administration. Discussions of congressional oversight of administration usually focus on congressional aggressiveness in oversight and bureaucratic resistance to it. Depending on the point of view, congressional aggressiveness is either praised or condemned, and the bureaucratic resistance is described as dastardly or heroic.

The position advanced here is different, however. It is argued that the bureaucratic-congressional relationship is at the center of public policy development in the United States and that cooperation characterizes this relationship far more than conflict. Basically, members of Congress and members of the bureaucracy have valuable items to trade and, unless the terms of trade strike one party or the other as outrageous there are strong incentives to keep the relations smooth, cooperative, and devoid of disruptive conflict. Conflict can be costly to both sides and so both sides are reluctant to initiate it. Conflict does arise and should be noted, but the more usual situation is one of relative peace and harmony.

As members of a congressional committee and officials of a bureau interact, mutual support can be offered in several forms. The committee can provide the bureau with favorable decisions on budget, authority, jurisdiction, procedure, organization, and reorganization. Committee members also provide bureaucrats with rewards in the form of public praise for jobs well done. Bureaus can provide committee members with "good" policy (that is, policy in accord with the preferences of the committee members) and with special treatment for the states, districts, and constituents of committee members on matters involving the application of regulations, the location of facilities, or the priority given a specific matter. Bureaucrats can also provide public support for senators and representatives by deferring to them as experts in given areas. A classic case of committee-bureau interaction in which virtually all of the above supports were traded occurred during the 1950s and 1960s between the National Institutes of Health and appropriations subcommittees chaired by Senator Lister Hill (D-Ala.) and Representative John Fogarty (D-R.I.).

The instances of conflict that do occur usually stem from genuine differences of opinion over what is good policy, disputes motivated by partisan considerations, or personal dislikes. The running dispute for several decades between the foreign aid agency and a House appropriations subcommittee chaired by Otto Passman (D-La.) provides an example of continuously hostile relations based on policy differences and personal considerations.

From the congressional point of view the danger of close cooperation is that it may, in fact, amount to cooptation by a bureau with a more numerous staff and more complete information about the subject matter of its own programs. The danger of generating programmatic conflict is that the benefits that the bureau can offer to committee members may be withheld or withdrawn.

In general, then, influence over the development of public policy is shared (unevenly, in most instances) by the president and individuals in the institutional presidency, members of the House and Senate, civil servants in the bureaucracy, and lobbyists representing various interests. In any given policy area various coalitions may emerge involving these basic participants. One particularly strong link is that between Congress and the bureaucracy—specifically, between a subcommittee or two and the top officials in a specific bureau. When this nexus adds a few supportive interest group representatives it becomes exceptionally powerful and can often withstand even pressure from the White House.

Congressional Involvement in Policy-Making: Patterns of Interaction with The Executive Branch

Congress, because of both its constitutional position and the activity of its members, is involved in one way or another in every area of policy in which the federal government is active. But the nature of congressional activity varies from issue to issue and from time to time. Generalizations that Congress is losing power to the president and has been since the beginning of the twentieth century may make exciting rhetoric but reveal almost nothing about the nature of congressional involvement in policy-making. The reality of congressional involvement is much more complicated and cannot be caught in a facile general statement.

There are four analytical models that are useful in understanding congressional involvement in policy-making. Congress never follows a single model at any given time. Rather it usually is involved in all four models simultaneously in different issue areas. It may be that trends develop in specific areas—that is, with Congress consistently moving from one model to another one—but any comprehensive generalization about the trend of congressional involvement is bound to be so general that most important variations will be obscured.

The first model can be labeled *executive dominance*. In this model the principal source of initiation for legislative ideas comes from the executive branch. The executive, usually the president on major matters, sets the agenda for Congress to consider. Congressional participation in shaping the details of specific programs is generally low. Not only does the executive serve as the principal source of initiation but it also produces the details of proposals which are, for the most part, ratified by Congress. Congress simply legitimizes what the executive proposes. Thus there is a final legislative product that is broadly acceptable to both the executive branch (which gets what it wants without much change) and Congress (which seems quite content to approve the details of what the executive wants).

There are a number of easy generalizations in the literature that the whole of foreign policy and defense policy are typified by the executive dominance model. More careful examination, however, suggests that this generalization is only selectively true, as will be seen in chapter 11. The original proposal for a "war on poverty" in 1963–64 through programs such as community action, the job corps, the neighborhood youth corps, and operation headstart, provides a closer fit to the executive dominance model.

The second model is *joint program development*. In this model the principal source of legislative initiative can be either the executive branch or Congress or it can be a joint initiative either coordinated and planned or fortuitous and unplanned. Both the executive and Congress are heavily involved in decisions about details. There may be some conflict over these details but there is also a high degree of willingness both within Congress and the executive to compromise so a final product broadly acceptable to both can emerge.

A great variety of matters in the economic field—taxes, for example —seem to fit this model reasonably well. Additional examples include the "depressed areas" programs (Area Redevelopment and Economic Development) of the 1960s and the Model Cities program of the late

1960s. These programs were both aimed at promoting economic development—the first in primarily rural areas and the second primarily in inner city ghettos.

The third model is *congressional dominance*. In this model the principal source of initiation comes from within Congress; congressional involvement in shaping details is high. The executive branch in this case is willing to participate in the shaping of details in only a marginal way. The executive is also willing at least to acquiesce to the congressional initiative and decisions on details and may even be eager to embrace the congressional solution. Whatever the motivation and whatever the degree of eagerness, a final legislative product emerges because the important individuals in the two branches reach some form of agreement.

In recent years policies and programs relating to atomic energy, air pollution, and water pollution all seem to fit this model. In large part these programs fit this model because of aggressive members of Congress with decided policy views and institutional positions from which to push those views successfully.

The fourth model is *stalemate*. In this model there may be initiative in either branch, or there may be competing initiatives undertaken simultaneously in both branches. Both branches also get heavily involved in the attempt to shape details, but again their simultaneous efforts run counter to each other. Finally, all of this activity bears no immediate fruit because neither side is willing to yield to the views of the other or even compromise to reach some mutually agreeable solution.

The controversy over the supersonic transport in the early 1970s seems to fit this model. The executive branch was pushing federal funding for the development of the SST and Congress was balking. As a result some initial funds were spent but the entire project was finally cancelled. Oftentimes debate in an area will fit this model for several years and then a different model will finally apply as some form of compromise is reached. For example, in the late 1950s a large number of areas fit this model: aid to education, area redevelopment, medicare, and manpower development and training. But in the 1960s agreement was reached and measures passed. As this example suggests, the fourth model is often the product of partisan differences between Congress and the White House; it is most likely to appear in those periods when the major elective parts of the government are not in the hands of a single party. In general, it can be said that the same policy area can move between any combination of models over time. It is far too simple to think of a single dimension of presidential "strength" or "weakness" as explaining patterns of relative influence over all policy.

Table 1–1
Models of Congressional Involvement in Policy-Making

Model	Principal Source of Initiation	Degree of Congressional Participation in Shaping Details	Degree of Executive Participation in Shaping Details	Production of Final Legislative Product
Executive Dominance	Executive	Low	High	Yes
Joint Program Development	Executive or Congress or Both	High	High	Yes
Congressional Dominance	Congress	High	Low	Yes
Stalemate	Executive or Congress or Both	High	High	No

Table 1–1 summarizes the models of congressional involvement in policymaking.

* * *

This chapter has introduced a number of themes that will recur throughout the rest of the book: the substantive importance of Congress, the ability of the members to shape both the impact and the nature of the institution, and the centrality of the relations with the executive branch.

The place of Congress in government is fixed only in the sense that it is likely to remain important. But the details of the congressional role and the quality of congressional performance are not fixed. They will be determined in part by events outside the control of the members; but in large part they will also be determined by the deliberate choices made by the members.

2

CONGRESSIONAL

DEVELOPMENT

THE MODERN CONGRESS HAS BEEN INTRODUCED IN BROAD TERMS
in the preceding chapter. The origins and development of that
institution are the concerns of this chapter.

Although Congress has changed—especially in response to a developing presidency, the growth of the bureaucracy, and the vast expansion of the tasks undertaken by the federal government—it has
always been an important force in the governing apparatus of the
nation. In this it was following a tradition well-rooted in the colonial
period of the seventeenth and eighteenth centuries. Beginning with the
establishment of the Virginia House of Burgesses in 1619, legislatures
played an important part in the colonies. This development was not
surprising since the early settlers left a country whose Parliament was
well-established and contending with the Crown for governmental
power. Thus it can be said that the existence of powerful legislative
assemblies in the colonies and in the United States was never an open
question; the concept and practice of legislative representation arrived
on the ships with the new settlers and has never been seriously questioned throughout our entire national history.*

---

* This paragraph, of course, vastly oversimplifies British history. The final outcome of the contention between Parliament and Crown was in doubt at least

THE CONSTITUTIONAL MANDATE

Much lively debate and many detailed compromises characterized the decisions made by the members of the Constitutional Convention in 1787 that stated the powers Congress would possess.* But the principle that there would be a powerful national legislature was never jeopardized. The numerous provisions and clauses throughout the Constitution that refer to Congress, especially those in Article I, section 8, make evident the intent of the framers to have such a legislature. In that section Congress is given a variety of specific powers, including the power to tax, borrow and coin money, regulate foreign and interstate commerce, establish a post office, establish federal courts in addition to the Supreme Court, declare war, and provide for the creation and maintenance of armed forces. And, in the event that these grants did not prove sufficient, the framers of the Constitution also granted Congress the power "To make all Laws which shall be necessary and proper for carrying into Execution the foregoing Powers, and all other Powers vested by this Constitution in the Government of the United States, or in any Department or Officer thereof."

Two central decisions made by the framers in Philadelphia have shaped all of Congress's subsequent history and development: first, the decision to make the legislature bicameral, with equal houses representing different constituencies, and second, the decision to interweave the powers of the president and Congress thoroughly while maintaining their very distinct identities.

Another important decision made in Philadelphia was to create a separate and independent judiciary that could serve to check both the president and Congress. The policy interaction between the federal courts and Congress has been sporadic and has mainly involved a few congressional statutes struck down as unconstitutional in whole or in part, an event that has occurred more than eighty times, although usually on rather minor matters. The courts have also had a major impact on Congress through their role in redistricting (treated in chapter 7).

---

until the Glorious Revolution of 1688. Contending philosophical strains (symbolized by Hobbes vs. Locke) and contending political forces continued to keep British political life fluid. One of the most successful claims made by the rebellious American colonists was, of course, that they were not receiving adequate representation in the government of Great Britain and so could not be expected to support that government by taxes and in other ways. In this claim they were supported by such leading British political figures as Edmund Burke.

* On the Constitutional Convention's decisions about Congress and for "founding fathers" interpretations of those decisions see Max Farrand, *The Framing of the Constitution of the United States* (New Haven: Yale University Press, 1913); and Alexander Hamilton, John Jay, and James Madison, *The Federalist* (New York: Random House).

Bicameralism

The decision to have two houses of the national legislature followed the precedent set by the British Parliament and ten of the thirteen colonies. The Convention opted for a two-house national legislature with little debate.

There was debate, however, over the basis on which the two houses should be organized and elected. There was only minimal sentiment against having at least one house popularly elected (a "popular" electorate by the standards of the eighteenth century included a large proportion of all adult white males although some white males might be denied the vote on the grounds of not having sufficient property). The delegates also assumed that the House of Representatives (as the popularly elected branch was called) would represent "democratic" interests—that is, measures favored by the majority of the voters that were widely expected to be "radical." The institution of slavery was protected even in the House, however, because representatives were apportioned to the states on the basis of their white population plus three-fifths of their slave population, even though slaves could not vote. Thus southern states received extra seats in the House because of their large populations of black slaves. This compromise marked the first attempt to deal with a subject that would eventually tear the Union apart.

The Senate (as the second house of the legislature was called) was expected to serve as a check on the impetuosity of the House. But how the Senate should be organized and elected was a subject of some debate, although there was virtually no sentiment for having it popularly elected. It was expected to be representative of more privileged interests in society that presumably would be badly treated in the House. But the delegates could not find a way of defining interests other than in terms of states. Thus every state was given two senators and the power of their election was lodged in the state legislatures.

The overly simple assumption that individuals elected by what passed for a mass electorate in 1787 to represent "the people" would be radical and that individuals elected indirectly to represent states would be more conservative and solicitous of economic interests was not borne out in practice. Certainly there have been numerous important policy disagreements between the two houses. But relative degrees of "conservatism" and "liberalism" have fluctuated. In the last several decades, for example, the Senate has tended to be more consistently concerned about federal aid for urban problems than the House, in part because most senators have at least one large urban area in their states with problems of which they are personally aware.

In contrast, many members of the House come from totally rural or suburban districts, where these problems are far less visible.

In 1913 the seventeenth amendment to the Constitution changed the mode of election of senators so that they too would be elected by a mass electorate. The electoral system had been moving toward popular election for some time. Even during the period of election by state legislatures, senatorial candidates had often involved themselves in the campaigns of candidates for the state legislatures so that citizens were informed who their senator might be when they made their choice among state legislative candidates.*

In theory, the Constitution made the two chambers equal partners in the making of laws, although some special functions were reserved for each house: the Senate was given sole power to try impeachments, ratify treaties, and approve presidential nominations; the House was given the sole power to bring impeachments and to initiate tax bills (by custom this has also included the sole power to initiate appropriations bills). In practice, the two houses have remained generally equal, although at various points in American history one house has seemed to overshadow the other one. Throughout most of congressional history it has also been true that as individuals senators have had more prestige than representatives; many representatives have willingly left the House to run for the Senate while virtually no one has gone the reverse route. Nevertheless, prestige is not "power" or "influence." Equality may vary between substantive fields and over time, but the fact of equality is real: both bodies are jealous of their independence and their impact on public policy. This means that both houses will usually seek to have an impact in virtually all important areas of legislation. No substantive fields become the exclusive property of one house or the other. Relative importance of the two houses varies from area to area but rarely is either house devoid of influence.†

Congress and the President

The second crucial decision made by Constitutional Convention involved the nature of the relationship envisioned between the Congress and the executive. The two were formally separated, each with particular "checks and balances" on the other, yet there are also some shared functions, and policy-making on a large scale is impossible

---

* On the interweaving of senatorial campaigns and state legislative campaigns see William H. Riker, "The Senate and American Federalism," *American Political Science Review* 49 (1955): 452–469.

† For evidence of vacillations in relative impact of the two chambers on legislation, see David J. Vogler, *The Third House* (Evanston: Northwestern University Press, 1971): 110–111.

without sustained close cooperation between Congress and the president. In Article II, section 3, the Constitution formally charges the president to give "to the Congress Information of the State of the Union, and recommend to their Consideration such Measures as he shall judge necessary and expedient." The president is also given the power to call special sessions of either or both houses. Finally, he can veto a measure passed by both houses if he feels it is unsound or otherwise improper.

Congress, however, is responsible for either passing or rejecting various proposals for laws—proposals coming from the president or from any other source. Although the president is commander-in-chief of the armed forces, only Congress can formally declare war. All operations of the executive branch are dependent on the appropriation of money that can be made only by Congress. And the resources from which those appropriations are made come from taxes that are imposed only after proper congressional action. Two-thirds of the voting members of both houses can override a presidential veto. Treaties and nominations made by presidents are subject to congressional veto.

A president can be removed from office by Congress. This is extremely difficult to achieve because most members fear the negative consequences for the stability of the political system and a majority of the House and two-thirds of the Senate must agree in separate actions in order to effect the removal of the president. Only two serious attempts have been made to impeach presidents in the whole course of American history. In 1868 President Andrew Johnson was impeached by the House but the Senate fell one vote short of conviction.

In 1974 Congress was well on the way to impeaching and convicting President Richard Nixon when he resigned. The House Judiciary Committee spent a number of months sifting the evidence against Nixon and committee members from both parties recommended impeachment of the President on three different counts (articles) to the full House. These articles involved obstruction of justice, abuse of presidential powers, and contempt of Congress—all in connection with the attempt by Nixon to cover up the White House role in the break-in at the Watergate headquarters of the Democratic National Committee in June 1972, and, in the case of the second article, with the attempt by the president to use federal agencies to harass political "enemies." It seemed very likely that the House would support at least the first two articles and that the Senate would vote to convict on at least those two articles. The case became moot when Nixon, in effect, admitted to ordering a cover-up of Watergate activities six days after the break-in by releasing information not previously available to the Judiciary Committee. The reaction to this admission was so overwhelmingly negative that it took only three days (from the admission on 5 August 1974, until 8 August 1974) for Nixon to decide that resigning would be preferable to certain impeachment and conviction.

Article II, section 4 of the Constitution provides that "The President, Vice President and all Civil Officers of the United States, shall be removed from Office on Impeachment for, and Conviction of, Treason, Bribery, or other high Crimes and Misdemeanors." There is no specific definition either in law or precedent of what constitutes "other high crimes and misdemeanors." In the case of a president it certainly seems likely that offenses against the Constitution and oath of office to support it as interpreted by a majority of the House and two-thirds of the Senate could bring impeachment and conviction even though those offenses might not literally involve acts for which the president could be tried and convicted in a court of law. Before Nixon's final disastrous admission his defenders on the House Judiciary Committee had argued that impeachable offenses should be narrowly defined to those for which criminal conviction could be obtained in a court but their position was in a minority of about two-to-one in the Committee.

Presidents are chosen by the House if the electoral college does not provide a majority. This happened after inconclusive elections in 1800 and 1824. In the first instance the House chose Thomas Jefferson over Aaron Burr and in the second John Quincy Adams over several rivals including Andrew Jackson. On another occasion, following the election of 1876, Congress created an Electoral Commission that, in effect, determined the results of the election, probably contrary to the will of the majority of the electorate. Thus Rutherford B. Hayes became president instead of Samuel Tilden. The Senate is responsible for choosing the vice-president following an inconclusive election. This has happened only once, in 1837. When the vice-presidency is vacant, a majority of both the House and Senate must confirm the president's nominee. If a president declares himself able to resume his duties after a period of disability and the vice-president and a majority of the cabinet disagree, Congress must settle the issue.

In effect, no matter what the vision of the president is about the shape of public policy, the implementation of that vision is dependent on Congress. Congress can also take considerable initiative in shaping public policy according to some collective vision possessed by a large number of its members. Congress is also deeply involved when those policies are implemented through the bureaucracy. Thus both Congress and the president legislate, and both Congress and the president administer. Yet they are part of a governmental system in which their entities and their roles—that is, what is expected of them—are kept separate and distinct. They are mutually interdependent in producing results; but they are separate and independent in defending institutional prerogatives.

THE EMERGENCE OF THE MODERN CONGRESS

In the early part of the nineteenth century Congress bore only a partial resemblance to the institution with which we are familiar today. The electorate for representatives had not yet stabilized (in some states restrictions on voting on the basis of property continued through the first few decades) and state legislatures elected senators. Not all representatives were elected from specific districts; until 1842 states were free to elect all representatives on a statewide basis and many did. Congress dealt with only a few aggressive presidents (chiefly Washington, Jefferson, and Jackson) before the Civil War. Even more important, the workload of the government was not very demanding. The main business of Congress consisted of debates on tariff policy every decade or so and two major efforts to preserve the federal union without civil war in 1820 and 1850.

By mid-century and particularly following the Civil War new conditions emerged. The remaining restrictions on voting based on property disappeared and black male citizens were added to the electorate by the fourteenth and fifteenth amendments to the Constitution. Virtually all representatives now came from districts that were only part of a state. Lincoln revived the tradition of a consistently aggressive president that had been dormant since the days of Jackson. And his successful prosecution of the War left little doubt that the government could be mobilized to pursue national policy. His immediate successors did not appear aggressive—in part because Congress had adopted an aggressive stance particularly with regard to Reconstruction. By late in the century Cleveland and McKinley began to revive the presidency and, in a sense, prepare it for the burst of activity that would come in the twentieth century. Following the Civil War the government—both executive and legislature—had a great deal more to do as the nation industrialized rapidly and the government sought to cope with the consequences of that development.

It is here argued, then, that roughly before the immediate post-Civil War period of the 1870s and 1880s Congress was in a "pre-modern" phase. After the 1870s and 1880s the "modern" Congress emerged. Naturally, change existed before the 1880s and has continued since then. But the process of emergence was rapidly accelerated for a few decades in the late nineteenth century.

The difference between the pre-modern Congress and the modern

Table 2–1
Primary Differences between Pre-Modern Congress and
Modern Congress

Pre-Modern Congress	Modern Congress
High turnover of membership	Low turnover of membership
Many contested elections	Few contested elections
Short sessions, relatively light workload	Long sessions, heavy workload
Chaotic floor proceedings	Orderly floor proceedings
High turnover of committee personnel; shifting criteria for assignment	Low turnover of committee personnel; stable criteria for assignment
Undeveloped political party structures	Well developed political party structures

Congress can be illustrated in six important areas: 1) turnover of membership; 2) finality of electoral decisions; 3) workload and length of sessions; 4) orderliness of floor proceedings; 5) stability of committee memberships and criteria for assignments to committees; and 6) the level of party development within the House and Senate. Table 2–1 summarizes the differences and succeeding sections discuss them.

These features were chosen because, collectively, their impact in the modern Congress has been to promote professionalism and stability in contrast with the relative amateurism and instability in the pre-modern era. As indicated in chapter 1, institutional stability has both costs and benefits in terms of maximizing substantive congressional policy impact. Congress can still consciously promote change, but it cannot recreate the radical instability of the pre-modern period.

Turnover of Membership

In the pre-modern Congress, members came and went rapidly. There were few senior members. Life in Washington was not pleasant, Congress did not seem very important, and the unstable party situation often made re-election difficult to achieve. In the modern Congress, members began serving for much longer periods of time. They became wedded to the notion of a career in Congress. This new desire stemmed from several factors: the strengthening of the parties and the emergence of one-party states and districts after the Civil War making re-election easier; the emergence of national problems raised a legislative career to a new level of importance; and the demonstration by Congress after Lincoln's death that it intended to be an aggressive part of the government.

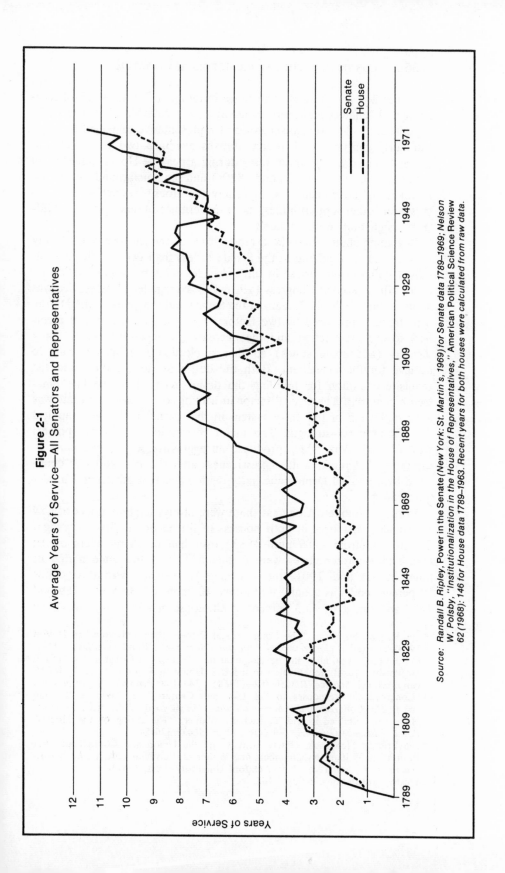

Figure 2-1

Average Years of Service—All Senators and Representatives

Source: Randall B. Ripley, Power in the Senate (New York: St. Martin's, 1969) for Senate data 1789–1969; Nelson W. Polsby, "Institutionalization in the House of Representatives," American Political Science Review 62 (1968): 146 for House data 1789–1963. Recent years for both houses were calculated from raw data.

Figure 2–1 summarizes this change in terms of average years of service for all senators and representatives since 1789. Until the 1880s the experience of the average senator and representative remained at a low and fairly constant level—representatives averaged two years (after a higher level of around three years during a peak of House influence on national policy in the 1810s and 1820s) and senators around four years. Members of both chambers, especially the House, routinely left Congress for other opportunities, both governmental and private. Midterm resignations were common.

Beginning about 1880 the average years of service rose dramatically in both houses, doubling in the Senate in less than two decades and almost tripling in the House in three decades. This trend has continued: in the Ninety-second Congress (1971–72) average length of service was at an all-time high: 11.5 years in the Senate and 9.8 years in the House. This trend is produced by two factors: the desire on the part of members to seek re-election and the decreasing competitiveness of many districts (and some states) so that re-election is relatively easy to achieve for the incumbent. Both the desire for long service and the requisite condition for fulfilling the desire emerged in the late nineteenth century.* The critical factor in helping to produce safe seats was a strengthening of the party system in that period and a geographical division of party strength. The major reason for these developments was the Civil War, which produced an aggressive Republican party in the north that retained its aggressiveness after the War and was countered by a revived Democratic party, with a strong southern and border state base.†

In the pre-modern Congress there were always large numbers of new (freshmen) members in both houses. In fifteen of the first forty-eight Congresses (from 1789 until 1883) over half of all members of the House of Representatives were freshmen. During the same period of time (in fact, until 1901) the percentage of freshmen was never below 30 percent and was usually well above 40 percent.° Between 1789 and 1899 an average of 45.3 percent of all House members were freshmen

---

* See H. Douglas Price, "The Congressional Career—Then and Now," in Nelson W. Polsby (ed.), *Congressional Behavior* (New York: Random House, 1971). On the general point of the development of a "career" in Congress see Nelson W. Polsby, "Institutionalization in the U.S. House of Representatives," *American Political Science Review* 62 (1968): 144–168; Samuel P. Huntington, "Congressional Responses to the Twentieth Century," in David B. Truman (ed.), *The Congress and America's Future* (Englewood Cliffs, N.J.: Prentice-Hall, 1973, 2nd ed.); and T. Richard Witmer, "The Aging of the House," *Political Science Quarterly*, 79 (December 1964): 526–541.

† See Eric L. McKitrick, "Party Politics and the Union and Confederate War Efforts," in William N. Chambers and Walter D. Burnham (eds.), *The American Party Systems* (New York: Oxford University Press, 1967).

° Polsby, "Institutionalization," 146.

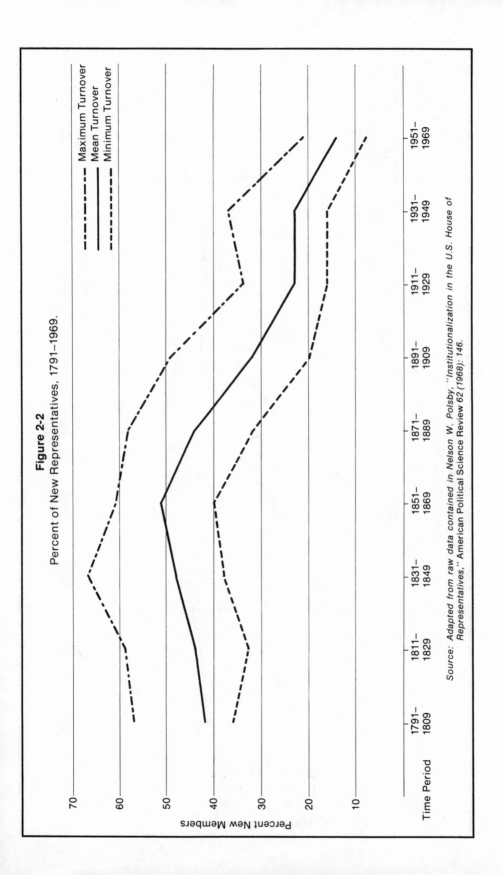

Figure 2-2

Percent of New Representatives, 1791–1969.

Maximum Turnover
Mean Turnover
Minimum Turnover

Percent New Members

70
60
50
40
30
20
10

Time Period

1791–1809   1811–1829   1831–1849   1851–1869   1871–1889   1891–1909   1911–1929   1931–1949   1951–1969

Source: Adapted from raw data contained in Nelson W. Polsby, "Institutionalization in the U.S. House of Representatives," American Political Science Review 62 (1968): 146.

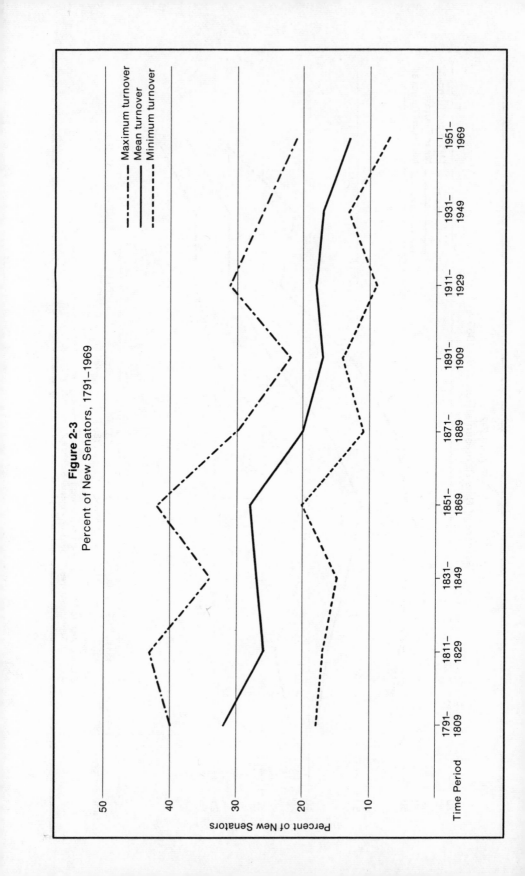

Figure 2-3
Percent of New Senators, 1791–1969

Maximum turnover
Mean turnover
Minimum turnover

Percent of New Senators

Time Period

1791–
1809

1811–
1829

1831–
1849

1851–
1869

1871–
1889

1891–
1909

1911–
1929

1931–
1949

1951–
1969

50

40

30

20

10

in each Congress. Because length of service has been increasing there are fewer vacancies and hence the number of new members has decreased. Since 1899 (until 1971) the average number of freshmen has been only 20.4 percent.

Figures 2–2 and 2–3 summarize the percentage of representatives and senators coming for the first time to their respective chambers since 1791 (the Second Congress) through the Ninety-first Congress (1969) in twenty-year periods. The First Congress is not included because, of course, all members were freshmen. In 1971 the figures were very close to the means reported on the graphs for 1951–69: 11 percent in the House and 14 percent in the Senate. These graphs show a dramatic and continuing drop in turnover in the House beginning in the 1870s and continuing to the present. In the Senate the major drop in turnover occurred in the 1870s and 1880s and has continued somewhat sporadically since, particularly in the last two decades. Before the Civil War the turnover in both houses was very high: between one-quarter and one-third of every Senate was composed of freshmen senators and close to half of every House was composed of freshmen representatives. In the last two decades those figures have shrunk to between one in every seven or eight in both houses. Again the emergence of relatively strong parties with different geographical bases in the late nineteenth century is a powerful factor to explain the initial change.

Finality of Electoral Decisions

In the pre-modern Congress members were subject to challenges to their election. These challenges, on the grounds of electoral irregularities, were especially frequent from the end of the Civil War to the turn of the century. Virtually all contests were decided by the House and Senate on strictly partisan grounds.* Each seat was particularly valuable in the late nineteenth century because it was a period of close competition between the parties both in the electorate in terms of close elections and in Congress in terms of shifting control and small majorities. Partisan election contests in both houses dropped dramatically around the turn of the century, and have continued to decline since. Members who wanted to make careers in Congress—now a majority instead of a small minority—could no longer afford to tolerate arbitrary threats to their goal. Figure 2–4 summarizes the percentage of seats challenged in the House and Senate by decade.

---

* Price, "Congressional Career," reports that only 3 of 382 contested seats in the House were given to the minority party candidate from 1789 to 1908.

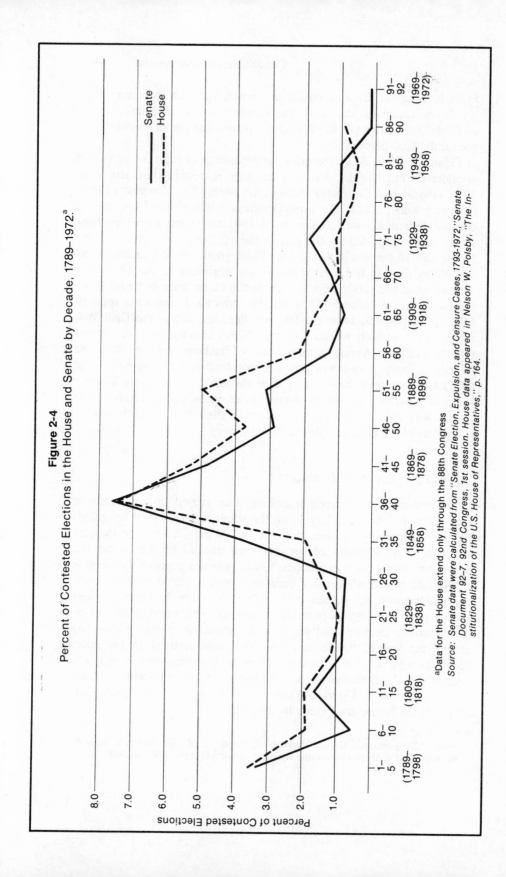

Figure 2-4

Percent of Contested Elections in the House and Senate by Decade, 1789–1972.[a]

[a]Data for the House extend only through the 88th Congress

Source: Senate data were calculated from "Senate Election, Expulsion, and Censure Cases, 1793-1972," Senate Document 92-7, 92nd Congress, 1st session. House data appeared in Nelson W. Polsby, "The Institutionalization of the U.S. House of Representatives," p. 164.

Workload and Length of Sessions

The pre-modern Congress did not meet much of the time because it did not have a great deal to do. In fact, until early in the twentieth century Congress met less than twelve months out of every two years. Except for the First Congress, which met seventeen months for the purpose of creating a governing apparatus, and the Civil War and Reconstruction Congresses, which met between ten and twenty-two months, the length of sessions remained consistently short until roughly 1911. Since that time Congress has met over twelve months out of every twenty-four. In the last three decades Congress has been in session most of the time. This feature of the modern Congress has required that a large proportion of the members become full-time legislators. The reason for this change is primarily that the workload of the entire national government has increased steadily since the Civil War. Since Congress is a central unit in the governing apparatus its workload has also increased steadily. Gradually, Congress became involved in the whole range of foreign and domestic policies outlined in chapter 1.

Figure 2–5 summarizes the growth in the length of the Congressional session.

Orderliness of Floor Proceedings

In the pre-modern Congress, particularly in the House, floor proceedings were chaotic. H. Douglas Price described the House of the nineteenth century: "Members often used bitter and outrageous language, scathing ridicule, and sarcasm. Outbreaks of physical violence were not infrequent, and guns and knives were on occasion carried into the chamber." Neil MacNeil reports a number of instances of violence on the House floor and duels outside the House between members. In one famous encounter before the Civil War, Preston Brooks, a South Carolina representative, beat Charles Sumner, a Massachusetts senator, senseless on the Senate floor. Even more important, the rules of the House and Senate did not allow the orderly conduct of business.*

In the modern Congress decorum replaced raucousness and rules evolved that allowed Congress to dispatch large amounts of business on the floor rapidly. The development of such rules in the House was particularly important. The major developments came between 1876 and 1899 and were largely the result of the work of four Speakers: Samuel

---

* Price, "Congressional Career," 18; Neil MacNeil, *Forge of Democracy* (New York: McKay, 1963): 306–309. See also Malcolm E. Jewell and Samuel C. Patterson, *The Legislative Process in the United States* (New York: Random House, 1973, 2nd ed.): 49–50.

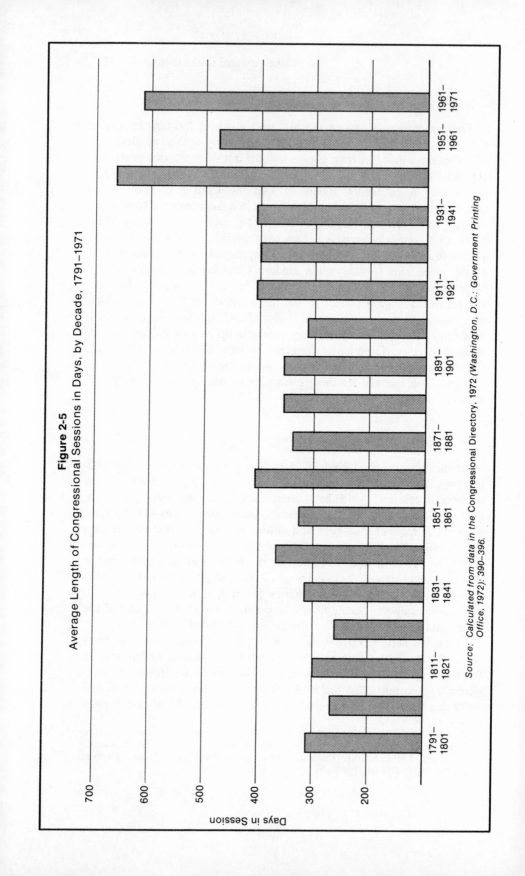

Figure 2-5

Average Length of Congressional Sessions in Days, by Decade, 1791–1971

Source: Calculated from data in the Congressional Directory, 1972 (Washington, D.C.: Government Printing Office, 1972): 390–396.

J. Randall (1876–1881), John G. Carlisle (1883–1889), Thomas B. Reed (1889–1891; 1895–1899), and Charles F. Crisp (1891–1895). Randall made the power of recognition absolute and not subject to appeal, obtained a general revision of the rules, and strengthened the Rules Committee, of which he was chairman. Carlisle was particularly astute in using the power of recognition and he further developed the Rules Committee as an instrument of party government. Reed had the House pass rules effectively outlawing dilatory motions and filibustering in the House. He also continued to use the power of recognition for party ends. Crisp extended the jurisdiction of the Rules Committee to bills still pending in standing committees. The Rules Committee also began to grant special orders or "rules" that would allow legislation to be brought to the floor more systematically.

The Speaker himself was shorn of some of his power acquired during this period in a House revolt against Speaker Joseph Cannon (1903–1911) that took place in 1909–1911 and reached a dramatic peak on the House floor on 19 March 1910. In 1909 the House established a consent calendar (which provided for the orderly consideration of bills to which there was no important opposition) and agreed to call the standing committees every Wednesday for consideration of business on the Union or House calendars (calendars are simply lists of bills ready for floor action; different calendars include different types of bills). These changes limited the Speaker's arbitrary power to control the flow of business. In the March 1910 revolt the Speaker was removed from the Rules Committee, which was enlarged and made elective rather than appointive. Later that year, a method of discharging bills from standing committees was approved that gave the majority of the House the right to bring a bill to the floor even if it was opposed by a committee chairman and the Speaker. In 1911 the rules were changed to provide for the election by the full House of all standing committees and their chairmen. In practice, this led to the establishment of committees on committees (see chapter 4).

The Senate, which established decorum earlier than the House, has continued to take a more leisurely pace on the floor. But even in the Senate the wasting of time on the floor has declined. In the pre-modern period Congress could afford to waste time because the workload was so light. Once the workload grew and was attended to by professional legislators, time became valuable and procedures were invented to prevent gross waste of it.

Committee Membership: Stability and Assignment Criteria

In the pre-modern Congress there were shifting processes for assigning members to standing committees, and no consistent criteria were applied when such assignments were made. High turnover occurred in the membership of specific committees every two years, in part simply because turnover in Congress itself was so high. In the House the appointment power early gravitated to the Speaker, but it was not used with any consistency to promote policies he favored. Henry Clay, for example, the Speaker for eight years between 1811 and 1824, seems to have used this power merely to make friends and continue his tenure in the Speaker's chair.*

In the Senate even the location of appointment authority kept changing. The Senate had no standing committees until 1816 when eleven were authorized. Until 1823 the members of these committees were chosen by ballot by the whole Senate. From 1823 to 1833 the method of choice alternated between ballot, appointment by the president pro tempore of the Senate, and, for one short period, appointment by the vice-president. During much of the period before 1833 seniority for initial assignments and for rank on committees was so unimportant that chairmanships were rotated.

After 1833 the Senate again resorted to balloting for all members. Chairmanships ceased to rotate, and party control of assignments began to appear. Committees began to divide on predictable ideological lines, and minority reports were written whereas previously only majority reports were written. Party control was firm enough by 1846 that, although the formal requirement of balloting remained, the committee assignment lists supplied by the parties were routinely approved.

As the old parties split under the strain of dealing with the slavery question, the Senate found committee assignments more difficult to make. From 1849 to 1857 the president pro tempore again became the appointing agent, although the parties did not relinquish their influence. The southern Democrats dominated the committee chairmanships because of their number in the party. They supported the hardening of seniority to protect their position so that they could defend slavery. Democrats defended a version of the principle of seniority (not removing sitting committee members because of their experience) in an 1857 debate over proposed committee assignments. The Republicans had challenged the assignments as unfair; they had not been consulted by the Democrats when the assignments were made. When the Republicans became the majority in the Senate in 1861 they consulted the Democrats in that year but then ceased consulting them, instead filling all committee places themselves. This situation prevailed until the Democrats became numerous enough after the Civil War to force, in

---

* James S. Young, *The Washington Community, 1800–1828* (New York: Columbia University Press, 1966): 132–133.

effect, the adoption of a seniority criterion.* Since then memberships on committees have been relatively stable—the same members tend to serve on the same committees term after term and develop both their own legislative career and the capacity of Congress to cope with the professionalism of the bureaucracy. Long service on specific committees has accompanied long service in the House and Senate as a whole.

Committee Chairmanships: Appointment Criteria

In the pre-modern Congress chairmen were selected by the same variety of methods by which other members were selected. And a variety of criteria for choice were used—including personal loyalty to the appointing authority. Turnover of chairmen was frequent.

In the modern Congress seniority developed as a virtually automatic rule for apportioning committee chairmanships.† In the Senate, seniority became well-established very quickly in 1877, when the Senate again had a minority party large enough to pose a threat to the policy preferences of the majority party. Between 1865 and 1877, when vacancies occurred in the chairmanships of ten of the most important standing committees in the Senate the Republican party filled those vacancies only about one-quarter of the time on the basis of seniority. Since 1877 the seniority rule for chairmanships has been basically sacred, with only scattered violations.° The evidence suggests that the Democrats had begun to use seniority in the four Congresses preceding the Civil War (at which time most of them left the Senate). In the period after the War, until 1875, there were only a few Democrats in the Senate. When they reappeared in sizeable number seniority was rarely violated.‡

In the House the development of seniority occurred more gradually. Speakers were struggling to get control of the House in the 1880s and 1890s and they frequently ignored seniority in the appointment of committee chairmen and ranking minority members in order to assure that

---

* The preceding three paragraphs are taken from Randall B. Ripley, *Power in the Senate* (New York: St. Martin's, 1969): 22–23. The brief review is based on George Lee Robinson, "The Development of the Senate Committee System" (Ph.D. dissertation, New York University, 1954).

† On this subject see Barbara Hinckley, *The Seniority System in Congress* (Bloomington: Indiana University Press, 1971); Michael Abram and Joseph Cooper, "The Rise of the Seniority System in the House of Representatives," *Polity* 1 (1968): 53–85; Nelson W. Polsby, Miriam Gallaher, and Barry Spencer Rundquist, "The Growth of the Seniority System in the U.S. House of Representatives," *American Political Science Review,* 63 (1969): 787–807; and George Goodwin, Jr., "The Seniority System in Congress," *American Political Science Review* 53 (1959): 412–436.

° Ripley, *Power in the Senate:* 43–44.

‡ Ibid., 45.

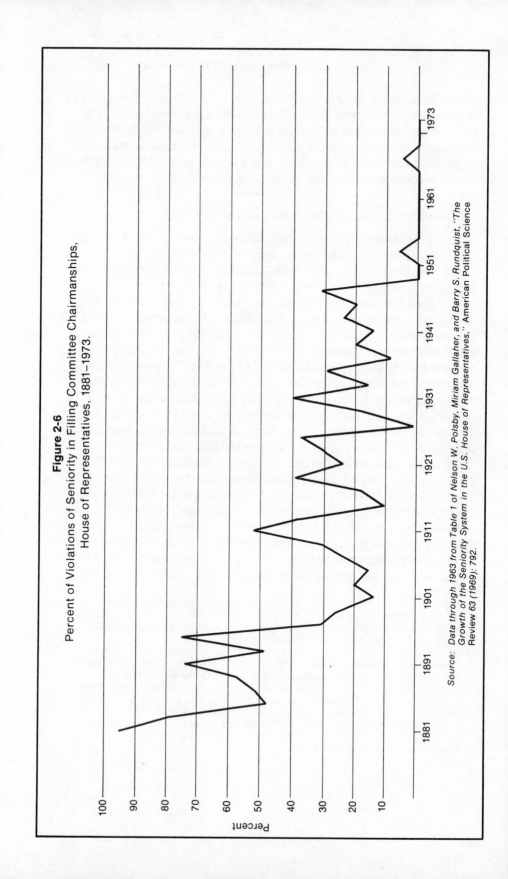

Figure 2-6

Percent of Violations of Seniority in Filling Committee Chairmanships, House of Representatives, 1881–1973.

Source: Data through 1963 from Table 1 of Nelson W. Polsby, Miriam Gallaher, and Barry S. Rundquist, "The Growth of the Seniority System in the U.S. House of Representatives," American Political Science Review 63 (1969): 792.

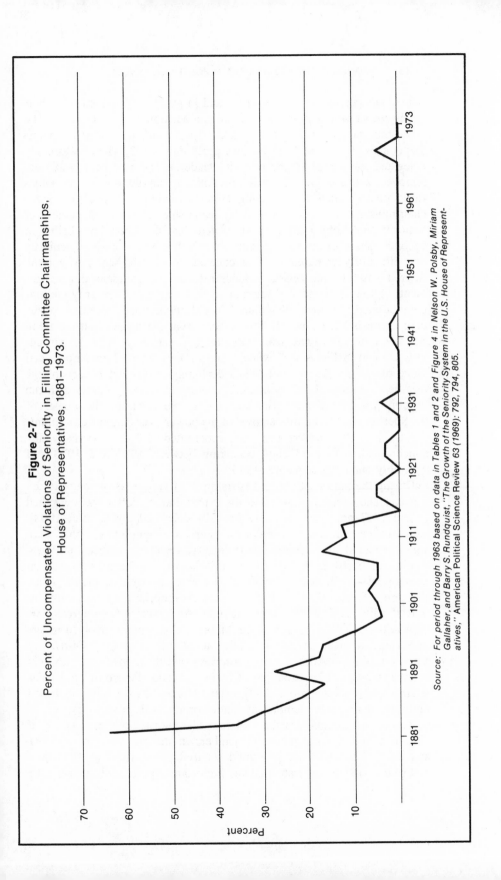

Figure 2-7

Percent of Uncompensated Violations of Seniority in Filling Committee Chairmanships, House of Representatives, 1881–1973.

Source: For period through 1963 based on data in Tables 1 and 2 and Figure 4 in Nelson W. Polsby, Miriam Gallaher, and Barry S. Rundquist, "The Growth of the Seniority System in the U.S. House of Representatives," American Political Science Review 63 (1969): 792, 794, 805.

individuals personally loyal to them and in general agreement with their policy views would hold key committee positions. (It should also be noted that, at least in formal terms, the Speaker made minority appointments as well as those from his own party until 1903, when he formally delegated the power to the minority leader.) The members who were removed or passed over in these non-seniority appointments were sometimes compensated by receiving better assignments, equal or better chairmanships, or positions of party leadership. However, a number of seniority violations went uncompensated—that is, a member eligible to become chairman or ranking minority member on the basis of seniority was effectively demoted and someone else with less seniority got the desired position; the senior member received no compensating assignment. Figures 2–6 and 2–7 summarize all violations of seniority and uncompensated violations of seniority in the appointment of House chairmen between 1881 and 1973. It is clear from the figures that the trend has been steadily away from violations of seniority. This is particularly evident in Figure 2–7, which shows a high level of uncompensated violations in the 1880s and 1890s declining in the first decade of the twentieth century. There is a spurt of uncompensated violations in the turmoil just before and after the drastic reduction of the power of the Speaker (including the removal of his power over committee appointments in 1910) and by 1921 uncompensated violations virtually disappear—with a total of eight occurring between 1921 and 1973 and with only one occurring since 1943.

During the period of the highest number of violations of seniority the Speaker and minority leader (to the extent that the latter was consulted before 1903 and used his more formally delegated power after 1903) were selective in the non-seniority criteria for appointment that were used. Personal and programmatic loyalty, regional balance, and promotion of party unity were used most heavily in the most important committees—those deeply involved in politics as well as major policy decisions (Rules, Ways and Means, and Appropriations) and those involved with major policy (for example, Agriculture, Commerce, Foreign Affairs, Judiciary, and Naval Affairs). Committees involved in less important or relatively minor policy areas (for example, District of Columbia, Indian Affairs, and Territories) and those involved with only routine matters (for example, Claims, Invalid Pensions, and War Claims) were much more likely even before 1911 to have chairmen and ranking minority members appointed on the basis of seniority.

Table 2–2 summarizes the violation of seniority in the choosing of chairmen and ranking minority members in the House between 1881 and 1919. The data are presented separately for 1881 to 1911 and 1911 to 1919 to illustrate that an important change did in fact take

Table 2–2
The Violation of Seniority in Chairmanship and Ranking Minority
Member Appointments for Selected House Committees, 1881–1919.

	Percent of Appointments that Violated Seniority							
	Chairmen				Ranking Minority Members			
Type of	*1881–1911*		*1911–1919*		*1881–1911*		*1911–1919*	
Committee	%	*(N)*	%	*(N)*	%	*(N)*	%	*(N)*
Political	65	(17)	0	(4)	73	(15)	40	(5)
Major Policy	49	(37)	17	(6)	28	(37)	0	(14)
Minor Policy	25	(24)	40	(5)	10	(31)	14	(7)
Routine	37	(19)	33	(3)	18	(22)	0	(7)
All Committees	43	(97)	22	(18)	20	(105)	9	(33)

Source: Based on raw data contained in Michael Abram and Joseph Cooper, "The Rise of Seniority in the House of Representatives," Polity 1 (1968): 52–85.

place in 1911 (after the Speaker lost the appointment power) but that the change was gradual rather than immediate. This confirms the data presented earlier in Figures 2–6 and 2–7. Note that in both periods violations of seniority were much more frequent when a chairmanship was involved than when only the ranking minority position was involved.

Table 2–3 shows that before 1911 the violation of seniority was very similar in both parties. In the 1911–1919 period the differences between

Table 2–3
The Violation of Seniority in Selected Committee Leadership
Appointments by Democratic and Republican Parties in the
House of Representatives, 1881–1919.

	Percent of Appointments That Violated Seniority							
	Republicans				Democrats			
Type of	*1881–1911*		*1911–1919*		*1881–1911*		*1911–1919*	
Committee	%	*(N)*	%	*(N)*	%	*(N)*	%	*(N)*
Political	75	(20)	40	(5)	58	(12)	0	(4)
Major Policy	30	(50)	0	(14)	25	(24)	17	(6)
Minor Policy	12	(34)	14	(7)	24	(21)	40	(5)
Routine	27	(26)	0	(7)	27	(15)	33	(3)
All Committees	32	(130)	9	(33)	31	(72)	22	(18)

Source: See Table 2–2.

the parties may be attributed almost wholly to the fact that the Democrats were the majority party and the Republicans the minority. Thus the Democrats made all of the chairmanship appointments and, in a period of transition after the decision to limit the powers of the Speaker, had more at stake in filling chairmanships. But by 1921 both parties virtually rejected any criteria other than seniority for appointing committee chairmen and ranking members (and all other seats too). Bypassing seniority after 1921 came only in the most extraordinary circumstances—for instance, when the person under consideration supported a presidential candidate of the opposition party.

The rise of seniority as the single criterion for advancement toward committee chairmanships is explained principally by the emergence of a large number of career legislators. Because committee work is an important factor in the creation of a congressional reputation, career legislators could not tolerate arbitrariness in this area. Therefore, they supported—or perhaps demanded—an automatic role of advancement that would protect an orderly career development.

Development of Party and Leadership Structures

Pre-Modern Congress. In the pre-modern Congress there were few identifiable party leaders or institutions in either House. Members would occasionally rise to prominence in one House or the other, but this was usually a result of personal accomplishments, not of holding any position. The one institutional position that did have a number of influential incumbents was the speakership of the House (the only congressional office specified in the Constitution), but a large number of Speakers were figureheads *—either serving as pawns for others or purposely apolitical. There were no majority leaders or minority leaders or whips—positions that evolved well after the Civil War, either late in the nineteenth or early in the twentieth centuries. The few individuals who were widely recognized in their time as leaders came and went quickly, were often very junior at the time of their rise to eminence, and often voluntarily left Congress for other pursuits. Pre-Civil War Speakers such as Henry Clay and a host of individuals long since forgotten serve as examples. The speakership itself offers a good index in support of the point. Table 2–4 summarizes differences in years of service before becoming Speaker and in years of life after leaving the House for Speakers before and after 1875.

---

* See Mary P. Follett, *The Speaker of the House of Representatives* (New York: Longmans, Green & Co., 1896).

Table 2–4
The Aging of the Speakership.

	Years of service prior to assuming the speakership	Years of life after leaving the House
Pre-1875 Speaker (N = 27)	6.5	16.7
Post-1875 Speaker (N = 17 or 19) [a]	19.5	5.6

[a] The one living ex-Speaker and the incumbent are included for column 1 but excluded from column 2.

Source: *Adapted from data in Nelson W. Polsby, "Institutionalization in the U.S. House of Representatives," American Political Science Review 62 (1968): 148, 150–151.*

It is clear from the table that the average Speaker before 1875 had relatively few years of previous experience and tended to leave the speakership early in life (most lived about seventeen years after leaving the House). Since 1875, however, Speakers have had a great deal of legislative experience and have remained in the speakership until late in life, living an average of only six years after leaving the House.

"Careerism" in the speakership has grown. Table 2–5 presents information on the occupations of Speakers immediately following their

Table 2–5
Occupations of Speakers of the House of Representatives Immediately after Leaving the Speakership.

	Career Speakers [a]	"Higher" [b] Office	"Lesser" [c] Office	Private Business
1789–1875	2	8	16	1
1875–1972	12	4	0	1
Total	14	12	16	2

[a] These were individuals who died as Speaker, remained in the House but not as Speaker because their party lost control of the House, or simply retired because of old age or election defeat.

[b] This category includes the presidency (1), the vice-presidency (2), and the Senate (9).

[c] This category includes all other elective and appointive offices.

Source: *Adapted from Nelson W. Polsby, "The Institutionalization of the U.S. House of Representatives," pp. 150–51.*

speakerships. Before 1875 only two (Nathaniel P. Banks and William Pennington) out of twenty-seven Speakers finished their working lives either in the speakership, in the House (losing the speakership only because of a party turnover), or in retirement. And neither of them really made a career in the House. After 1875 71 percent of the Speakers have been "career" Speakers. Before 1875 sixteen of the twenty-seven Speakers (almost 60 percent) left the speakership for some office that today would be regarded as distinctly inferior: for example, a receiver-general of the Pennsylvania Land Office, a state treasurer of Virginia, and a minister to Russia were all men fresh from the speakership. After 1875 no Speaker left office to take a lesser office, three left for the Senate, one (John N. Garner) left to become vice-president, and the only other, Thomas B. Reed of Maine, was in most ways a career Speaker but left the speakership to practice law when he became disgusted with the policies (and personality) of President McKinley.

Parties in the pre-modern House and Senate were not well developed or influential entities. At least until the Jacksonian era party influence on voting patterns in both houses was far outweighed by regional influences and the influence of groups that lived and ate in the same Washington boardinghouses. James Young offers a persuasive description of congressional parties in the era before Jackson:

> If the party did not meet, neither did it attain, but momentarily, the status of an organized group in the congressional community. What degree of formal organization the party did achieve was only for the brief duration of its convocation as a nominating caucus [for President]. . . . In the periods intervening between caucuses the party had no officers, even of figurehead importance, for the guidance or management of legislative processes. Party members elected no leaders, designated no functionaries to speak on their behalf or to carry out any legislative task assignments. The party had no whips, no seniority leaders. There were no Committees on Committees, no Steering Committees, no Policy Committees: none of the organizational apparatus that marks the twentieth-century congressional parties as going enterprises.*

A similar lack of formal organization and consistent leadership persisted until late in the nineteenth century, although greater party unity in roll call voting emerged in the 1830s and 1840s and disintegrated only slowly in the 1850s as the slavery issue produced a national party realignment.†

---

* Young, *Washington Community:* 126–127.
† See Thomas B. Alexander, *Sectional Stress and Party Strength* (Nashville: Vanderbilt University Press, 1967); and Joel H. Silbey, *The Shrine of Party* (Pittsburgh: University of Pittsburgh Press, 1967).

Party membership was loose and unbinding even on the supposed members. There was little party cohesion even in voting for Speaker.* Party labels changed; before the Civil War the Whigs, National Republicans, Democratic Republicans, and Federalists came and went as major parties. In some Congresses there were no readily identifiable parties at all but merely pro-administration and anti-administration groups of members. In the period between 1830 and 1870, there were often sizeable numbers of minority (third-party) party members in Congress. But after the Civil War the two-party system crystallized nationally and congressionally.

Modern Congress. In the modern Congress, parties emerged as much more structured parts of the congressional apparatus, although their policy importance has fluctuated. In the period between the Civil War and the present both parties in both houses have identified formal leaders and established a variety of party committees. The sequence varied in the two houses, however. Since 1789 the Speaker of the House had been at least a nominal leader of the majority party; he became consistently important after 1869 (with the single major exception of 1919–1925, when internal politics in the House Republican party produced a Speaker explicitly elected because he agreed to be a figurehead). A formal minority leader emerged in the early 1880s and has been a consistently important figure in his party. In terms of status and function he has been parallel to the speaker for his own party.

In the period between 1897 and 1911 both parties in the House added additional central leadership positions as partisan conflict became more intense and the maintenance of party unity more difficult. Both the Speaker and the minority leader needed assistance. The majority leader became a formal and important leader in 1899 and has been generally influential in both parties since then. Both parties appointed their first whips in the last few years of the nineteenth century. Men in these positions were sporadically active until the 1930s. In the early 1930s both parties developed large whip organizations that have helped to make most chief whips more important figures. These organizations are heavily involved in the distribution and collection of information for the central leaders and in securing the most favorable attendance on the floor from a partisan standpoint. Their emergence in the 1930s was related to the vast increase in the congressional agenda as the New Deal responded to the Depression.

Both parties created important party committees after 1910–1911, when the speakership was substantially reduced in terms of potential

---

* See Appendix C of Follett, *The Speaker of the House of Representatives.*

influence. Chairmen of some of these committees have occasionally been prominent figures in the party.

In the Senate the development was reversed and the timing changed. The party committees and organizations emerged in both parties after the Civil War and became important in the decade between 1885 and 1895; no easily identifiable formal central leadership positions were created until the period between 1911 and 1915, although powerful leaders began to emerge after 1885.

The difference in the timing of Senate and House developments is largely explained by the development of the "career senator" several decades before the development of the "career representative." The professionalization of the Senate career occurred simultaneously with the centralization of power, whereas in the House the centralization of power preceded the professionalization of the representative career. Thus in the Senate there was a reluctance on the part of senators to trust single powerful leaders because their decisions could be so important (and so potentially harmful) to individual senators who wanted to stay in the Senate for the rest of their political lives. Seniority hardened at the time in the Senate in order to offer some protection to career senators. Party committees and organizations were thought to be less threatening than single leaders and they were first entrusted with leadership functions. Only after the Senate went through a period of leaderlessness in the early years of the twentieth century were senators willing to admit the need for strong single leaders.

In the House, power was centralized in the hands of the Speaker and minority leader before the career began to develop. When it did the members of the House demanded restrictions on the central leaders (symbolized by the revolt against Speaker Cannon in 1910) and seniority and party committees were established as protections for the career-oriented House members.

Table 2–6 summarizes the chronology of the two separate developmental histories.

Table 2–6
Party Development and Related Events in House and Senate

Event	House	Senate
Centralization of Power	1875–95	1885–95
Professionalization of Career	1890–1910	1875–95
Hardening of seniority as criterion for advancement on committees	1911–25	1885–95
Creation of central leadership positions	1897–1900	1911–15
Creation of party committees and organizations	1919–present	1885–95

The majority leader in the Senate emerged as a formal and readily identifiable party leader in both parties in the period between 1911 and 1915. The minority leader emerged at the same time. After some dominant personalities left the Senate in the first few years of the new century the Senate experienced a period during which arriving at decisions had become very difficult. It also had experienced an aggressive president in the person of Theodore Roosevelt. Both party leaders have remained influential in the affairs of their respective parties since then. The majority and minority whips were created in the same period to aid the floor leaders, but these individuals have not been major figures in their parties until the last several decades. From 1935 to 1944, in fact, the Republicans did not bother to fill the position because they were such a small minority in the Senate.

Important party committees—the equivalents of policy committees and committees on committees—developed in both parties during the 1870s and were the vehicles used to centralize power in both parties in the Senate in the 1880s and 1890s by men who did not bear formal leadership titles but who were highly influential and effective leaders.

Table 2–7 summarizes the establishment of various formal leadership positions and party committees on a continuing basis in both houses.

Table 2–7
The Establishment of Formal Party Leadership Positions and
Committees in Congress.

House [a]	Year of Creation on a Continuing Basis	
	Republicans	Democrats
Majority Leader	1899	1911
Minority Leader	1883	1889
Whip	1897	1900
Policy Committee [b]	1919	1933
Committee on Committees	1917	1911
Senate		
Floor Leader (Majority Leader and Minority Leader)	1913	1911
Whip	1915	1913
Policy Committee	1874	1879
Committee on Committees	1865	1877

[a] Positions in addition to the Speakership.

[b] The House Republican Policy Committee has been only sporadically important; the House Democratic Policy Committee (called Steering Committee) has never been important.

The activities of these leaders and committees in the modern House and Senate will be discussed in chapter 5.

By the beginning of the twentieth century, parties were an obvious, influential, and permanent feature of life in Congress. The development of strong parties in the electorate following the Civil War was reflected in Congress. When the national parties weakened again in the twentieth century the congressional parties also weakened although, given the vital procedural role of the leaders in providing order for a busy legislature, the pre-modern situation was not recreated.

Since the late nineteenth century members have been very clear about which party they belonged to and who the formal leaders of their parties were. Third parties have almost vanished. Speakers have been elected by a straight party vote. There were still some major centrifugal forces in both houses—particularly the orientation of members to serving constituency interests before party interests when the two were perceived to clash—but well-organized parties became firmly enough entrenched to counteract such forces at least some of the time.

Much of the debate over "reform" in Congress centers around the role of parties and party leadership. Parties clearly have the apparatus to centralize much of the policy-making in the Senate and particularly in the House; whether their leaders have the will or the opportunity to develop such centralization is always an open and important question.

*   *   *

The above description and analysis points to one conclusion: on all of the criteria discussed the modern Congress has become both professional and stable. The professionalism has allowed Congress to cope with its increasing workload and also to face the fact of a powerful executive branch in such a way as to keep a considerable amount of legislative influence. The stability has permitted the processing of the workload in reasonably good and timely order.

On the other hand, stability also has its costs. It may be deemed necessary by a group of career-oriented professionals—such as most senators and representatives—but it may also lead to seemingly permanent alliances on segments of public policy between the professionals in Congress and the professionals in the executive branch and in the interest groups. These alliances may result in good policy or bad policy, in programs that work or in programs that fail. But, in any event, such alliances are not likely to view dramatic changes in policy as necessary or useful. Such changes might threaten the existence of the alliances themselves and thus threaten the security of the members of those alliances, including the congressional members. Some would argue this is a wise way to make public policy—with any changes widely agreed on and only relatively minor in scope. Others would argue that such excessive stability and concern with preserving the status quo inhibits the government's ability to meet pressing national problems.

3

CONGRESSIONAL
DECISION-MAKING

A S THE MODERN CONGRESS MAKES DECISIONS IN THE MANY SUBSTANTIVE fields for which it is responsible, its members have to face three central facts that have shaped the character of the institution: (1) the fact that they are elected representatives, 2) the fact of an enormously powerful presidency, and 3) the fact of a vast professional bureaucracy. In the following sections the congressional response to this environment is outlined. More detailed attention is paid to the central processes—both formal and informal—by which Congress makes specific decisions. These processes include the inculcation of general norms, the giving and receiving of behavioral cues, and the formal rules and procedures of the House and Senate.

THE BROAD CONGRESSIONAL RESPONSE
TO INSTITUTIONAL ENVIRONMENT

All members of the House and Senate are elected from individual constituencies (with the relatively insignificant exception of a few senators who may hold short-term appointments from governors to fill vacant seats). Virtually all of them are genuinely concerned with the way they "represent" their constituents. Virtually all of them bear one of two party labels both in the electoral process and in Congress. These labels, however, are associated with a national party system that is weak and somewhat mythical and with congressional parties that are only sporadically cohesive and demanding. This combination of circumstances allows individual members a maximum of freedom as they make up their minds on substantive questions. They can easily rationalize whatever behavior they decide on in terms of representation of constituents despite the competing demands of the president, party leaders, committees, interest groups, or bureaucrats.

Given that most members prize the independence they derive from this situation there is a strong norm in Congress that legitimizes a member's policy stances and behavior as long as that member justifies them in the name of representation. At the same time, the norm does not demand rigorous attention to ferreting out "real" constituency opinion, so that members are free to provide their own definition of the interests and opinions that deserve attention. Members can maximize their freedom of action in Congress by playing off presumed constituency pressure against pressures brought by party leaders in Congress, the executive branch, or committees. If, for example, the president and party leaders actively advocate a gun control bill, a member opposed to the bill can claim in talking with a leader urging him to vote for it that he would like to but that constituency opinion prohibits a "yes" vote. The leader will neither check (because he has no way) nor rarely even challenge the member's assertion about the views of his constituents. This freedom is not granted members simply for its own sake; the main point of allowing members such latitude is to maximize their chances of re-election—a goal virtually all members have in common.

Congress must also confront a president endowed by the Constitution with enormous powers that have been expanded in practice through the aggressiveness of a number of specific presidents and the attentions of the media and the public. On selected issues the president can appeal directly to the electorate for support, thus pressuring Congress for a favorable response. John Kennedy made such an appeal on tax reform, Lyndon Johnson did the same on civil rights, and Richard Nixon took a similar route in promoting revenue sharing. The institutionalization of the presidency has also enhanced its potential for influence.

The existence of a powerful chief executive has stimulated the development of elaborate Congressional leadership structures and apparatus, the function of which is not only to centralize congressional response to presidential proposals but also, importantly, to mediate between the rank-and-file members (and sometimes the chairmen and senior members) and the president. The leaders are channels for information and presumed influence flowing both ways. If the members have a grievance or a strongly felt position the leaders are expected to so inform the president. If the president has a strongly held position the leaders (at least of his party) are expected to communicate that position to the members. There is a natural tension surrounding the positions of leadership: the president tends to view the leaders of his party as his lieutenants; members often prefer to think of the leaders as being responsible for defending congressional autonomy against the encroachments of the president and executive branch.

The professional bureaucracy that Congress must face is nominally under the control of the president but is, in practice, a set of independent forces. The presence of such a bureaucracy, which administers the programs Congress legislates, has contributed to the growth and entrenchment of a well-developed structure of relatively autonomous committees and subcommittees with fixed jurisdictions and fairly stable memberships. In addition, the presence of the bureaucracy helps determine the functions that the committees will perform: oversight (review of bureaucratic activities), authorization of new programs or renewals of existing programs, and appropriation of funds are all carried on with specific reference to parts of the bureaucracy. To facilitate oversight of existing programs and consideration of new legislation the subject matter division of labor among the committees roughly parallels that in the bureaucracy. Within the committees the workload is further divided among subcommittees whose jurisdictions often parallel the responsibilities of specific units in the bureaucracy. For example, in 1973–74 the House Foreign Affairs Committee had separate subcommittees on five different geographical regions that exactly paralleled the State Department's regional bureau structure. The Foreign Affairs Committee also had the Subcommittee on International Organizations and Movements which paralleled the State Department's Bureau of the International Organization Affairs. The Subcommittee on Foreign Economic Policy paralleled the Bureau of Economic and Business Affairs, the Special Subcommittee for Review of Foreign Aid Programs paralleled the office of the Inspector General of Foreign Assistance, and the Subcommittee on National Security Policy and Scientific Developments partially paralleled the Bureau of International Scientific and Technological Affairs.

The advantage of this consistent method of division of labor is that it encourages members to become knowledgeable and expert in particular issue areas and enables them to compete with the experience and expertise of the bureaucrats with whom they interact. The disadvantage of this same division of work, particularly when coupled with the fact that committee memberships are stable, is that it encourages the formation of cozy relationships between a small number of bureaucrats and legislators who come to see eye-to-eye on matters in their particular policy sphere. This results in policy that does not change much.

An additional effect of the large bureaucracy has been that Congress has turned to the use of professional staff in an effort to compete with the bureaucrats' generally superior command of information about programs. Individual members simply have too many responsibilities to delve deeply into all of them, and they need assistance to match the advantage that size alone gives the bureaucracy. Thus they have created a sizeable group of knowledgeable staff members who possess considerable technical competence in a variety of legislative fields. Many of these individuals become permanently tied to a committee regardless of personnel or even party turnover.

NORMS AND SOCIALIZATION

Norms are simply standards that prescribe acceptable and unacceptable behavior in an organization. They are "informal rules, frequently unspoken because they need not be spoken, which may govern conduct more effectively than any written rule. They prescribe 'how things are done around here.' " *

Norms do not appear in Congress by magic. Rather, they stem from institutional process and interaction. By the same token, they are not immutable. They change when personnel, times, and the issues confronting Congress change. The single most important source of change in norms is turnover in personnel.

New people are rarely socialized perfectly into an institution in the sense that they both understand and accept its norms totally. The greater the number of newcomers to an institution the more likely that the norms will change. Newcomers bring their own views to an institution. These views are the result of differing ideologies, ages, and societal norms acquired during childhood and young adulthood. New members may affect the views of more senior members toward congressional norms, particularly if the senior members sense a widespread feeling in support of some changed views.

A classic example of changing norms and the differences those changes make is provided by the Senate in the 1950s and 1960s. Observers of the Senate during the late 1940s and 1950s concluded that that body was in the grip of norms that produced an ideologically conservative bias in the decisions it made.† It was implied that these specific

---

* Barbara Hinckley, *Stability and Change in Congress* (New York: Harper and Row, 1971): 59.
† See William S. White, *Citadel* (New York: Harper and Brothers, 1956); and Donald R. Matthews, *U.S. Senators and Their World* (Chapel Hill: University of North Carolina Press, 1964).

norms—that junior members should act as apprentices, work hard mainly on legislative details, defer to the wisdom of senior members (who also happened to be the most conservative senators), and that all senators should approach the task of legislating in a sober spirit that would produce only minor changes from a status quo—were permanent features of Senate life.

Subsequent studies of the Senate, however, have pointed out that the norms of the Senate differed both before and after the particular period of the 1950s. The norms of that era were not fixed nor was the stance of the Senate.* In the 1960s and 1970s it became clear that junior members, often of an aggressively liberal persuasion, could also wield substantial legislative influence and produce important changes from the status quo that were not to the liking of the senior, conservative members. The norms changed to become less restrictive.

Predominant Norms in the House and Senate †

Four norms or clusters of norms dominate life in the House and Senate. The norms in the two chambers appear very similar although some differ in specific details between the two houses. The fact of similarity is hardly surprising considering the large number of ex-representatives in the Senate. For example, of the 100 senators in 1972, 40 had been members of the House.

Institutional Loyalty. Both houses have strong norms demanding the loyalty of the members to their respective institution. This means that members should not, by and large, make public criticisms of their fellow members or of the functioning of their institution, although considerable deviation from this norm is tolerated during election campaigns. Members should take the place of the House or Senate in the governmental scheme seriously and make this seriousness evident. For the most part members are expected to anticipate a career in the House or Senate, although many House members are eager to obtain Senate

---

* See Ralph K. Huitt, "The Outsider in the Senate: An Alternative Role," *American Political Science Review* 55 (1961): 566–575; Ripley, *Power in the Senate;* and Nelson W. Polsby, "Goodbye to the Inner Club," *Washington Monthly* (August 1969): 30–34.

† For the fullest discussion of Senate norms, see Matthews, *U.S. Senators and Their World,* chapter 5; and Matthews, "The Folkways of the United States Senate: Conformity to Group Norms and Legislative Effectiveness," *American Political Science Review* 53 (1959): 1064–1089. On the House see Richard F. Fenno, Jr., "The Internal Distribution of Influence: The House," in David B. Truman (ed.), *The Congress and America's Future* (Englewood Cliffs, N.J.: Prentice-Hall, 1973, 2nd ed.): 83–90. For another useful discussion of norms, see Hinckley, *Stability and Change in Congress:* 59–69.

seats. Members are expected to defend the institution against the encroachment of the president or the bureaucracy and are expected to defend the prerogatives of their own chamber against perceived imperialistic behavior of the other chamber.

Most of the few senators and representatives who have been disciplined by the House and Senate by removal or by loss of seniority or committee assignments were guilty mainly of bringing discredit to their chamber. In two of the most celebrated recent cases—the censure of Senator Joseph McCarthy in 1954 and the refusal to seat Representative Adam Clayton Powell in 1967—it seems clear that one of the prime offenses of both was that they brought the "good name" of the Senate and House, respectively, into public question. McCarthy was censured because of excesses connected with his chairmanship of the Permanent Investigations Subcommittee and his refusal to testify before the Senate Rules Committee in connection with accusations he and another Senator, William Benton of Connecticut, had made against each other. Powell was excluded from his House seat because of misuse of funds of the committee he chaired, refusal to pay a New York libel judgment, and noncooperation with House committees investigating his behavior.

In the last few years a number of senators and representatives have felt free to criticize the decline of congressional power. Included in this general criticism are specific allegations that outmoded procedures may help relegate Congress to a subordinate position. This criticism is tolerated because the motivation behind it is the desire to restore Congress to its "rightful" place in the governmental scheme—a place in which it cannot be dominated by the president and bureaucracy.

Seniority and Apprenticeship. The grip of seniority—both formal and informal—is strong in both houses. Yet it is not inflexible. In 1973 all four congressional parties talked about a variety of modifications for the seniority system for selecting committee chairmen and some modifications were adopted. For example, the House Democrats made it necessary for persons nominated for chairmanships by the Committee on Committees to receive a majority vote in the caucus. This created the potential for rejecting the most senior member of a committee as chairman. None of these changes were dramatic and none were likely to have any immediate tangible effect—but at least they signified a willingness to challenge the sanctity of seniority. It is still true—and is always likely to be true—that senators and representatives with more service will have more influence. But that truism does not mean that relatively junior members, even first-termers, have no influence.

Related to the grip of seniority is a norm of apprenticeship: the belief that junior members should serve for a period of time as apprentices before beginning to speak out and take an active role in legislative matters. This has meant that junior members should be restrained in speaking on the floor, offering bills, offering amendments, and, in general, becoming visible on legislative matters. This norm has also been applied to behavior on specific committees.

The general (non-committee specific) norm of apprenticeship seems to have weakened considerably in both House and Senate, and in most of the Senate committees and some of the House committees. Again, no doubt there is some truth (and probably some inevitability) in the proposition that the more experienced members are going to be more visible, verbal, and influential, both on the floor and in the various standing committees. But, in recent years, this truth has not necessarily meant that junior members are effectively excluded from the legislative process.

One study based on a large number of interviews and roundtable discussions with senators concluded:

> Virtually all senators can acquire substantial legislative influence. Those who do not have it usually have disqualified themselves by violating the Senate's code of acceptable conduct that is understood by most members. The code is not highly restrictive, and only repeated violations bring sanctions.

> The Senate is not composed of a few omnipotent and happy senior senators and a great many impotent and unhappy junior senators. Most senators are content with their lot. Most of them feel that they have a considerable amount of legislative potency, at least in selected fields.*

Several recent studies of the House have also shown the norm of apprenticeship to be weakening its hold on freshmen members. Herbert Asher has written that

> the need for a lengthy inactive apprenticeship no longer seems to be accepted; freshmen appear to be participating more frequently and earlier in their careers than the traditional description of the newcomer would lead one to expect. . . . The objective measures did suggest an improvement in the committee assignments given to freshmen.†

In both houses it remains true that, despite improvements in the committee assignments of junior members, some seniority is generally

---

* Ripley, *Power in the Senate:* 185.
† Herbert B. Asher, "The Changing Status of the Freshman Representative" (unpublished paper, 1972): 15. See also Asher, "The Learning of Legislative Norms," *American Political Science Review* 67 (1973): 499–513.

still necessary to get the best assignments. One study of committee as-signments in the House concluded, "The apprenticeship model is useful in understanding committee assignments despite the changing values of some of the variables in the assignment process." * Some committees re-tain a relatively strict apprenticeship system.

Specialization. In both the House and the Senate, members are ex-pected to specialize in one or a few legislative areas. The House norm is more restrictive because there are more members there than in the Senate and therefore each member has fewer committee and subcommit-tee assignments. Concomitant with this norm is an additional norm that legislative work should be taken seriously. Members of both houses are expected to pay serious attention to their legislative duties and to work hard. Again this norm is more fully developed in the House than in the Senate, where it is recognized that the pressures on the time of the average senator are such that he or she may have to spend a lot of time and energy on non-legislative matters. Many House members and some senators choose their specialties to coincide with important interests in their districts or states. This is not made mandatory by the norms, but is certainly approved behavior.

Reciprocity and Accommodation. The House and Senate process a vast number of bills each year. Each bill must go through a large num-ber of stages. It is imperative that senators and representatives help each other or very little would be accomplished. It is expected of all members that they will learn to be mutually helpful, to accommodate themselves to each other's needs, and to bargain in a way that always leaves room for compromise. This norm necessarily requires an extensive amount of mutual courtesy and deference, particularly on matters in which one in-dividual is reputed to be expert. This norm also tends to reduce extreme partisanship, which makes bargaining and accommodation more difficult.

In short, the normative mandates to senators and representatives in the 1970s can be summarized as follows:

1. Speak well of Congress and particularly of your own chamber. If you criticize, do it constructively and in a way designed to make clear that your goal is to strengthen the institution.

2. Be sure you have something to say before saying it, but do not let the fact of relatively junior status inhibit you from contributing to the legislative process.

3. Specialize in a few substantive areas and work hard in those areas.

---

* Charles S. Bullock III, "Apprenticeships and Committee Assignments in the House of Representatives," *Journal of Politics* 32 (1970): 720.

4. Respect your fellow members—both as individuals and as experts in specific substantive areas. Deal with them openly and courteously in ways that will lead to the maximum achievement of their goals and your own. Do not let party or ideological stances get in the way of making mutually agreeable and profitable bargains.

It should also be remembered that all of these norms are set in the context of the all-encompassing norm of taking representation seriously.

The Process of Transmitting Norms: The Socialization of Freshmen

Freshmen members of Congress seem to know the general norms of the House or Senate before they even arrive in Washington. One study observed that freshman representatives are conversant with congressional norms simply because these norms parallel the codes of behavior common to many institutions.*

This is not to argue, however, that freshmen have nothing to learn. They certainly need to learn how the system actually operates: what committees do what, which individuals have what kinds of influence, what specialization means in practice, and so on. This kind of information often fleshes out the bare bones of norms, and to acquire it, new freshmen observe and talk to such knowledgeable people as senior colleagues, staff members, and the press when they come to Washington.† Freshmen also spend a considerable amount of time with each other, sharing experiences, observations, and the information they have picked up. Likewise, they tend to hire at least some experienced staff members who are able to pass on relevant information to them.°

Freshmen members also begin to learn where to look for cues on how to vote on the floor. It has been found that in the House, they initially look to their state delegations; as the session wears on they broaden their search for cues to members of relevant committees.‡

The best evidence is that freshmen in both the House and Senate are now incorporated into the life of those two bodies very quickly. The new members come to Washington already aware of the norms of the chamber in which they will sit; they learn additional details quickly and soon

---

* Asher, "The Learning of Legislative Norms," 512.

† See Richard F. Fenno, Jr., "The Freshman Congressman: His View of the House," in Nelson W. Polsby (ed.), *Congressional Behavior* (New York: Random House, 1971): 125–135.

° On these two sources of information see Irwin N. Gertzog, "The Socialization of Freshmen Congressmen: Some Agents of Organizational Continuity" (paper prepared for delivery at the meeting of the American Political Science Association, September 1970).

‡ Herbert B. Asher, *Freshmen Representatives and the Learning of Voting Cues,* Sage Professional Paper in American Politics 04–003 (Beverly Hills: Sage, 1973).

are assimilated into the institution. Their voting does not distinguish them from others, nor do their committee assignments, except for scarce representation on the most prestigious committees.*

The Consequences of Observing or Not Observing Norms

A great deal of attention has been given to the impact of norms in the Senate. One view of the Senate is that it is dominated by a "Club" or "establishment", membership in which requires complete acquiescence to the principal norms—including seniority and apprenticeship. The Club is portrayed as conservative in ideology and dominated by southerners, who tend to be very senior and highly adroit at legislative maneuvering.†

The consequences for any individual senator of not adopting the norms of the Club are decreased legislative success and fewer career benefits. One study of committee assignments in the Senate between 1949 and 1964 gives empirical support to the proposition that senators who were non-conformists in terms of ideology and who often failed to support established rules and procedures received desirable committee assignments less frequently and later, if at all, in their Senate careers than the senators who did conform.°

Another study ‡ found that senators who spoke least on the floor and specialized the most highly (presumed to be norms highly favored by the Club members) were also the most "effective" in terms of the proportion of bills they introduced that were passed on the floor of the Senate. Although the measure of effectiveness used has limits, the general finding is still notable: those who conformed to the norm of specialization were the most successful.

A second view is that the Senate distributes influence unevenly, that some of the conservative tendencies identified by those who believe in the existence of a club are present, but that the Senate is also highly

* On voting see Theodore Urich, "The Voting Behavior of Freshmen Congressmen," *The Southwestern Social Science Quarterly* 39 (1959): 337–341; William Mishler, James Lee, and Alan Tharpe, "Determinants of Institutional Continuity: Freshmen Cue-taking in the U.S. House of Representatives" (unpublished paper); and J. Richard Emmert, "Freshmen Congressmen and the Apprenticeship Norms," *Capitol Studies* 2 (1973): 49–64. On assignments of freshmen to committees see Charles S. Bullock III, "Freshmen Committee Assignments and Re-Election in the United States House of Representatives," *American Political Science Review* 66 (1972): 996–1007.

† For discussion concerning the existence of the Club, see Matthews, *U.S. Senators and Their World;* White, *Citadel;* and Joseph S. Clark and other senators, *The Senate Establishment* (New York: Hill and Wang, 1963).

° Wayne R. Swanson, "Committee Assignments and the Non-Conformist Legislator: Democrats in the U.S. Senate," *Midwest Journal of Political Science* 13 (1969): 84–94.

‡ Matthews, *U.S. Senators and Their World:* 114–115.

tolerant of deviant behavior and does not really punish it with loss of influence. In a study of the behavior of Senator William Proxmire, who is a Wisconsin Democrat and an avowed "Outsider," Ralph Huitt concluded:

> What happens inside the Senate to the Outsider? Not much; . . . the Senate is not a body disposed to impose sanctions on any behavior but the most outrageous. . . . The Senate is of all official bodies . . . perhaps the most tolerant of individualistic, even eccentric, behavior.

The evidence is strong that the Senate accepts as legitimate a wide range of behavior. Its members advance without hindrance to the perquisites of seniority, and some of the most powerful committees have had rather odd chairmen. Relations among subgroups appear to be easy; an Outsider who fights with only a handful of friends on one issue may, because of personal expertness on the subject, be chosen by the leadership to lead the party on a crucial measure the next week.

If this analysis is correct, an assumption of role consensus in the Senate is incorrect; there is variability not only in the behavior of occupants of the senator position but in the expectations—the "ideal patterns"—of behavior to which members may conform. The Outsider therefore is not a deviant but an alternative role. It would be a mistake also to assume, without empirical justification, a bimodal distribution of acceptable behaviors—the Inner Club members and the Outsider.*

The Senate's capacity to tolerate deviant behavior is evident in another study that concluded that even "Bolting the party ticket in a presidential election is not usually punished in the Senate by loss of rank or membership on committees." †

A third view of the Senate is that although the Club may have been in existence in the 1940s and 1950s, by the mid-1960s it was pretty well gone.° Power and influence seemed to be well distributed—although not necessarily equally so—by the mid-1960s and has remained so. For example, when committee assignments were announced in 1973 every Democratic senator, even the freshmen, received the chairmanship of at least one subcommittee.

On balance, the evidence seems to be that at present the Senate is a legislative body that punishes no one for his or her behavior unless it is

---

* Ralph K. Huitt, "The Outsider in the Senate: An Alternative Role," *American Political Science Review* 55 (1961): 573.

† Ralph K. Huitt, "The Morse Committee Assignment Controversy: A Study in Senate Norms," *American Political Science Review* 51 (1957): 329.

° See Ripley, *Power in the Senate;* and Polsby, "Goodbye to the Inner Club."

so outrageous as to call into question the good name of the body. This is also true even within Senate committees. The third view outlined above has the most empirical support.

Less empirical work has been done on the observance or non-observance of norms in the House. In general, it seems reasonable to assert that in some committees divergence from the norms might result in at least some psychological pressure on wayward junior members. In the House as a whole, psychological pressure may also be applied to deviant cases. This is true of individuals who consistently oppose their party.*

It can also be argued that in both houses the basic norms—particularly specialization and reciprocity and accommodation (even if apprenticeship is waning)—give added support to the dominance of substantive decisions by the standing committees. This may not have a conservative effect in terms of substance in all cases but it has a conservative effect in the sense that it helps make centralized leadership very difficult except for short periods of time. Thus coordinated programs of legislation are less likely to emerge from a number of committees simultaneously in response to leadership requests. Scattered bills are reported on a sporadic basis but central direction of a range of measures is rare.

The Impact of the Norms on Congressional Behavior

Many of the operating norms of the House and Senate acknowledge the members' concern with representation and re-election, and allow them considerable freedom in balancing perceived constituency pressure against pressure from party leaders. The consequence of these norms is that the power of the party system in Congress to command and receive cooperation from party members in policy matters is limited. There are other factors contributing to a relatively weak and decentralized party system; none, however, is more critical than the recognition of each member's need to vote in accord with the presumed interests of his constituency.

Because many of the governing norms are oriented toward promoting a stable membership, this means that the norms operate against handling controversial (that is, potentially politically damaging to at least some incumbents) matters openly. If they are handled at all an effort is made to arrive at compromises that either defuse explosive issues or at least minimize the political costs of the detonation.

---

* See Randall B. Ripley, *Party Leaders in the House of Representatives* (Washington, D.C.: Brookings, 1967): 158–159.

CUES FOR INDIVIDUAL BEHAVIOR

Members of the House and Senate are called on to make a very large number of decisions each year. They must vote publicly several hundred times on the floor. They must vote many more times on the floor by voice vote or in other less visible ways. They must vote in committee and subcommittee. They must make a raft of other decisions in committee and subcommittee on which no formal vote is taken. They are basically asked to be familiar enough with everything the government does to make intelligent choices.

Obviously, no single individual can become even semi-expert in everything on the governmental agenda. Therefore, members seek shortcuts as they try to make up their minds. They seek cues for how to behave and how to vote on a great variety of policy matters. They want sources for those cues whose judgment they trust and who will lead them to "proper" decisions—that is, decisions that will help the senator or representative reach his own goals: whether they be re-election, ideological consistency, the "public good," personal status, or a combination of these goals.

Figure 3–1 portrays, in highly simplified fashion, the pressures (or cues) involved in the decision process by which an individual senator or representative makes up his mind on what position to take on any specific policy.

In this figure, pressures from outside Congress include those stemming from the public (mass opinion, the opinion of various specialized publics, and the opinion of voters as registered in their electoral decisions), interest groups, the various parts of the executive branch

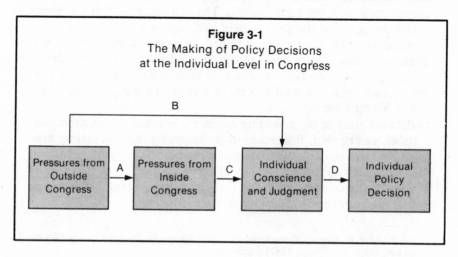

Figure 3-1
The Making of Policy Decisions
at the Individual Level in Congress

(the presidency and bureaucracy), and state and local officials. These pressures have an impact on the institutional clusters within Congress (relationship A in the figure) and also have an impact on the individual member directly (relationship B).

Pressures from inside Congress include those generated by party leaders, committee delegations, state delegations, informal clubs and groups, and staff members. These pressures impinge on the individual senator and representative (relationship C). It should also be noted that these sources of outside and inside pressure have a vast array of inter-relations among themselves.

Once the individual legislator has received the various outside and inside pressures he views them through the filters of his conscience and judgment and reaches his decision on his position (relationship D).

A number of studies have attempted to determine the cues to which members respond. Typically, these studies examine the relationship between potential cues and roll call voting on the floor. They do not prove causality in the sense that a member consciously searches for a cue, receives it, and behaves accordingly; instead they infer that patterns of behavior reflect patterns of cue-giving and cue-taking.* Such studies of the House have outnumbered those of the Senate, but it is reasonable to assume that senators and representatives share similar thought processes.† They are also confronted with approximately the same

---

* For discussions relying specifically on an analysis of decision-making, cue-giving, and cue-taking see Donald R. Matthews and James A. Stimson, "The Decision-Making Approach to the Study of Legislative Behavior: The Example of the U.S. House of Representatives," (paper prepared for delivery at the American Political Science Association meeting, September 1969); Matthews and Stimson, "Decision-Making by U.S. Representatives: A Preliminary Model," in S. Sidney Ulmer (ed.), *Political Decision-Making* (Cincinnati: Van Nostrand Reinhold, 1970); and Aage R. Clausen, *How Congressmen Decide* (New York: St. Martin's, 1973). Other relevant studies include Cleo H. Cherryholmes and Michael J. Shapiro, *Representatives and Roll Calls* (Indianapolis: Bobbs-Merrill, 1969); Aage R. Clausen and Richard B. Cheney, "A Comparative Analysis of Senate-House Voting on Economic and Welfare Policy: 1953–1964," *American Political Science Review* 64 (1970): 138–152; James W. Dyson and John W. Soule, "Congressional Committee Behavior on Roll Call Votes: The U.S. House of Representatives, 1955–64," *Midwest Journal of Political Science* 14 (1970): 626–647; Thomas A. Flinn and Harold L. Wolman, "Constituency and Roll Call Voting: The Case of Southern Democratic Congressmen," *Midwest Journal of Political Science* 10 (1966): 192–199; Lewis A. Froman, Jr., *Congressmen and Their Constituencies* (Chicago: Rand McNally, 1963); David R. Mayhew, *Party Loyalty Among Congressmen* (Cambridge: Harvard University Press, 1966); Leroy N. Rieselbach, "The Congressional Vote on Foreign Aid, 1939–1958," *American Political Science Review* 58 (1964): 372–388; W. Wayne Shannon, *Party, Constituency and Congressional Voting* (Baton Rouge: Louisiana State University Press, 1968); and David B. Truman, *The Congressional Party* (New York: Wiley, 1959).
† Clausen, *How Congressmen Decide.*

workload. There is evidence that "Senators are less subject to constituency pressures and more independent of partisan constraints," * because most states have more diverse constituencies than most House districts and because Senate party leaders are usually less demanding than House party leaders. But these differences are not so great as to suggest that completely different decision-making processes exist in the two houses.

A number of studies have tried to assess the impact of constituency on individual decision-making. The patterns that emerge from these studies are less than crystal clear. The safest conclusion seems to be that in terms of socio-economic characteristics, certain kinds of districts (for example, poorer urban districts) are more likely to elect Democrats, other kinds of districts (for example, relatively well-off suburban districts) are apt to elect Republicans, and that some ideological and programmatic differences are built into the basic difference between "Democratic districts" and "Republican districts." † The effect of typical constituency characteristics on the voting habits of congressmen is not at all clear.°

Occasionally constituency interests (as opposed to constituency characteristics) will clearly be a factor accounting for changed voting patterns. Southern Democratic attitudes about foreign trade, for example, changed markedly from free trade to protectionism as the southern states industrialized and brought in industries concerned with protection—particularly the textile industry. At a more general level, of course, it can be argued that constituency characteristics (for example, percent blue collar workers, percent Catholic) reflect constituency interests (higher minimum wages, urban renewal, aid to parochial schools).‡

A number of cue-givers inside the House have also been identified. Usually they have been studied in isolation—that is, the impact of state delegations as a separate topic, the impact of committee delegations as a separate topic, the impact of party leaders as a separate topic, and so on. But recently several studies have looked at these influences simultaneously in order to compare them. One of the most interesting studies was done by Matthews and Stimson on the period between 1957 and 1964.§ They investigated the relative potency of state party delegations, the president, party leaders, party majority,

---

* Clausen and Cheney, "A Comparative Analysis of Senate-House Voting," 151.
† See Froman, *Congressmen and Their Constituencies:* 95; and Shannon, *Party, Constituency, and Congressional Voting:* chapter 9.
° See Shannon, *Party, Constituency, and Congressional Voting:* 178.
‡ Flinn and Wolman, in "Constituency and Roll Call Voting," make this argument.
§ Matthews and Stimson, "Decision-Making by U.S. Representatives."

Table 3–1
Cue Sources for Congressmen, 1957–1964.

| | Average Cue Scores | | | |
| | Democrats | | Republicans | |
Cue Source	1957–60	1961–64	1957–60	1961–64
State Party Delegation	.42	.43	.37	.38
President	.04	.32	.13	−.16
Party Leaders	.27	.34	.26	.28
Party Majority	.34	.37	.35	.37
House Majority	.31	.39	.20	.23
Committee Chairmen	.19	.31	−.05	−.09
Ranking Members	−.05	−.01	.08	.19
Democratic Study Group	.29	.35	−.09	−.09

Source: Adapted from Donald R. Matthews and James A. Stimson, "Decision-Making by U.S. Representatives: A Preliminary Model," in S. Sidney Ulmer (ed.) Political Decision-Making (Cincinnati: Van Nostrand Reinhold, 1970): 31.

majority of the House, committee chairmen and ranking committee members, and the Democratic Study Group as cue-givers.

Matthews and Stimson summarize their principal findings succinctly:

> The consistently most important single cue-giver in both parties is the member's state party delegation. . . . Two additional collective cues—the party majority and the House majority—are also potent, especially among the Democrats (who were in the majority all eight years). The President as a *direct* cue-giver is seemingly less significant, although Kennedy and Johnson did considerably better among Democrats than Eisenhower did among Republicans as a direct source of cues.*

Table 3–1 summarizes the Matthews-Stimson findings. It should be noted that the possible variation in the figures reported ranges from .50 (perfect agreement between the average Democratic or Republican congressman and a cue-giver) to −.50 (perfect disagreement). Thus figures greater than .30 are quite high. The table reports two periods: 1957–1960, when a Republican was president, and 1961–1964, when a Democrat was president.

State party delegations were the most important cue-givers in both parties, although they were more important for the Democrats than for the Republicans. The president was an important positive cue-giver for the Democrats when he was a Democrat and a relatively important

---

* Ibid., 31–32.

negative cue-giver for the Republicans. The Republican president was only moderately important as a cue-giver for the Republicans and was about neutral as far as the Democrats were concerned.

Party leaders, particularly for the Democrats under a Democratic president, were important cue-givers. The party majority was consistently and about evenly important for members of both parties. The House majority was, predictably, a more important cue-giver for the members of the majority party throughout the period.

Committee chairmen were important as cue-givers for the members of their party and provided some negative cues for the members of the other party. Like the party leaders, they were most important when a member of their party was also president. This underscores the point that the party becomes most important when the president and congressional majority are of the same party.

Ranking minority members are not quite the mirror image of committee chairmen. They provided mildly negative cues for the members of the majority party, but were only moderately important in providing positive cues for the members of their own party. They were also more important in this regard when a Democrat was president, lending support to the image that the Kennedy-Johnson term was much more partisan in Congress than the second Eisenhower term.

The Democratic Study Group did about as well providing cues to the Democrats as the party leaders and party majority, largely because the views of the DSG were similar to the views of most Democrats except the southern conservatives. The DSG also provided mildly negative cues for the Republicans.

There is valid evidence that members of the House and Senate take stable positions over time on general classes of policy issues. Clausen has identified five predominant policy dimensions: government management, social welfare, international involvement, civil liberties, and agricultural assistance.* He found that in the 1950s and 1960s members' positions on these issues exhibited great stability. He also found that the influential factors on the five dimensions remained quite stable: party influence dominated the government management dimension, a combination of party and constituency influence dominated the social welfare and agricultural assistance dimensions, constituency influence dominated the civil liberties dimension, and a combination of constituency and presidential influence dominated the international involvement dimension. These findings suggest that the Matthews-Stimson analysis would be even more potent if it were done separately for the different policy dimensions. In any event, the work of Matthews-

---

* See Clausen, *How Congressmen Decide.*

Stimson and Clausen suggest that cue-giving and cue-taking is not a random matter in Congress but that patterns of regularity and predictability do exist. The varying sources of influence will be examined in detail in subsequent chapters.

THE SUBSTANTIVE IMPACT
OF RULES AND PROCEDURES

The general impact of the rules in both the House and the Senate is the same: the rules protect the power and prerogatives of the standing committees of the House and the Senate by making it very difficult for a bill that does not have committee approval to come to either floor and by making it very difficult to amend bills reported from committee (this is particularly true in the House).* Thus the centrifugal impact of stable standing committees is enhanced and perpetuated.

The rules create a situation in which there are multiple "veto points" through which every piece of legislation must pass. Every item that finally becomes a statute must usually be acted on affirmatively by two subcommittees (one in each house), two committees (one in each house), the House Rules Committee, the entire House, the entire Senate, a conference committee, and the president. At each step in the congressional process there are opportunities for delay and/or defeat. There are also opportunities for amendment that may render the final product unrecognizable to the original sponsors. Ultimately, a statute may also face review by federal courts on constitutional questions. Some statutes and portions of statutes are declared unconstitutional and, therefore, void.

The rules of the House and Senate underscore the necessity of bargaining if anything is to be accomplished in Congress. The rules are structured to prevent domination of the process by any one person or small group. An unavoidable result of the rules is that coalitions must be built for positive action to be taken.

The Sanctity of Committee Decisions

The House. Ordinarily no legislation can come to the floor of the House unless it has been considered and reported on by a standing committee. There are ways around the committee system but they are cumbersome and rarely successful. For example, a discharge petition to

---

* For excellent discussion of the impact of the rules see Lewis A. Froman, Jr., *The Congressional Process* (Boston: Little, Brown, 1967); and Leroy N. Reiselbach, *Congressional Politics* (New York: McGraw-Hill, 1973); chapter 5. The following discussion incorporates some of the insights of these works, but for information on details, these books should be consulted.

remove a bill from a committee and bring it to the floor requires the signatures of an absolute majority of the House (218 individuals). Between 1937 and 1960 only two bills became law by that route and only 10 percent of the discharge petitions that were filed (212) obtained the required signatures.

A procedure called suspension of the rules can also be used to circumvent House committees, but this procedure requires a two-thirds vote and thus controversial bills have a difficult time passing under it. The Rules Committee can also bring any bill to the floor regardless of committee action. It rarely does so, because its members properly perceive that they too have a stake in preserving the sanctity of the committee process.

When bills come to the House floor through the regular committee process they may have special safeguards to insure their prompt consideration and perhaps their passage. Appropriations and tax bills, for example, may come to the floor as privileged business at any time, although the Appropriations Committee and Ways and Means Committee may prefer to go through the Rules Committee in order to obtain conditions they deem favorable placed on the debate.

The rules of the House plus the actions of the Rules Committee make it difficult for committee bills to be amended. Debate on amendments is strictly limited. Amendments rejected in the Committee of the Whole (a procedure used to facilitate floor debate) cannot be made subject to a formal roll call after the Committee has risen; but amendments that are passed in the Committee of the Whole can be retested on a roll call. On most bills the minority party is, in effect, limited to one major effort to amend or kill the bill—the recommittal motion that immediately precedes the vote on final passage. Thus if the majority party members of the committee are in agreement with a large part of the majority party in the House the committee version of a bill is likely to pass unchanged.

The Senate. The Senate rules have a discharge provision that is very difficult to use. But there are other provisions, easier to use, that can bypass a committee stage and produce floor action. The Senate suspension of the rules procedure is easier to use than the House procedure and requires only a majority vote; it is used mainly for appropriations bills. Non-germane amendments (also called "riders") can also be added to Senate bills through the normal amending procedure in committee or on the floor, again unlike the House, which has a strict rule of germaneness. With some frequency, important measures reach the Senate floor as riders to trivial bills. Finally, bills passed in the House can be brought directly to the Senate floor without consideration by a Senate committee. Civil rights bills have sometimes been kept out of the hostile Judiciary Committee in this way.

All of these measures are unusual; but their greater availability suggests that the Senate is less dedicated to protecting the sanctity of the committee stage than is the House. Similarly, on the floor even those bills coming through the normal committee procedure (the vast majority of bills) are less protected against amendment than in the House. Senators have a number of committee assignments; in some ways this helps lead them to attach less negative symbolism to the amendment of committee products.

Multiple Vetoes

In both houses there are a number of points at which a few determined members (or perhaps even a single determined member) can stop or at least significantly delay the passage of a piece of legislation. Committee procedure and floor procedure are both very complex. As a bill travels between houses and from the committee to the floor in either house (particularly the House) there are other dangers. Table 3–2 summarizes the points at which delay or defeat may occur in the House

Table 3–2
Points at which Delay or Defeat May Occur in the House.

Delay	Defeat
Committee inaction in referring to a subcommittee	Committee inaction
Subcommittee inaction (prolonged hearings; refusal to report)	Negative vote in committee
	Subcommittee inaction
Committee inaction (prolonged hearings; refusal to report)	Negative vote in subcommittee
	Rules Committee inaction
Rules Committee inaction (refusal to schedule hearings; prolonged hearings; refusal to report)	Negative vote in Rules Committee
	Defeat of rule on the floor
Slowness in scheduling the bill	Motion to strike enacting clause
Floor action (demanding full requirements of the rules)	Motion to recommit
reading of the journal	Final passage
repeated quorum calls	
refusing unanimous consent to dispense with further proceedings under the call of the roll	
prolonging debate	
various points of order	

Source: Lewis A. Froman, Jr., The Congressional Process *(Little, Brown, 1967): 18.*

alone. The same table would apply to the Senate with the deletion of the references to the Rules Committee, some minor changes in the details of stalling action on the floor, and the significant addition of the filibuster as a weapon for either delay or defeat.

The Special Case of the Senate Filibuster

The right of senators to engage in "unlimited debate" unless two-thirds of their fellows vote to deny them that right is regarded as the oldest of the rules of Congress by the public and, in many ways, by senators themselves. The filibuster has been used by minorities that, knowing they were in the minority position, were nonetheless so intense in their opposition to some issue that they were willing to disrupt the normal proceedings of the Senate in an effort to prevent the action they found abhorrent.

Filibusters sometimes will go unchallenged and thus succeed. This is most true at the end of a session, particularly at the end of a Congress, when time simply has run out. Since 1917 the Senate has provided a cloture mechanism by which filibusters can be ended. From 1917 to 1949 and since 1959 this rule has provided for cloture by two-thirds of those senators present and voting. Between 1949 and 1959 the rule was interpreted to mean that two-thirds of the entire Senate had to vote for cloture before it could be imposed.

Between 1917 and 1972 sixty-three cloture votes were taken, of which only twelve were successful. But the pattern of usage has varied. In the early years in which the rule was in effect (1917–1929) the procedure was used ten times and was successful four times. None of these votes involved civil rights questions. However, in the next three decades (1930–1959) the procedure was used only twelve times; eight of those occasions involved civil rights questions, and none of the cloture motions were successful. It was during this period that the reputation of the filibuster as the absolutely unbeatable southern weapon against civil rights legislation was established. However, the 1960s and 1970s have seen a very different attitude toward cloture emerge, in terms of frequency, subject matter, and success. During the 1960s cloture was attempted twenty-three times, only eleven of which involved civil rights matters. (Four of the twenty-three motions were successful, and three of the four successes were on civil rights bills.) In the first three years of the 1970s alone eighteen additional cloture attempts were made and four were successful. Only three of the votes were on civil rights matters and one of them was successful (and the two that failed were on the same bill—so the filibuster did not succeed in its purpose of preventing the bill). In the first four months of 1974 six more votes were taken and three successfully imposed cloture. None of these votes involved civil rights. In short, in the 1970s senators have been relatively uninhibited about using the filibuster on a range of matters in addition to civil rights. Senators have also been more willing to impose cloture and limit the previously sacred right of unlimited debate.*

Filibusters are not only used to kill legislation. One study of the filibuster in fact tends to dismiss them as effective weapons even on civil rights in the 1940s and 1950s:

(1) Filibusters have been so unthreatening to various presidents' legislative programs that the actual postwar occupants of the White House either have remained aloof from attempts to curb this presumed impediment to their power or have even covertly helped defeat and distract such efforts. (2) With one possible exception, in no case between the war and 1966 was the filibuster responsible for the death of a civil rights bill supported by majorities in Congress.†

The threat of a filibuster is also used to gain concessions even if the filibuster itself is not invoked. Often, the proponents of a bill will agree to amendments that weaken the bill in order to build a two-thirds majority for cloture. Thus, filibusters may well achieve part of their aims even if cloture is voted. Sometimes just the threat of a filibuster may bring forth the desired concessions.°

Rules, Bargaining, and Coalition-Building

The rules in both houses are such that they enhance the influence of both the skilled parliamentarian and the skilled bargainer and coalition-builder. Three recent cases illustrate a number of points about the relationship between the rules of the House and Senate and the processes of bargaining and coalition-building.

---

* For additional details on the use of the filibuster and cloture see *Congressional Quarterly's Guide to the Congress of the United States* (Washington, D.C.: Congressional Quarterly, 1971): 84–85; and *Congressional Quarterly Weekly Report* (September 16, 1972): 2363.

† Raymond E. Wolfinger, "Filibusters: Majority Rule, Presidential Leadership, and Senate Norms," in Wolfinger (ed.), *Readings on Congress* (Englewood Cliffs, N.J.: Prentice-Hall, 1971): 305.

° See, for example, Howard E. Shuman, "Senate Rules and the Civil Rights Bill: A Case Study," *American Political Science Review* 51 (1957): 955–975.

Food Stamps, Tobacco, Wheat, and Cotton: House Action in 1964.*
In 1964 Congress passed a food stamp act making permanent a program that had begun under executive order a few years earlier. The passage of that bill in the House illustrates how the rules and procedures of the House are used to affect substantive outcomes.

In early February 1964 the House Agriculture Committee voted to table the administration's food stamp bill by a vote of nineteen to fourteen. The fourteen Republicans had been joined by five Democrats (four southerners and a Missourian) in favor of the tabling motion. All fourteen opposed to it were Democrats. The chairman of the Committee had favored the bill (and opposed the tabling motion). He was not personally enthusiastic about the food stamp bill but was willing to support the administration, which had worked very hard in December 1963 to help him get a cotton bill through the House.

Liberal Democrats both on and off the Agriculture Committee sought a lever to persuade the committee to reconsider the tabling motion. They chose to use a bill the committee had reported that would authorize public funds for the support of a study of tobacco and health. The Agriculture Chairman, Harold Cooley, from a large tobacco-growing district in North Carolina, had a special interest in having the tobacco bill passed. A moderate California Democrat on the Rules Committee, B.F. Sisk, determined that he would work to prevent the Rules Committee from granting a rule to the tobacco bill until the Agriculture Committee had reported out the food stamp bill favorably. He was successful in this maneuver, although he reserved a motion to reconsider the tobacco bill, implying that it could be saved given favorable Agriculture Committee action on the food stamp bill.

The Agriculture Committee responded as Cooley and Sisk hoped it would: three of the dissident Democrats changed their votes and the Committee reported the bill. (Sisk kept his end of the implied bargain and the tobacco bill came out of the Rules Committee soon thereafter.)

The involvement of the food stamp bill in trades involving the House rules did not end there, however. In early March the Senate had added a wheat program to the cotton program passed by the House the preceding December. The administration feared that the wheat-cotton bill would lose in the House because of solid Republican opposition and the defection of some liberal northern Democrats. Agriculture Department officials, Cooley, and the House Democratic leaders wanted to arrange a trade in which northern liberals would vote

---

* The discussion of the food stamp program is based on Randall B. Ripley, "Legislative Bargaining and the Food Stamp Act, 1964," in Frederic N. Cleaveland and Associates, *Congress and Urban Problems* (Washington, D.C.: Brookings, 1969): 279–310.

for wheat-cotton if southern conservatives (*very* interested in cotton) would vote for something important to the liberals. Until the House on 12 March defeated a pay raise bill for government employees (including members of Congress) there had been talk that the pay raise and wheat-cotton bills might be linked. However, votes by rural representatives had helped kill the pay raise, which increased the antagonism of the urban Democrats toward agriculture bills.

Gradually, during late March, it became clear that the hoped for trade would involve the food stamp bill and the wheat-cotton bill. No formal announcement was made of such a trade. Indeed, no formal meeting was held at which leaders of urban-liberal and rural-conservative blocs agreed on it. Instead, as is typical of the implicit bargaining that takes place in Congress, a favorable psychological climate developed. The more the individual members and the press talked about a specific trade of southern rural votes on food stamps for northern urban votes on wheat-cotton, the more firmly the exchange became implanted in the minds of the members. Individual lobbying efforts by the Agriculture Department and the House leaders reinforced this attitude.

The Rules Committee granted rules to both bills and the House leaders scheduled them back-to-back in early April. Liberals insisted that the food stamp bill go first, as they were mistrustful of their southern colleagues.

When debate ended on the food stamp bill the Republicans used a familiar delaying tactic: a Republican demanded an engrossed copy of the bill (that is, a bill printed with all amendments) before the final vote could be taken. The Democrats had anticipated this ploy and had alerted the printer ahead of time so that he could accomplish the task in a few hours. In the interim the Speaker of the House let debate on the rule for the wheat-cotton bill begin. Within a few minutes liberal Democrats realized that this might mean that the final vote on wheat-cotton would come before the final vote on food stamps. They protested to the Speaker and he, employing a power that had been temporarily granted to him earlier that day for an entirely different purpose (paying respects to the remains of General Douglas MacArthur in the rotunda of the Capitol), declared a recess so that the "proper" ordering of the bills could be re-established. When the House resumed its deliberations both bills passed, adjournment coming near one o'clock the next morning.

In this case the liberal proponents of food stamp legislation used the rules to cement an ad hoc coalition that allowed their position to prevail. They skillfully used the existence of the Rules Committee and the procedures under which the House votes on the floor to give themselves every chance of success. If the leaders of this group had not been thoroughly familiar with House rules and procedures they might have let success slip away from them.

The Senate and Legislative Reapportionment, 1964–1966.* Shortly after the Supreme Court declared in 1964 that both houses of state legislatures had to be reapportioned on a one-man, one-vote basis, Senator Everett Dirksen, Illinois Republican and the Senate minority leader, introduced a constitutional amendment that would remove federal court jurisdiction over legislative reapportionment cases. Constitutional amendments are time-consuming and require two-thirds majority votes; therefore, Dirksen also introduced a bill that would provide a two-year stay of federal court decrees involving reapportionment. The subsequent debate illustrates how delays possible under Senate rules can be used to defeat seemingly popular initiatives. This case is particularly interesting because "liberals" used the delaying tactics and "conservatives" were eager for action.

Dirksen got approval for the bill from the Judiciary Committee but then offered it on the floor as a rider to the foreign aid bill. A liberal coalition announced its intention to filibuster, and the filibuster began. Dirksen advocated cloture but this move failed. Then another senior Republican moved to table the rider. He anticipated—correctly—that the Senate would defeat his motion. This would show that a majority of the senators favored the bill but were being frustrated by the filibusterers. It would also presumably force Majority Leader Mansfield to find a way out of the impasse. This Mansfield did by offering a sense of Congress resolution (not literally a law but simply a formal statement of opinion passed by a majority) that was not binding on federal courts and was inapplicable to the Supreme Court but which counseled moderation in application of the basic decision. Dirksen found this language unacceptable but the liberals picked up enough moderate support to pass it (effectively, it had no impact on the courts) and win the battle in 1964.

In 1965 Dirksen resumed his drive for a constitutional amendment. The liberals' first tactic was to prolong discussion of the proposal (and several variants that appeared throughout 1965 and 1966) in the subcommittee of the Judiciary Committee handling the bill. Then in the full committee the liberals were able to gain a tie, which prevented the bill from being reported out favorably. Dirksen succeeded in bringing the amendment to the floor by substituting it for a joint resolution

---

* The following account is based on Edward Keynes, "The Senate Rules and the Dirksen Amendment: A Study in Legislative Strategy and Tactics," in Lawrence K. Pettit and Edward Keynes (eds.), *The Legislative Process in the U.S. Senate* (Chicago: Rand McNally, 1969): 107–145.

proclaiming National American Legion Baseball Week on the floor. This is a rarely used procedure in the Senate but it got the Dirksen amendment to the floor in 1965. Dirksen had a majority of the Senate in support of his proposal but did not have the necessary two-thirds. Thus the Senate defeated the amendment fifty-seven to thirty-nine.

Dirksen submitted a watered-down version of his amendment to the Judiciary Committee. In a trade with the president, Dirksen allowed an immigration bill important to the president to be reported out by the Judiciary Committee (of which Dirksen was a member); in exchange, one anti-Dirksen Democrat on the committee changed his vote so that the Dirksen amendment could be reported out by the committee. This new version also failed to get the needed two-thirds vote on the floor in 1966 (the vote was fifty-five to thirty-eight).

Keynes' conclusions about the whole process are instructive:

> In the two-year struggle over state legislative reapportionment, the strategic needs of the two coalitions determined the selection of relevant and appropriate rules of procedure. While the members of the Dirksen coalition were confronted with the problem of promoting congressional action before too many state legislatures were reapportioned under court order, the liberals attempted to delay action and ultimately defeat any legislation designed to undermine the Reynolds decision.

> Both sides employed the rules to affect the timing of decisions. The liberals delayed action in the 88th Congress by selectively filibustering H.R. 11380 (as amended) until the closing days of the session. In the 89th Congress they structured events in the Senate Judiciary Committee to delay floor action until the beginning of August 1965. Senator Dirksen also employed the rules in the 89th Congress to circumvent the Judiciary Committee, thereby expediting floor action on his constitutional amendment (S.J. Res. 66, as amended). The very timing of the decision, as both sides realized, was important in determining the final outcome of the struggle.

> The rules were also employed as tools in the legislative process to bargain over substantive changes in the proposed legislation. Senator Dirksen offered a series of substantive concessions or 'sweeteners' to attract additional support for his measure. By bargaining down an initially untenable position Dirksen hoped to expand the base of his Senate coalition. The liberals, however, met each concession with still further demands for changes in the proposed resolutions. The liberals used the rules to slow down the momentum of the legislative process in the Senate and to bargain for substantive changes in the Dirksen legislation.*

---

* Keynes, "The Senate Rules and the Dirksen Amendment," 139.

The 1973 Farm Bill. In 1973 Congress passed a comprehensive farm bill that included sections on feed grains, wheat, cotton, dairy products, and food stamps. It was a very complex bill that engendered a great deal of controversy and debate. Various disputes erupted in various locations: in the Agriculture Committees of the House and Senate, on the Senate floor, in conference, between the administration and various members of Congress, between interest group representatives and members of Congress, and, above all, on the floor of the House. These disputes illustrate how the rules allow compromise to be worked out on the floor. They also illustrate that when final compromise cannot be reached at any one stage the matter under consideration can usually be shunted on to a succeeding stage (in this case, the conference committee) with the hope that the elusive winning bargain can be struck there.

When the bill first came to the House floor on 10 July 1973 it was already in tenuous shape. Its ultimate success depended on ratification by the House of an agreement reached by the senior members of the Agriculture Committee and the administration whereby the committee members agreed to remove a provision that would have increased price support payments as production costs increased (a provision opposed by the administration as too expensive and inflationary) in exchange for administration support of other key provisions including, critically, those on cotton supports. On July 10 and 11, however, the roof fell in on the committee, particularly the senior southern Democrats most solicitous of cotton interests. First, the House refused to remove the escalator clause for price support payments. Then the House itself turned on cotton interests and limited the amount of subsidy that could be paid to any individual farmer to $20,000 (many large cotton growers receive a great deal more); it also deleted a $10 million subsidy to a private organization engaged in research and promotional work for cotton. On July 12 the chairman of the Agriculture Committee, W. R. Poage of Texas, used the rules of the House to give himself some more time to put a winning combination together again. He moved to postpone consideration of the bill until further notice and the House agreed.

Four days later, on July 16, Poage was ready to try again. In the interim a presumably winning bargain had been struck between cotton interests and organized labor. Labor spokesmen agreed to support an amendment eliminating all specific references to cotton in the bill (this would effectively eliminate the ceiling provision on subsidy amounts) if cotton interests would agree to oppose an amendment to the bill that would prevent the families of individuals on strike from using food stamps. Presumably, conservative members from cotton districts would support labor's position on the food stamp amendment in return for the support of liberal members from heavily unionized districts in the north for cotton's position on subsidy ceilings. But only some of the southerners voted with the labor bloc when three separate votes were taken on the question of stamps for strikers, even though a majority of the northern Democrats had gone along with an earlier successful motion to strike all references to cotton from the bill. The conservative position, with a majority of southerners supporting it, triumphed. Thus when the cotton questions again came up the northerners defected and the anti-cotton provisions were reinserted in the bill. Now the bill was satisfactory to neither the northern pro-labor Democrats nor to the pro-cotton southerners. The rules had permitted an incredible chain of amendments and amendments to amendments as the various interests sought to negotiate their varied interests on the House floor itself. But the bargain simply did not hold.

However, the rules, in effect, permitted one more appeal—to the conference committee. With neither of the major Democratic blocs happy but with a large number of members still having considerable interest in other provisions of the bill (food for peace, the other provisions for food stamps, and the other crops) the leadership on the bill frankly appealed to the House to pass the bill even in its unsatisfactory form so that more quiet and private negotiation could take place in the conference committee. The hope was that the combination of senior senators and representatives on that committee could quietly satisfy all of the major interests and thus insure the ultimate adoption of the conference report. And, in fact, the conference committee did succeed and deleted or modified the provisions offensive to organized labor and the cotton interests.

Thus, in a single case, the rules of the House were used first to stall when time was needed for working out an agreement between interests, second to allow elaborate extensive amendment designed to implement the agreement, and third to send the bill to conference for a second chance at satisfying all major interests when the agreement could not be successfully implemented on the House floor.

* * *

This chapter has outlined the setting in which both Congress as an institution and senators and representatives as individuals operate. In general, a number of regularities in congressional behavior, both individual and collective, are visible. These regularities have been explained primarily in terms of major environmental features—the electoral and representational system, the nature of the executive branch, and the nature of the workload. These features impinge on individual members directly and are also transmitted through the norms of behavior in the two houses, the cue-taking patterns used by the members, and the nature and impact of the rules and procedures of both houses.

The norm of specialization is a reaction to the existence of a specialized bureaucracy and a large and demanding workload. It also serves to promote narrow constituency interests. The norm of reciprocity and accommodation also facilitates the representation of those interests as well as making feasible the processing of an extensive agenda.

Among the cue-givers that have the most impact on patterns of congressional decisions, the constituency (including state delegations) and the president stand out, in addition to political parties and party leaders in the House and Senate. This fact highlights both the importance of the constituencies and president in the congressional environment and the complex role of the congressional parties as entities that in some ways serve the interests of the constituencies and president but in other ways are the main potential rallying points for a genuinely *congressional* point of view on policy.

The rules also afford members the opportunity to respond to perceived constituency interests (as, for example, with filibusters on civil rights bills) if they so desire. At the same time, skillful parliamentarians can also maximize their responsiveness to the president or to some party position on policy. These activities are allowed by the rules, even though in general the rules also promote the relatively orderly disposition of the large workload. At times, however, orderliness takes second place to serving constituency, president, or party.

PART II

The Internal
Environment
for
Congressional
Policy-Making

4

COMMITTEES

IN MID-NOVEMBER 1973 THE SENATE AND HOUSE UNANIMOUSLY passed S. 2408, a bill authorizing almost $2.8 billion in military construction for fiscal year 1974 (the period between 1 July 1973 and 30 June 1974). The passage of this bill through the legislative process was unspectacular and routine; it went virtually unnoticed except by those directly involved in the process. The brief and undramatic story of this bill illustrates a number of general points about the congressional impact on public policy: that even legislation involving a great deal of money (and $2.8 billion is still a sizeable sum despite rapid inflation) does not necessarily attract wide attention; that Congress often passes legislation for a specific time period after that time period has already begun (the bill was signed by the president over four months after the fiscal year had begun and the bill did not actually supply money, it only authorized subsequent appropriations); that Congress is generally responsive to executive branch requests but also makes some substantial alterations, even in the area of national defense; that foreign policy and domestic policy are intertwined; that there is poor coordination between related issues; and, above all, that the standing committees of Congress effectively make most of the substantive desions for the entire body.

In early 1973 when the president's budget was submitted it included a request for an authorization of $2,992,513,000 for military construction for fiscal 1974. The Senate Armed Services Committee acted on this request first. After holding hearings the committee issued a unanimous report in September that cut about $150 million from the Pentagon's request. The cuts were scattered and had no major importance in substantive terms. The main action of interest in the committee was the provision of almost $120 million to begin construction of a Trident submarine base—even though the funds for research and development of the submarine had not yet been approved and had been virtually eliminated by specific congressional action the year before.

Senate floor action produced no debate on the basic package of over $2.8 billion recommended by the committee. Instead, some senators took the occasion to grumble about the shutdown of bases (always a sore point) and, by voice vote, the Senate added an amendment providing for an additional $213,000 for housing construction at an air base in Montana—an amendment offered by Senator Mansfield of Montana, who also happened to be the majority leader of the Senate. But on anything major the senators were simply willing to accept uncritically the work of their Armed Services Committee.

The House Armed Services Committee also held hearings and unanimously recommended a bill authorizing a little over $2.7 billion—a figure about $120 million below the Senate figure and an 11.4 percent cut from the Pentagon request. The bill contained the full amount for the Trident base. The House passed the bill without amendment and virtually without debate by a roll call vote 359 to 28.

The few differences between the two bills were quickly and easily resolved in the conference committee and final agreement came unanimously and without debate. As almost always, the Congress of the United States had made a major commitment of the nation's resources primarily on the unquestioned recommendation of that tiny fraction of its membership sitting on the two committees with jurisdiction in the area.

Virtually since its beginning, Congress has conducted its business through committees. The modern Congress is characterized by a stable system of standing committees with fixed jurisdictions and relatively unchanging memberships. This committee structure is at the heart of all congressional activities; it embodies the principal congressional response to the subject specialists in the bureaucracy and to its own heavy workload. Without resorting to this labor-saving device, a body of 535 members would be incapable of processing the extensive amount of legislation necessary to govern this nation. And yet the very device that permits the legislature to legislate contains the potential for dilution of congressional impact: individual committees and subcommittees can become highly responsive principally to selected interests. When allowed to operate with virtual autonomy, the committee structure becomes a fragmenting force—the numerous specialized clusters of individuals each proceed on their separate courses never united by any common vision of national policy goals. However, the presence of party leaders, and the types of interaction that must occur between the leaders and the committees help curb the fragmenting tendency of committees. When working in accord with the party leaders, the committee system offers Congress its principal opportunity to shape national policy in detail.

An Overview of the Present Committee System

There are several different kinds of committees in Congress. By far the most important are the *standing committees* and their *subcommittees*. These are committees that exist from Congress to Congress, with stable memberships and jurisdictions. The entire range of legislation that Congress considers is parceled out to the standing committees. At present there are twenty-one standing committees in the House and seventeen in the Senate. The jurisdictions are relatively well denoted by the names of the committees. In general, the two houses have parallel committee structures, although they use slightly different titles for some committees (for example, Ways and Means in the House and Finance in the Senate have roughly the same jurisdiction —basically both deal with taxes; Education and Labor in the House and Labor and Public Welfare in the Senate have about the same jurisdictions). The House has four committees that the Senate does not have: Internal Security (these matters are handled by the Judiciary Committee in the Senate when they are handled at all), Merchant Marine and Fisheries (these matters are handled by the Commerce Committee in the Senate), Rules (this is a committee unique to the House because of its rules of procedure), and Standards and Conduct (this is a select committee in the Senate). Table 4–1 lists the committees of the House and Senate along with the size of their memberships and the number of subcommittees each has.

There is a wide range in size, and House committees are generally larger than Senate committees. There is also a wide range in the number of subcommittees established by any given committee. Some have none and conduct all of their business in full committee; others have many and conduct virtually all of their business through them.

Table 4-1
Standing Committees of Congress, 1972.

Committee in House of Representatives	Number of Members	Number of Subcommittees	Parallel Committee in Senate	Number of Members	Number of Subcommittees
Agriculture	36	10	Agriculture and Forestry	14	6
Appropriations	55	13	Appropriations	24	13
Armed Services	41	6	Armed Services	16	14
Banking and Currency	37	7	Banking, Housing, and Urban Affairs	15	6
District of Columbia	25	4	District of Columbia	7	3
Education and Labor	38	7	Labor and Public Welfare	17	15
Foreign Affairs	38	10	Foreign Relations	16	9
Government Operations	39	7	Government Operations	18	4
House Administration	25	7	Rules and Administration	9	7
Interior and Insular Affairs	38	7	Interior and Insular Affairs	16	7
Internal Security	9	0	—	—	—
Interstate and Foreign Commerce	43	5	Commerce	18	10
Judiciary	36	5	Judiciary	16	15
Merchant Marine and Fisheries	37	6	—	—	—
Post Office and Civil Service	26	7	Post Office and Civil Service	9	3
Public Works	37	7	Public Works	16	5
Rules	15	0	—	—	—
Science and Astronautics	30	6	Aeronautical and Space Sciences	11	—
Standards of Official Conduct	12	0	—	—	0
Veterans' Affairs	26	5	Veterans' Affairs	9	4
Ways and Means	25	0	Finance	16	0

Source: Compiled from data in *Congressional Directory*, 1972.

Table 4–2
Select and Special Committees in Congress, 1972.

Name of Committee	Number of Members
House of Representatives	
Committee on the House Restaurant	5
House Recording Studio	3
Select Committee on Crime	11
Select Committee on the House Beauty Shop	3
Select Committee to Regulate Parking	3
Select Committee on Small Business	19
Senate	
Select Committee on Equal Educational Opportunity	15
Select Committee on Nutrition and Human Needs	15
Select Committee on Small Business	17
Select Committee on Standards and Conduct	6

Source: Compiled from data in Congressional Directory, 1972.

Both houses make some use of *special* and *select* committees. Table 4–2 lists these committees for 1972 and indicates their size. The importance of these committees varies. The two Select Committees on Small Business have had considerable importance.* So have the Senate Select Committee on Nutrition and Human Needs and the Senate Special Committee on Aging. At the other end of the spectrum, the House Select Committee on the House Beauty Shop probably has not handled matters vital to the welfare of the republic.

Congress has also established some *joint* committees made up of equal numbers of senators and representatives. In 1972 nine such committees existed. Table 4–3 lists them and their size. Three of these committees are particularly important. The Joint Committee on Atomic Energy virtually runs the atomic energy program of the nation and is unusual among joint committees in that it has authority to report legislation to the House and Senate floors.† The Joint Committee on Internal Revenue Taxation is important mainly for the work of its staff in the tax field.° The Joint Economic Committee produces a series

* Dale Vinyard, "Congressional Committees on Small Business," *Midwest Journal of Political Science* 10 (1966): 364–377.
† Harold P. Green, "The Joint Committee on Atomic Energy: A Model for Legislative Reform?" in Ronald C. Moe (ed.), *Congress and the President* (New York: Goodyear, 1971).
° See John F. Manley, "Congressional Staff and Public Policy-Making: The Joint Committee on Internal Revenue Taxation," *Journal of Politics* 30 (1968): 1046–1067.

Table 4-3
Joint Committees of Congress, 1972.

Name of Committee	Number of Members
Joint Committee on Atomic Energy	18
Joint Committee on Congressional Operations	10
Joint Committee on Defense Production	10
Joint Committee on Internal Revenue Taxation	10
Joint Committee on the Library	10
Joint Committee on Navajo-Hopi Indian Administration	6
Joint Committee on Printing	6
Joint Committee on Reduction of Federal Expenditures	12
Joint Economic Committee	20

Source: Compiled from data in Congressional Directory, 1972.

of reports and holds hearings that receive considerable publicity and help shape thinking about economic policy.

Congress uses *conference* committees to resolve differences between the House and Senate versions of bills. These committees are appointed only for the duration of the discussion of a single bill; they disband once their report has been accepted by both houses and the bill is forwarded to the president for his signature. The same members may serve on a large number of conference committees in any given session. Typically, senior members are assigned to many more conference committees than junior members.

The ratio of Republicans to Democrats on most committees is determined by approximating the ratio of Republicans to Democrats in the whole House or Senate. There are a few committees in the House with fixed ratios: two to one for the majority party on the Rules Committee and three to two for the majority party on Ways and Means (this ratio was changed to about two to one during 1965–66 and again in 1975–76, when the Democratic majority in the House was about two to one).

There are pressures to expand the size of the most sought after committees in order to increase the number of choice seats open. During the period 1947 to 1972 there was an increase in total number of seats on all standing committees in the Senate from 203 to 247. The increase for all standing committees in the House in this period was from 484 to 668. Some of this increase stemmed from the creation of two new standing committees in each house during the period, but most reflected the increasing size of existing standing committees. The largest increases in the House tended to come in the most sought after

Table 4–4
Growth of Committee Size, 1947–1972.

	Number of Members		Net Change
	1947	*1972*	
House Committees			
Agriculture	27	36	9
Appropriations	43	55	12
Armed Services	33	41	8
Banking and Currency	27	37	10
District of Columbia	25	25	0
Education and Labor	25	38	13
Foreign Affairs	25	38	13
Government Operations	25	39	14
House Administration	25	25	0
Interior and Insular Affairs	25	38	13
Internal Security	9	9	0
Interstate and Foreign Commerce	27	43	16
Judiciary	27	36	9
Merchant Marine and Fisheries	25	37	12
Post Office and Civil Service	25	26	1
Public Works	27	37	10
Rules	12	15	3
Veterans' Affairs	27	26	–1
Ways and Means	25	25	0
Senate Committees			
Agriculture and Forestry	13	14	1
Appropriations	21	24	3
Armed Services	13	16	3
Banking, Housing, and Urban Affairs	13	15	2
Commerce	13	18	5
District of Columbia	13	7	–6
Finance	13	16	3
Foreign Relations	13	16	3
Government Operations	13	18	5
Interior and Insular Affairs	13	16	3
Judiciary	13	16	3
Labor and Public Welfare	13	17	4
Post Office and Civil Service	13	9	–4
Public Works	13	16	3
Rules and Administration	13	9	–4

Source: Congressional Directory.

Note that some committees had different names in 1947. Committees created after 1947 are not included in this table.

committees. In the Senate the most attractive committees expanded and the least attractive and relatively unimportant shrank. Table 4–4 summarizes the growth of committee size from 1947 to 1972. As this table shows, nearly all of the standing committees have grown. Only five committees in the House and three in the Senate either shrank or did not change size.

COMMITTEE ASSIGNMENTS

Each of the four parties in Congress (House Democrats, House Republicans, Senate Democrats, and Senate Republicans) uses slightly different methods for assigning members to vacancies in standing committees.* The House Democrats used the Democratic members of the Ways and Means Committee to recommend assignments to the Democratic caucus through 1974. Beginning in 1975, this recommending power was transferred to the Steering and Policy Committee. The caucus possesses the final authority to accept or reject the recommendations. Complete acceptance is usually routine.

The House Republicans have a special committee on committees comprised of a member from every state having at least one Republican. The actual work of making assignments, however, is done by an executive committee that always includes representatives of the states with the largest Republican delegations (New York, California, Ohio, Pennsylvania, Michigan, and Illinois). Since voting is on the basis of the number of Republicans from a state, those states with the most Republicans dominate the process.

The Senate Democrats have a steering committee appointed by the floor leader that makes the Democratic appointments. The steering committee is comprised of the senior members of the party (many of them committee chairmen); once on the committee they are automatically reappointed. The decisions of this committee are limited by the unwritten rule that all Democrats should have one choice assignment before any Democrat is given two (this is called the "Johnson rule" because it was first implemented in the early 1950s when Lyndon Johnson was the Democratic floor leader).

The Senate Republicans have a committee on committees that makes initial assignments on the basis of seniority. They are limited, however,

---

* Still the best treatment of committee assignments in the House is Nicholas A. Masters, "Committee Assignments in the House of Representatives," *American Political Science Review* 55 (1961): 345–357. See also "Politics of House Committees: The Path to Power," in *Congressional Quarterly Weekly Report* (February 10, 1973): 279–283.

by a rule adopted by the Republicans in 1965 that no Republican can hold seats on more than one of the four most desired committees (Appropriations, Armed Services, Finance, and Foreign Relations) before every Republican senator at least has a chance to refuse such a seat.

Many criteria are used in making initial assignments to committees. These include seniority, region, ideology, preferences of the individual members, and—at least in some cases—religion and race. In general, all of the parties use the same mix of criteria. Additional factors that affect committee assignments include the expressed preferences of individuals such as party leaders, senior committee members, and, occasionally, representatives of groups. In general, the assigning authorities are amenable to the argument that a particular assignment will help a member retain his seat in forthcoming elections. This is the most commonly used criterion and the most persuasive argument a member can make.

But the criteria change from year to year, from committee to committee, and from member to member. A veteran member of the House, Jim Wright (D-Tex.) provides a nice summary:

> Being appointed to the committee of one's choice is a matter of application and luck. The freshman member should certainly make his wishes known to the Speaker (if he is of the same political faith) and the leaders of his party in the House in either event. He also should try to line up as much support as he can muster among the colleagues of his own state delegation.
>
> Sometimes, however, even the most careful plans will not avail an aspirant. Naturally, if a freshman is to be successful in his quest there must be a vacancy on the desired committee, and generally there must be no one with seniority from his own geographic zone and in his own political party who wants this particular assignment. . . .
>
> But other considerations might prevail. During President Eisenhower's Administration, for instance, the conservative bloc of the Republican Party in the House controlled the party leadership. They would not permit any Republican member to be appointed to the powerful Ways and Means Committee unless he *opposed* Eisenhower's liberal position on reciprocal trade. On the other hand, while Sam Rayburn held sway as Speaker, no Democrat was chosen to this committee unless he agreed to *support* the reciprocal trade program.*

Policy or ideological biases are built into the bargaining process for

---

* Jim Wright, *You and Your Congressman* (New York: Coward-McCann, 1965): 131.

some committees. Over the years, for example, both parties in the Senate have assigned their more conservative members to the Finance Committee. Senate Democrats have also tended to put an unusually large proportion of conservatives on the Appropriations, Armed Services, and Judiciary Committees.* A systematic study of the progress of senators through shifting committee assignments supports the claim that at least for the period from 1947 through 1963, Senate Democrats regularly discriminated against liberal senators who were anxious to change the rules of the Senate.† This discrimination in favor of conservatives has moderated since the mid-1960s, however, and liberal Democrats who apply for the best openings are less likely to be rebuffed.

In the House the evidence seems to suggest that the more liberal Democrats get the better committee assignments or are at least more likely to get their preferences.° In the House Republican party the more conservative members seem to get the better assignments and a larger share of their requests.

Since both the House and Senate have equally elaborate committee and subcommittee structures it is inevitable that senators will have more assignments than representatives (unless the size of Senate committees were kept very small). In the Ninety-third Congress (1973–74) each member of the House had an average of 1.6 assignments to standing committees and 3.5 subcommittee assignments. Every senator, however, had an average of 2.6 standing committee assignments and 9.7 subcommittee assignments.‡

The Impact of Seniority

In general, the impact of the seniority system is limited.§ The distribution of chairmanships is regionally biased, but these biases are not necessarily attributable to the operation of the seniority rule itself. Many may be due to initial decisions made about assignments to the committee. Only in the case of southern overrepresentation in the Democratic party in the House and Senate is an obvious tie between

---

* See Ripley, *Power in the Senate:* chapter 3.
† Wayne R. Swanson, "Committee Assignments and the Nonconformist Legislator: Democrats in the U.S. Senate," *Midwest Journal of Politics* 13 (1969): 84–94.
° See Ripley, *Party Leaders in the House of Representatives* (Washington, D.C.: Brookings, 1967): 60.
‡ The figures come from Herbert B. Asher, "Committees and the Norm of Specialization," *Annals of the American Academy of Political and Social Science* (January, 1974): 68.
§ For support of this view see Barbara Hinckley, *The Seniority System in Congress* (Bloomington: Indiana University Prees, 1971).

Table 4–5

Regional Distribution of Democratic Committee Chairmen, 1947–1968.

Region [a]	House (%)	Senate (%)
East	22	4
Midwest	9	4
South	59	60
West	10	33
	(N = 176)	(N = 140)

[a] The East includes the six states of New England, plus New York, New Jersey, Delaware, Maryland, and Pennsylvania. The South includes the eleven states of the Confederacy plus Oklahoma and Kentucky. The Midwest includes Ohio, Indiana, Illinois, Michigan, Wisconsin, Minnesota, Iowa, Missouri, North Dakota, South Dakota, Nebraska, and Kansas. The West includes the rest of the states.

Source: Adapted from George Goodwin, Jr., The Little Legislatures (University of Massachusetts Press, 1970): 127.

the seniority system and regional overrepresentation present. Given the conservatism of most southern Democrats, this tie means that the Democratic committee leadership of Congress has a more conservative cast than the party membership as a whole. Table 4–5 summarizes the regional distribution of chairmanships for Democrats from 1947 through 1969. Table 4–6 traces the changing patterns of southern overrepresentation in the Senate from 1941 to 1971. Overrepresentation is still present but has been declining in recent years.

One of the most obvious impacts of the seniority system is, of course, that chairmen are older than the average member of Congress. The mean age of all members has hovered around fifty-two for the House and fifty-six for the Senate for several decades. Yet 30 percent of the committee chairmen in both houses from 1947 to 1967 were over seventy and almost two-thirds were over sixty.* There may be a commonly held assumption that the older members are necessarily more conservative but empirical data on members of Congress in support of the point are not available.

The conclusion of a recent careful study of the policy impact of seniority is that Democratic committee chairmen are more conservative than the average Democrat but that Republican committee leaders on the average are quite representative of the policy views of most Republicans. The Democratic bias towards conservatism is fostered

---

* See George Goodwin, Jr. *The Little Legislatures* (Amherst: University of Massachusetts Press, 1970): 126.

Table 4-6
Southern Democratic Representation on Senate Committees and Subcommittees, 1941–1971.

Percentage of Southerners [a] among:

Congress (Year)	All Democratic Senators	Committee Chairmen	Three Highest Ranking Democrats on All Committees	All Democrats on Four Choice Committees [b]	Three Highest Ranking Democrats on Four Choice Committees [b]	Subcommittee Chairmen [c]
77th (1941)	33	62	48	36	67	—
79th (1945)	39	50	44	35	50	—
81st (1949)	41	40	42	54	67	—
83rd (1953)	47	47 [d]	56	56	67	—
85th (1957)	45	53	44	58	58	45
87th (1961)	34	56	48	46	67	41
89th (1965)	29	62	52	43	83	35
90th (1968)	30	56	46	37	67	31
92nd (1971)	31	53	37	38	58	28

[a] Those from the eleven states of the Confederacy.
[b] Appropriations, Armed Services, Finance, and Foreign Relations.
[c] Accurate data on subcommittees are difficult to obtain before 1955.
[d] Ranking minority members (Republican Senate).

Source: Randall B. Ripley, "Power in the Post-World War II Senate," Journal of Politics 31 (1969): 475 (as updated in William J. Keefe and Morris S. Ogul, The American Legislative Process (Englewood Cliffs, N.J.: Prentice-Hall, 1973, 3rd ed.): 476.

Table 4–7
Average Party Unity Score for Chairmen (or Ranking Minority Members)
and All Party Members, 1947–1968.

	House		Senate	
	Democrats	Republicans	Democrats	Republicans
Average (mean) party unity score for chairmen or ranking minority members	66	76	64	71
Average (mean) party unity score for all members	73	76	71	72

Source: Adapted from Goodwin, The Little Legislatures: *133*.

not just by the existence of the seniority "rule" but also by the pattern of
initial committee assignments and change in committee assignments.*

Table 4–7 measures the party loyalty of senior committee members
compared to all party members. This is suggestive of policy differences
—since less loyal Democrats are more conservative than the average
Democrat and less loyal Republicans are more liberal than their fellows. These figures show that senior Democrats on committees are less
loyal to their party (and thus more conservative) than all Democrats;
but again the senior Republicans share the same traits of loyalty that
the majority of their party possess.

The Attractiveness of Committees

Committees vary in their attractiveness to the members of the House
and Senate. Some committees—such as Appropriations, Ways and
Means, or Finance—offer their members increased visibility as legislators. Some committees—such as Public Works or Agriculture—enable
the members to do things for their constituents that they might not
otherwise be in a position to do; this enhances the standing of the
member at home and may well increase the safety of his or her seat
at election time. Some committees—such as Foreign Relations, Foreign
Affairs, Education and Labor, or Labor and Public Welfare—allow the
members to maximize their ability to influence national policy in an
area of special interest to them.

Committee preferences of the members over a twenty-year period
have been aggregated and rank ordered in Table 4–8. The first column

---

* Hinckley, *The Seniority System:* 110–111.

Table 4–8

Preference Ranking of Congressional Committees, 1949–1968.

	Net Shifts	Net Transfers Per Unit of Membership	Ratio of Transfers In to Transfers Out
House Committee			
1. Rules	24	.182	4.0
2. Ways and Means	39	.157	8.8
3. Appropriations	59	.119	5.5
4. Foreign Affairs	34	.108	4.8
5. Armed Services	29	.079	4.2
6. Internal Security	7	.078	2.4
7. Interstate and Foreign Commerce	14	.045	1.6
8. Judiciary	12	.037	1.8
9. Agriculture	8	.024	1.4
10. District of Columbia	1	.004	1.0
11. Public Works	−2	−.006	.9
12. Education and Labor	−6	−.020	.7
13. House Administration	−5	−.020	.9
14. Government Operations	−10	−.033	.8
15. Interior and Insular Affairs	−15	−.050	.7
16. Banking and Currency	−15	−.050	.6
17. Merchant Marine and Fisheries	−20	−.067	.6
18. Post Office and Civil Service	−22	−.088	.5
19. Veterans' Affairs	−37	−.146	.3
Senate Committee			
1. Foreign Relations	28	.175	15.0
2. Finance	22	.141	8.3
3. Appropriations	31	.127	6.2
4. Judiciary	18	.122	4.6
5. Armed Services	15	.096	4.0
6. Commerce	15	.095	2.5
7. Agriculture and Forestry	0	.000	1.0
8. Interior and Insular Affairs	−1	−.006	.9
9. Labor and Public Welfare	−6	−.042	.6
10. Banking, Housing, and Urban Affairs	−10	−.069	.5
11. Public Works	−17	−.117	.4
12. Rules and Administration	−14	−.143	.5
13. Government Operations	−20	−.157	.3
14. Post Office and Civil Service	−21	−.184	.3
15. District of Columbia	−32	−.360	.2

Source: Adapted from Goodwin, The Little Legislatures: *114, 115.*

indicates whether a committee gained more members than it lost through voluntary shifts to other committees or vice versa. Since virtually all of these shifts were voluntary and made by members with at least two years of service, they offer a natural preference ranking expressed by a large number of senators and representatives. The second column in Table 4–8 is the result of dividing the number of net shifts for the period by the total number of seats open during the period. Most of these seats were, of course, filled by incumbent members of the committees. But the number in the second column provides an index to the magnitude and direction of movement. (The rank orderings in the table are based on this index.) It should be noted that at least some members voluntarily left even the most prestigious and sought-after committees for other assignments and even the least attractive committees drew at least some voluntary transfers. The third column on the table shows the ratio of transfers into a committee to transfers out of the committee. This is another way of measuring attractiveness and results in roughly the same rank ordering.

In large part the most attractive committees are the most important committees in terms of policy. This suggests that individual members take seriously their desire to influence policy. Finance, Ways and Means, Armed Services, and Appropriations also offer a number of opportunities to perform major services for constituents and for fellow members in terms of such items as special tax provisions, protection of defense installations against closing, and appropriation of funds for pet projects.

THE INTERNAL OPERATIONS OF COMMITTEES

The standing committees of the House and Senate vary in the way they work. Some of them seek internal integration that presumably enhances their autonomy and the chances that their policy decisions will go unchanged in the full House and Senate and in conference committees. Others are much more oblivious to any necessity for a high degree of integration. Some virtually eschew partisanship as they pursue agreement on policy statements and actions. Others not only carry general party disagreements into committee deliberations but also magnify and intensify them. Some, in effect, prescribe a period of apprenticeship for junior members. Others admit junior members to full participation immediately.

Integration

Integration refers to how well the parts of a committee (that is, the individuals and, to a lesser extent, the subcommittees) mesh as the committee operates from day to day. The classic example of a highly integrated committee is the House Appropriations Committee.* Individuals who are recruited for this committee are not passionate partisans and must maintain an aura of "responsibility" about them. These qualities are sought to perpetuate the dominant norms about the job of the committee: to cut the federal budget and guard the treasury. In general, committee members believe—regardless of party—that the proposals coming from the executive branch almost always contain some fat. Their job is to trim that fat while providing enough money to maintain federal programs, particularly those vital to constituents, at adequate levels. Agencies that receive the largest percentage of their requests from the committee are likely to be those with non-controversial tasks, stable workloads, and leaders held in high esteem by the committee. Agencies involved in controversy, with shifting workloads, and leaders held in low esteem by committee members are unlikely to fare very well. Agencies with strong support from external clientele groups are likely to grow more rapidly from year to year than agencies without clientele groups or with weak, apathetic, or hostile groups. Bureaus such as the Forest Service, Office of Education, and Soil Conservation Service are in a particularly strong situation because they have strong support from within and without the committee simultaneously. At the other extreme, agencies such as the Bureau of Mines, the Bureau of Reclamation, and the Census Bureau, have had neither external nor committee support.

Virtually all of the work of the committee is conducted in the appropriations subcommittees, and the full committee routinely accepts nearly all of their budget decisions. This means that individual members specialize in one or two specific areas and are expected to become experts on whom the rest of the committee (and the House) can rely for sound judgments. The prime integrating factors in this committee seem to be the mutual deference paid to one another by the various subcommittees and the widely shared vision of the central purpose of the committee.

Another highly integrated committee is the House Committee on Ways and Means.† The integrating mechanisms of this committee are different from those of the Appropriations Committee. The committee

---

* Richard F. Fenno, Jr., "The House Appropriations Committee as a Political System: The Problem of Integration," *American Political Science Review* 56 (1962): 310–324; and Fenno, *The Power of the Purse* (Boston: Little, Brown, 1966).

† John F. Manley, "The House Committee on Ways and Means: Conflict Management in a Congressional Committee," *American Political Science Review* 59 (1965): 927–939. See also, Manley, *The Politics of Finance* (Boston: Little, Brown, 1970).

is not united substantively: the tax matters (the tax code, social security and medicare, welfare, the tariff) that the committee handles have long had major partisan aspects that divide members both of the committee and of the House. On the other hand, the committee members do seem to be agreed that their task is to legislate so well and so thoroughly that their work will be accepted virtually without question by the House and, hopefully, by the Senate Finance Committee and the whole Senate, too. The chairman of the committee from 1958 through 1974, Wilbur Mills of Arkansas, was adept at managing the substantive policy tensions that are part of his committee's province. He showed great skill in emphasizing points of agreement and minimizing points of disagreement while treating all participants fairly.*

A classic example of Mills at work occurred in 1965 on the question of establishing a federal program supporting medical care for the aged (medicare). The administration was supporting a bill that was funded through a payroll tax but that provided mainly hospitalization costs and left other medical expenses largely uncovered. The ranking Republican on the committee had introduced a bill with a more generous benefits package but funded on the basis of voluntary enrollment supplemented by money from general federal revenues. After listening and helping guide the debate between the contending forces, Mills cleverly proposed a compromise that adopted the more generous benefits package of the Republican bill but retained the compulsory membership-payroll tax feature of the Democratic bill. Thus he left virtually all members of the committee with some reason for satisfaction and yet was instrumental in creating a program that was more far-reaching than anyone thought could come out of the Ways and Means Committee.

Yet another pattern of integration is evident in the House Committee on Agriculture.† The main work of the committee is conducted by subcommittees dealing with specific crops; the principal integrating factor is the mutual deference of these subcommittees to one another. The growers of all crops—particularly those important to the southern Democrats who have dominated the committee's majority party contingent for a number of years (for example, cotton and tobacco)—receive good treatment in the subcommittees; the full committee ratifies subcommittee decisions. When there are partisan issues before the committee that are not tied to specific crops, however, integration is likely to be diminished as the demands of partisanship take over.

---

* See Manley, "Wilbur D. Mills: A Study in Congressional Influence," *American Political Science Review* 63 (1969): 442–464.
† Charles O. Jones, "Representation in Congress: The Case of the House Agriculture Committee," *American Political Science Review* 55 (1961): 358–367.

The basic question of level of parity (the percent of a "fair market price" supported by governmental subsidy) has often been such a partisan issue.

The House Committee on Education and Labor provides an example of a committee not preoccupied with integration, probably because it would be virtually impossible to achieve.* The committee handles issues that not only provoke partisan differences (labor-management relations and federal aid to education, for example) but that also raise thorny racial and religious questions (federal aid to parochial schools, federal programs to force unions to open their ranks to black members). There is no agreement on the substance of what the committee should do (as in the case of Appropriations). There is the use of subcommittees but no mutual deference among them (as in the case of Appropriations and Agriculture). There have been no chairmen particularly skillful in muting conflict on partisan issues (as in the case of Ways and Means). And there has not even been agreement that the committee should aim for a product that will be accepted almost automatically by the House. Rather the expectation seems to be that the debate over the divisive aspects of the committee's work will continue on the floor and in the Senate and in conference committees.

Committee integration in the Senate presents a different picture from the House. The average size of Senate committees is smaller and the average senator has many more committee assignments. Whereas a House member becomes expert in a particular field and develops a personal stake in the most minute of outcomes, the individual senator develops a personal stake in only a few scattered items. He is much more reliant on staff than is the House member. Mutual deference to subcommittee decisions is widely accepted in the Senate as a norm, and is not a question that each individual committee must decide.

One study of Senate committee integration found that integration (measured by agreement of committee members in roll call voting on the floor) was related to similarity of members' constituencies (measured by income inequality) and to members' seniority in the Senate.† Committees whose members were relatively junior and who represented rather similar states were more highly integrated than committees whose members were more senior and represented states that differed. When integration was related to the members' success in getting their own bills reported from their committees, it was found that members on more integrated committees had greater success than

---

* Frank J. Munger and Richard F. Fenno, Jr., *National Politics and Federal Aid to Education* (Syracuse: Syracuse University Press, 1962).

† Lawrence C. Dodd, "Committee Integration in the Senate: A Comparative Analysis," *Journal of Politics* 34 (1972): 1135–1171.

members on less integrated committees. Pork barrel committees (those dealing primarily with tangible physical benefits—"pork"—for constituencies) were an exception to this finding.

What are the results of committee integration? Well-integrated committees are more likely to be able to offer inducements to members of the House and Senate that will lead them to seek membership on such committees (for example, members may receive important psychological gratification from seeing their efforts in committee result in successful legislation). Table 4–8 on member preferences for committee assignments lends support to this notion. Well integrated committees (Ways and Means, Appropriations) were more desired than a partially integrated committee (Agriculture,) which was, in turn, more desired than a relatively unintegrated committee (Education and Labor). There seems to be no convincing evidence, however, that better integrated committees "succeed" more on the floor.

Partisanship

It has already been suggested that committees vary in terms of their partisanship. Some, like House Education and Labor, are unabashedly partisan. Others, like Ways and Means, exhibit a restrained form of partisanship. Others, like Appropriations, are virtually nonpartisan. In general, in the House, reduced partisanship makes integration more likely. In the Senate there is less evidence about the extent and impact of partisanship within committees. There is, however, clearly a range of behavior. The Senate Appropriations Committee, for example, generally operates on a nonpartisan basis.* In general, most Senate committees have a tradition of minimizing partisan considerations whenever possible. No committees always split along party lines but there are occasions—predictable on the basis of the issues at stake and personalities of the most important committee members—in which committees will proceed on a highly partisan basis. The attitude of the chairman toward partisan questions is an important factor explaining the relative presence or absence of partisanship. Only a few Senate chairmen act as aggressive partisans. Most seek accommodation with at least a sizable part of the contingent from the minority party.

Virtually all of the committees in both houses rely on division of labor and specialization on the part of members. Only a few committees do not use subcommittees and even on those committees individual members develop reputations for expertise on specific matters that come under committee purview. Specialization is necessary for

---

* See Stephen Horn, *Unused Power* (Washington, D.C.: Brookings, 1970).

committees to process their generally heavy workloads and to compete with the level of information that bureaucrats possess.

Apprenticeship

In some committees specialization involves a differentiation between senior and junior members of the committee or subcommittees. The senior members are viewed as the genuine specialists and are given both formal and informal recognition (for example, more time for questioning during hearings) within the committee and on the floor of the chamber of which the committee is a part. On other committees junior members are accorded full rights virtually from the day they join the committee and they may, in fact, develop subject matter expertise that leads to deference very quickly. The apprenticeship norm is more prevalent in the House than in the Senate.

Committee Chairmen

Committee chairmen in the House and Senate are not the unfettered autocrats sometimes portrayed in the popular press; their roles, however, are crucial to the smooth functioning of the congressional machinery. Whether a committee operates on the basis of formal rules or on the basis of custom and tradition, the chairman has more influence than anyone else on the committee in shaping its policy decisions. Chairmen are influential either because they successfully exert independent judgment supported by their use of the resources they command or because they are faithfully reflecting the policy preferences of a number of committee members.

For well over a century in the Senate committee chairmen have almost all been chosen on the basis of their seniority in a given committee, as distinguished from their seniority in the Senate as a whole. The person in the majority party who has longest service on a committee at the beginning of any given Congress is designated as chairman; everyone below him in committee seniority is ranked accordingly for purposes of succession and, in some committees, for purposes of receiving subcommittee chairmanships. The minority party adopted the same pattern for choosing ranking minority members. The Civil War created some delay in the final consolidation of the seniority system but by the mid-1870s it was well established. Violations have occurred since but they have been rare.

In 1973 the Senate Republicans decided to make their ranking minority positions elective within the Republican delegation on each committee. Whether this announced policy will result in any violations of seniority remains to be seen; the presumption certainly has to be that the most senior members will continue to hold the ranking positions, even if formal "elections" are held. But at least the change gives the Republican senators on individual committees a weapon to use if they are actually confronted with an incompetent, senile, gravely ill, or tyrannical ranking member.

The principle of seniority has been used in the House by both parties for selection of committee chairmen with only a few exceptions approximately from World War I.

Chairmen are accorded deference in part because other members of committees hope to achieve seniority and chairmanships themselves and are often reluctant to participate in any activity that might permanently diminish a chairman's power, prestige, or position. A chairman also is deferred to because he is likely to have developed expert knowledge in the areas of concern to the committee. He can usually make a strong case for the position he favors and persuade a large proportion of the members to follow his lead.

Much of the influence of chairmen results from the discreet exercise of the formal and informal powers that come with the position and that can be used either to advance or stymie the legislative careers of their fellow committee members. The chairman, for example, controls the agenda of the committee and the scheduling of business, including hearings. Committee members with "pet" bills must rely on the support of the chairman to get their bills considered. Further, the chairman usually controls the allocation of staff resources. A member who wants formal assignment of a staff member or even a receptive attitude from the central committee staff is well advised to be in the good graces of the chairman.

A chairman assigns the members of his committee (at least of his party) to subcommittees. He can change the number and jurisdiction of subcommittees and appoint subcommittee chairmen without strict regard to seniority. The chairman also typically retains control of the budgets allocated to subcommittees.

Chairmen can offer the role of principal sponsor (the person for whom the bill is likely to be named) and/or floor manager (the person who manages the time allocated to the proponents of the bill on the House or Senate floor) to individuals on the committee. These roles confer additional prestige and recognition on the holders. And if the bill goes to a conference committee, chairmen appoint conferees, who help determine the final fate of a bill. Chairmen also appoint members to go on official trips, both domestic and foreign.

Despite his powers, the chairman's influence is not unlimited, nor is he immune to change. Chairmen who consistently antagonize committee members with tyrannical or erratic behavior may find themselves severely hemmed in by unwelcome new rules—an event that has occurred in recent years in the House Committees on Education and Labor, Post Office and Civil Service, and Government Operations.

In 1966 the House Education and Labor Committee reported a major anti-poverty bill (a series of amendments to the 1964 Economic Opportunity Act) on June 1. The Chairman of the Committee, Adam Clayton Powell, did not schedule the bill for floor action until September 26 and even suggested that it might not come to the floor until after the November elections. The great majority of the committee members—particularly his fellow Democrats—viewed this as the last straw in what they considered a history of irresponsible behavior on Powell's part since assuming the chairmanship of the committee. They were particularly critical of his high rate of absenteeism, and made allegations about arbitrary hiring and firing of committee staff, misusing committee funds, and simply refusing to report legislation favored by the committee. As a result the committee—by a vote of twenty-seven to one with three abstentions—adopted new rules for the committee that no longer left Powell in a position to thwart the majority of the committee. Among other things these rules set a regular weekly meeting that could be held even without the chairman, created six standing subcommittees not under the chairman's control, divided control of staff between the majority members as a unit, the minority members as a unit, and the subcommittees, guaranteed that bills approved by the committee would be reported to the floor, guaranteed that bills coming into the committee would be referred to a subcommittee, required reports on the use of committee funds, and specified that subcommittee members should sit on conference committees considering bills that had come from their particular subcommittee.

In 1973 and 1974 the Ways and Means Committee underwent major changes. Even before the departure of Wilbur Mills from the chairmanship he had held for seventeen years these changes had begun. Mills' dominance of the committee in favor of moderate policy positions was threatened. The House rejected a major Ways and Means compromise engineered by Mills involving cost-of-living increases in social security payments. A reform adopted by the Democratic caucus left room for opening committee bills to floor amendment, whereas previously most Ways and Means bills had been granted a "closed rule" (one that allowed no amendments on the floor of the House). The Republicans became less willing to cooperate with Mills and liberal Democrats seemed more demanding on issues such as tax reform and health insurance.

Then in October, 1974, the House required Ways and Means to establish subcommittees in the next Congress after defeating an effort to remove considerable jurisdiction from the Committee. And in December, 1974, the Democratic caucus removed committee assignment powers from the Democratic members of Ways and Means and increased the size of the committee from twenty-five to thirty-seven as a prelude to adding a number of new liberal Democrats in early 1975 when the Ninety-fourth Congress convened.

Subcommittees *

Most congressional committees use subcommittees to process their work. The natural tendency is for the subcommittees to move toward autonomy and for the full committees to ratify the work of the subcommittees almost automatically.

Committees can resist subcommittee autonomy in varying ways, however. A committee may elect not to use subcommittees at all. Three House committees and two Senate committees had no subcommittees in 1972. (See Table 4–1.) Subcommittees may exist but be given no clearly defined jurisdictions. Three House committees followed this path in the Ninetieth Congress (1967–68).† A full committee may also meet frequently both to conduct its own business and to review the work of subcommittees.°

In general, the substantive work of Congress gets done largely in subcommittees. This fact maximizes the impact of individual members (particularly the senior members of the subcommittees) on policy but it also opens the committee system to the special representations of the bureaucracy and interest groups. Every bureau and every interest group can seek out "its subcommittee," and if they can befriend the chairman and perhaps the ranking minority member they can help control federal policy in areas that interest them. In such a situation it is hard to say which persons in a triangular arrangement have the most influence: the senator or representative or the bureau chief or the lobbyist (or even, particularly in the Senate, a staff person for the subcommittee).

Subcommittee chairmanships are very widespread in the Senate; multiple chairmanships are normal. In the Ninety-third Congress (1973–74) thirty-nine of the fifty-seven Democratic senators chaired two or more subcommittees. At the same time only 9 House Democrats out of 238 (4 percent) chaired two subcommittees. At the other end

---

* See Goodwin, *The Little Legislatures:* 45–63; and Charles O. Jones, "The Role of the Congressional Subcommittee," *Midwest Journal of Political Science* 6 (1962): 327–344.

† Goodwin, *The Little Legislatures:* 49.

° Ibid.

of the spectrum only 2 Senate Democrats were without subcommittee chairmanships whereas 124 House Democrats—just over half—had none.* These differences between the two houses mean that junior senators are probably more influential and more content with their lot in terms of legislative influence than junior representatives. The differences also increase the power of staff members in the Senate since senators must necessarily delegate some of the large subcommittee burden they carry.

The Special Case of the House Rules Committee †

The House of Representatives operates under a much tighter set of rules on the floor than does the Senate. In large part this difference is dictated by the differing sizes of the two bodies. The much larger House must have a more orderly and restricted floor procedure in order to work effectively. To help govern the conditions under which specific measures are discussed on the House floor the House has long used a committee on rules. Centrally, the members of the Rules Committee set the time limit for the debate (time is always split evenly between those in favor of the bill and those opposed to it). They may leave the bill open to amendments, restrict the number of amendments, or eliminate the possibility of amendment altogether. The Rules Committee must also act to send bills to conference committees. The committee may, of course, refuse to grant a "rule" to a bill or a conference report, thus denying the House the opportunity to consider it unless some other measures are taken to countermand the position of the committee or bypass it.

From its creation in the nineteenth century until 1910, the Rules Committee was virtually the personal vehicle of the Speaker. He both appointed its members and served as its chairman. From 1910 until the late 1930s, although the Speaker could no longer sit on the committee and had lost the power of making committee appointments, the committee continued to be an instrument loyal to the wishes of the Speaker and other majority party leaders. The committee members from the majority party believed their main function was to assist the leaders of their party in the achievement of their legislative objectives.

---

* These figures are taken from Asher, "Committees and the Norms of Specialization."

† On the Rules Committee see James A. Robinson, *The House Rules Committee* (Indianapolis: Bobbs-Merrill, 1963); Douglas M. Fox, "The House Rules Committee's Agenda-Setting Function, 1961–1968," *Journal of Politics* 32 (1970): 440–443; and Douglas M. Fox and Charles Clapp, "The House Rules Committee and the Programs of the Kennedy and Johnson Administration," *Midwest Journal of Political Science* 14 (1970): 667–672.

From the late 1930s until the early 1960s, however, a group of conservative southern Democrats on the committee allied with the Republicans (who were all conservatives) to kill a number of liberal Democratic initiatives on domestic legislation. This legislative deadlock resulted in the committee becoming the focus of hot political division between liberals and conservatives. In 1961 the House agreed to increase the size of the committee temporarily in order to give the Democratic leaders a better chance of control of the committee; this increased size was made permanent in 1963. Almost immediately the stifling of major liberal Democratic initiatives by the committee ceased to be a problem—only measures of minor importance were killed. By the mid-1970s the Democrats on the Rules Committee had become reliable supporters of the leaders. It seems unlikely that party leaders would sanction committee appointments that might jeopardize future control of the committee by the majority party.

CONFERENCE COMMITTEES *

When the House and Senate pass two different versions of the same bill a conference committee is appointed to reconcile the differences and present a final product that both houses must ratify before sending the bill to the president for his signature. This committee is typically made up of a few senior members from the relevant standing committees in each house. Both parties are represented on the conference committee. The decision-making is not by majority vote of the whole committee but is by agreement of the majority of each of the two delegations.

Some committees routinely appoint the same members to all conferences. Others appoint the senior members of the relevant subcommittee (plus, usually, the chairman of the full committee and the ranking minority member). Some appoint all of the members of the relevant subcommittee. The senior members of the House and Senate clearly dominate the conference process.

It is expected that the delegations from each house will "fight to win" in any disagreements between the two contingents. However, it is also assumed that disagreements will have to be compromised so that a final bill can be produced that will be acceptable to both houses. Thus the conferees know that they will have to bargain and cannot

---

* On conference committees see David J. Vogler, *The Third House* (Evanston: Northwestern University Press, 1971); Gilbert Y. Steiner, *The Congressional Conference Committee* (Urbana: University of Illinois, 1951); Ada C. Mc-Cown, *The Congressional Conference Committee* (New York: Columbia University Press, 1927); and Fenno, *The Power of the Purse:* chapter 12.

expect to win all points in dispute. Sometimes, particularly in the Senate, committee leaders will accept amendments on the floor that they really do not favor so that later on, in conference, they will have trading chips that they can give away in order to save some provision they really care about.

Conference committees usually have considerable leeway in reaching final agreement. On some occasions they may even insert new legislative language in the bill, provisions contained in neither the House nor the Senate bill. On a few bills, however, they will receive specific instructions from their parent chamber on provisions on which they must insist.

Usually the conference reports are routinely accepted in both houses. Occasionally, one or both houses will reject a conference report; this necessitates a new conference committee (even though it may contain the same individuals). Conference committees almost always reach agreement; when they do not, the bill may die in conference; or the bill may be returned to the two houses in hopes that revisions will be adopted that allow the conference committee to agree. The few seemingly irreconcilable disagreements stem either from an issue on which basic House and Senate attitudes are poles apart (for example, the SST in 1970) or from personal rivalries between committees or individuals (for example, the 1962 dispute between the chairmen of the two appropriations committees that blocked a number of bills in conference for several months).

The evidence is solid that, since World War II, the Senate has dominated conference committees in terms of having more of its provisions adopted than those of the House. This represents a change from an earlier period between 1927 and 1949 when the House dominated conference committee results. But for the post-1949 period Richard Fenno found, for example, that when there were contested provisions in appropriations bills the Senate "won" almost two-thirds of the time in the sense of having the final figure closer to its own figure rather than being closer to the House figure. This pattern of dominance stretched across almost all issue areas. Fenno concluded that this pattern prevails because the Senate usually supports higher figures than the House and, late in the process, a presumption in favor of higher spending develops because all of the participants (interest groups, executive agencies, House and Senate members and the Senate Appropriations Committee and conferees) except the members of the House Appropriations Committee have reasons for wanting higher spending. All want to satisfy clients and constituents; only the House Committee members remain primarily concerned with the value of "economy in government" for its own sake.

Table 4–9
Percentage of Conferences Won by Senate by Policy Area,
1945–48, 1953–54, 1963–66.

Policy Area	Percentage of Senate Victories	Number of Conferences
Appropriations	78	119
National Security	67	21
Public Works and Resources	67	15
General Government	57	7
Agriculture	56	16
Education and Welfare	50	16
Foreign Policy	50	26
Taxes and Economic Policy	48	48

Source: David J. Vogler, The Third House *(Northwestern University Press, 1971): 59.*

In another study, based on five Congresses scattered between 1945 and 1966, David Vogler found that the pattern of Senate dominance extended to virtually all issue areas, although there were significant differences between the areas. Table 4–9 summarizes Vogler's findings.

That the Senate is more influential in conference committees does not signify that it dominates the congressional impact on public policy. On all appropriations bills and on many other bills the House acts first, which means that the Senate frequently is left in the position of amending the House bill and reacting to the agenda set by the House.

The vital role that can be played by conference committees is well illustrated by a conference in the summer of 1973. It worked for three months to produce a highway bill acceptable to a large number of competing interests and points of view—including those of mass transit proponents (primarily urban lobbyists and environmentalists) and pro-highway interests (road builders, concrete and asphalt makers, tire makers, car makers, and oil companies). Congress had failed to enact a highway bill in 1972 because of some of the same disagreements. When the House and Senate passed new bills in the spring of 1973 the same potential for irreconcilable disagreement existed because of the major differences between the two bills. Also complicating the work of the conferees was the threat of a presidential veto if the total amount of money in the bill was too large or if the bill provided for the subsidization of operating expenses of mass transit systems.

The most critical point of disagreement between the two houses had to do with whether Highway Trust Fund money could be diverted for use in mass transit facilities. (The fund had been created in 1956 to finance the construction of the interstate highway system. By 1973 about $5 billion was spent each year from the fund, which is replenished by taxes on gasoline, trucks, and other highway "user" taxes.) The Senate position was that the fund could be used for mass transit and the House position was negative. The conferees, over a period of three months, worked out an ingenious compromise that gave everyone a partial victory. In 1974 the inviolability of the trust fund for non-highway uses would be formally preserved (by an elaborate paper shuffle proposed by Jim Wright (D-Tex.), the central figure among the House conferees), in 1975 some limited diversion of money would be allowed for buses only, and in 1976 the Senate position became operative: money could be diverted for rail rapid transit as well as for buses. But the language was also written in such a way as to encourage the formation of a separate mass transit trust fund by 1976 or at least the creation of a single trust fund covering a wide variety of transportation needs.

The conferees also placated the administration by removing anti-impoundment language (but endorsing a court decision forbidding this practice by which the administration can refuse to spend money appropriated by Congress for specific purposes), by keeping spending levels within acceptable limits (in some cases below both the House and Senate versions), and by removing the operating subsidies section from the act. Mass transit proponents and pro-highway interests were at least partially satisfied because both got large subsidies.

In short, the conferees took a situation that looked very bleak and —by writing legislative language that appeared in neither the House nor the Senate bill—produced a winning compromise in three months.*

THE IMPACT OF COMMITTEES

Committee Success on the Floor

Committee bills usually pass on the floor of the House and Senate. In the ten years between 1955 and 1964, for example, 90 percent of all bills in the House that went through the normal committee process and came to a roll call vote passed. There were numerous other bills that were not the subject of roll calls that also passed.

Committees vary, however, in the ease with which their handiwork

---

* For a much more detailed description of the highway conference committee see Michael J. Malbin, "Transportation Report/Long Deadlock Ends in Compromise Opening Highway Trust Fund for Mass Transit," *National Journal* (August 11, 1973): 1163–1171.

is accepted on the floor. One study of roll call voting on committee bills in the House between 1955 and 1964 * showed that over the ten year period the most successful committees never had a bill that went to a roll call defeated (there were two such committees); the least successful committee had a little over 18 percent of its bills that went to a roll call defeated on the House floor.

The number of committee bills passed without amendment on the floor is another measure of committee success. The assumption is that amendments reflect a "second-guessing" of the judgment reported by the committee majority. Table 4–10 reports data on the passage of

Table 4–10
Percentage of Committee Bills Passing Unamended, 1963–1971.

	Percent of Bills Passing Unamended	Number of Bills
Senate		
All Senate Committees	65	1174
Top Three Committees		
Rules and Administration	92	25
Interior and Insular Affairs	88	80
District of Columbia	80	25
Bottom Three Committees		
Public Works	57	61
Armed Services	51	61
Appropriations	40	165
House		
All House Committees	70	1139
Top Three Committees		
Ways and Means	96	99
House Administration	93	29
Veterans' Affairs	93	27
Bottom Three Committees		
Banking and Currency	54	74
District of Columbia	47	17
Science and Astronautics	41	17

Source: Data compiled from Congressional Quarterly Almanacs, *1963–1971.*

---

* James W. Dyson and John W. Soule, "Congressional Committee Behavior on Roll Call Votes: The U.S. House of Representatives, 1955–1964," *Midwest Journal of Political Science* 14 (1970): 626–647.

House and Senate committee bills for the period from 1963 through 1971. The table supports the proposition that the House is somewhat more likely to pass the handiwork of its committees unamended than is the Senate (70 percent of the time as compared to 65 percent). The range of unamended bills is similar in both houses. In the Senate the three committees whose bills got amended most often are all pork barrel committees. This suggests that senators will tack on amendments to spread the benefits of governmental activity—whether public works, military installations, or appropriations in general—more widely. The parallel pork barrel committees in the House also ranked low—although not among the lowest three. (Armed Services was ninth, Public Works was fourteenth, and Appropriations was seventeenth.) In both houses the top three committees were in five cases out of the six either relatively minor committees or specifically concerned with housekeeping in the House and Senate themselves. The only important substantive committee in the top three was the House Ways and Means Committee; this can be explained largely because most bills from that committee are considered under a closed rule—that is, a rule that simply does not allow amendments.

The Content of Committee Impact

There are at least three major factors that help to explain why the policy statements and actions emerging from different committees vary.* First, the goals of the members in seeking membership on a committee are important. Second, the specific environment within which the committee works has a decided impact. Third, the basic decision rules adopted (perhaps unknowingly) by the committee help predetermine the kinds of policy statements and actions emerging from a committee. Table 4–11 summarizes the influence of these factors for six committees in the House. By discussing the general shape of the policy decisions emerging from each of the committees in the 1960s and early 1970s, one can see these factors at work.

The Appropriations Committee (in practice, its subcommittees) generally cuts budgets for all programs proposed by the executive branch by almost a fixed percentage (rarely greater than 10 percent and usually considerably lower), but the basic reliance is still on the executive request—the executive branch sets the agenda. Thus the committee responds to the executive-led coalitions and follows its basic decision rules of reducing executive budget requests while still providing adequate funding for the programs administered by the executive

---

* The following discussion is adapted from Richard F. Fenno, Jr., *Congressmen in Committees* (Boston: Little, Brown, 1973).

Table 4-11
Factors Related to Policy Decisions for Six House Committees

	Appropriations	Ways and Means	Foreign Affairs	Education and Labor	Post Office and Civil Service	Interior and Insular Affairs
Members' Goals	Maximize influence in the House	Maximize influence in the House	Maximize influence in a given policy area	Maximize influence in a given policy area	Maximize chances of re-election to the House	Maximize chances of re-election to the House
Environmental Constraints	Parent chamber coalitions led by executive agencies	Parent chamber coalitions led by partisan clusters in the House and by executive agencies	Coalitions led by executive agencies (mainly State Department and AID)	Coalitions led by partisan groups in and out of the House	Coalitions led by clients (civil service unions; and 2nd and 3rd class mailers)	Coalitions led by clients (many and diverse)
Basic Decision Rules	1. Reduce executive budget requests 2. Provide adequate funding for executive programs	1. Write bills that will pass the House 2. Allocate credit to majority party for policies adopted	1. To approve and help pass the foreign aid bill	1. Allocate credit to parties for policies adopted 2. To pursue individual policy preferences regardless of partisan implications	1. To support maximum pay increases and benefits for civil servants; and to oppose all postal rate increases 2. To accede to executive branch wishes if necessary to assure some pay and benefits increases	1. To secure House passage of all constituency-supported, member-sponsored bills 2. To balance the competing demands of conservationists and private users of land and water resources so as to give special benefits to users

Source: Adapted from Richard F. Fenno, Jr., Congressmen in Committees (Boston: Little, Brown, 1973).

branch. At the same time the power of the committee to cut at least some things selectively (and also the power to add some things selectively) helps the members realize their private goal of increasing their influence in the House.

The Ways and Means Committee passes carefully worked out versions of essentially majority party positions on the range of subjects within the committee's jurisdiction (principally trade, social security, and taxaton). The craftsmanship that goes into the final versions is designed to insure that the final product will pass the House. The majority party stamp is also clearly on that product so that, when it passes, the majority party can take most of the public credit for it, even though the minority party may have made a considerable contribution. The products coming from the committee show responsiveness to partisan coalitions, especially that within the majority party, and responsiveness to the views of the Social Security Administration, the president, the Treasury, and other parts of the executive branch coalitions. But the Ways and Means Committee rarely simply passes an executive request without putting its own stamp on it as it did in the case of welfare and trade in 1962, medicare in 1965, and major tax revisions in 1964, 1969, and 1971.

The highly visible nature of the issues with which the Ways and Means Committee deals and the important ramifications of these issues for constituents means that subject matter alone will make the members visible and sought after by their colleagues. This enhances their influence. In addition, until 1975 the Democratic members served as members of the Democratic Committee on Committees and were, therefore, accorded additional influence. Thus the committee members realize their goal of enhancing their influence in the House.

The Foreign Affairs Committee's major policy activities involve the annual foreign aid authorization bill. The committee always approves the bill in a form generally acceptable to the executive branch. Minor cuts and alterations may be made but the committee does not make major changes. This product obviously shows that the committee is responsive to the executive-led coalition and follows its basic decision rule of approving and helping to pass the foreign aid bill. To the extent that individual members go on the committee to help support foreign aid they perhaps can feel that they are maximizing their impact on this policy area, although that impact does not appear to be independent but rather dependent on the executive branch.

The Education and Labor Committee is in almost a constant state of partisan turmoil. Much of its policy activity consists of heated debates and arguments inside the committee over a whole range of controversial measures involving labor relations; and a variety of poverty, welfare, and educational aid measures. When agreement is possible among a majority of the committee members (usually composed almost entirely of members of the majority party), controversial measures are brought to the floor, although without the guarantee that they will be passed by the House. If the measures reported by the committee pass, then certainly the majority party will receive the bulk of the credit.

At the same time all members of the committee can pursue matters that interest them personally because there is no norm within the committee that winning on the House floor is very important. Therefore, if "teams" and majorities emerge that is fine, but if they do not, members can still pursue their own interests and have the feeling that they are maximizing their influence on policy areas that intrigue them. When a majority of the committee is able to agree on a major issue then it is responsive to partisan groups within the committee and within the House.

The Post Office and Civil Service Committee increases the pay of federal civil servants rather steadily. First class postage rates also increase fairly frequently. Commercial users of the mails (magazines and "junk" mailers) are protected by the committee and increases in their rates are more gradual. These policy activities by the committee reflect their basic decision rule of supporting pay raises. That postal rates also go up indicates that the executive branch basically demands such increases as part of the price for increasing pay rates; the committee accedes to at least some of these demands rather than jeopardizing the increased pay. Certainly the policy decisions made by the committee reflect their responsiveness to the civil servant and postal employee unions which are constantly pressing for higher wages and to the second and third class mailers who are constantly pressing for continued government subsidy of their mailing privileges with rates below cost. The favors that committee members do for federal workers (and every district has lots of postmen and many have other major federal installations) helps them maximize their chances for re-election by earning votes and also campaign contributions. The conversion of the Postal Service to corporation status has altered the jurisdiction of the committee and is likely to result in different patterns of behavior in the future.

The Interior and Insular Affairs Committee produces a mixture of legislation, some of it applauded by conservationists and sportsmen and offensive to the users of public resources (grazers, timbering interests, mining interests) and some of it favorable to the users and anathema to the conservationists and sportsmen. This mixed pattern of legislation reflects the conflicting pressures on the members of the committee, virtually all of whom come from western districts in which there are large numbers of users and increasing numbers of vocal conservationists.

These cross-pressured members seeking to maximize re-election chances naturally seek to turn out a balanced product that will placate all of the interests partially and offend none of them totally. The committee also gets involved in disputes between different geographical areas, particularly in the West when diversion of water is involved. In such instances the committee often tries to do something for all of the competing areas.

*   *   *

The standing committees and subcommittees of Congress are critical in determining the substantive impact of Congress on policy and also in determining which interests will have the most access to the policy process at the national level. Representatives of bureaus and interest groups know this and cultivate their contacts with individual members and staff members on committees and subcommittees important to them. Presidents and party leaders alike can be frustrated by their own relative lack of access to the committee system. Committees generally seek to conduct their business in relative privacy; since press coverage of committee business is limited, they generally succeed.

Such a situation is not inevitable. At times the party leaders have inserted themselves aggressively into the committee process. Certainly the leaders constitute the main centralizing potential in contrast to the generally decentralizing impact of the standing committee system. In the next chapter the relations between the leaders and the committees will be examined in some detail.

5

PARTY
LEADERSHIP

POLITICAL PARTIES IN THE HOUSE AND SENATE PLAYED A CENTRAL
role in the emergence of the modern Congress in the late nineteenth
century. In that period and in the first two decades of the twentieth
century it appeared as if an American form of strong party government
might become a permanent feature of Congress.

But, at about the time of World War I, support for consistently strong
parties and party leaders in Congress waned among the members.
Strong parties threatened the independence prized by the members.
Consequently, the type of congressional parties that have dominated in
Congress since World War I have been strong and effective shapers of
the policy impact of Congress only sporadically. They are still important elements in the working of Congress but have usually played a
more modest role than their predecessors between roughly 1890 and
1915.

The potential for change is always present in Congress, however.
Thus parties could again emerge as even more potent and central features of the congressional landscape, if the members put programmatic
considerations ahead of maximizing individual freedom from party
constraints.

THE GENERAL IMPORTANCE
OF CONGRESSIONAL PARTIES

A candidate who has been elected to the House or Senate is confronted immediately with a congressional party. This party is likely to have a much greater impact on him than either the national party under whose banner he ran for office or the state and local parties, whose organization may have helped him as he campaigned. Party leaders, caucuses, committees, and other elements impinge on his daily life and are responsible for items crucial to his congressional career such as committee assignments. They control floor business, so he must come to terms with his party if he desires success in pushing those bills and policies he favors through Congress. In short, congressional parties provide absolutely essential procedural controls over congressional business. Centrally, they provide order and efficiency in the legislative process.

Congressional parties also possess substantive content. Until the twentieth century, congressional parties generated their own substantive positions, but their attention during the course of a Congress was narrowly focused, mainly on changing tariffs and a few other areas (for example, roads, canals, and other internal improvements).

In this century the leaders of the party of the president have typically (and without exception since 1933) accepted most of his policies and program preferences as their own. The leaders of the president's party in the House and Senate usually lend support to these proposals without seriously questioning them. The president's preferences aggregated in his legislative program are generally consistent with the national party platform, although rarely identical to it.

When the president's program comes to the committees and the floor in each house of Congress it generally receives support from most of the members of his party. There may be considerable dissent over portions of his program, but the party label they share with the president helps motivate most members to avoid dissent when possible. Party label is both a symbol and a reality that provides a focus for loyal behavior on substantive issues. Shared experiences, friendships, party machinery all help reinforce the natural feelings of loyalty to the president and his program.

These natural ties to the president on the part of his party's members are most dramatically visible when the House or Senate considers the question of overriding a presidential veto. Typically, many members of the president's party who voted for the bill the first time it went through the chamber will change their vote and support the president's veto. For example, in the first half of 1973 President Nixon vetoed four bills:

Table 5–1
Republican Voting on Vetoed Bills, 1973

Bill and Chamber	Vote on Original Passage		Vote on Veto	
	Republican Voting	% Supporting Nixon Position	Republican Voting	% Supporting Nixon Position
Vocational Rehabilitation Act—Senate	35–2	5%	10–31	76%
Water-Sewer Program—House	105–48	31%	24–161	87%
OMB Confirmation—Senate	16–17	52%	14–22	61%
OMB Confirmation—House	20–164	89%	18–167	90%
Cambodia Bombing Halt—House	63–120	66%	53–133	72%

the Vocational Rehabilitation Act, the Consolidated Farm and Rural Development Act (with a provision directing the president to spend all funds authorized for water and sewer construction), a bill requiring Senate confirmation of the incumbent director and deputy director of the Office of Management and Budget as well as their successors, and a supplemental appropriations bill that contained a provision requiring the immediate cessation of bombing in Cambodia. The president had opposed initial passage of each of these bills, and when the veto was considered in Congress the president asked for support for that veto. Table 5–1 summarizes the voting of Republicans in the House and Senate on the first passage of the four bills and on the veto override. All four vetoes were ultimately sustained; only in the case of the Senate vote on the Office of Management and Budget confirmation bill did even one house vote to override. In all cases the Republican support for the president increased on the veto vote compared to the first time the chamber had passed the bill. In two cases—in the Senate on vocational rehabilitation and in the House on the water-sewer program—the change was dramatic. In the first instance a large majority of Republicans had voted against the president; on the veto vote a large majority voted with him. Even on the bills that directly raised the question of congressional powers in relation to presidential powers—the OMB confirmation bill and the prohibition of Cambodian bombing—some Republicans changed their mind and supported the veto.

The party that does not have a president in the White House has a difficult time in generating loyalty to a substantive program. This party can decide either to oppose the president and his party with or without proposing programmatic alternatives or to support partially the president's program or to try to participate in the development of some of it (an exceedingly difficult task). Typically, the party without the presidency has far less programmatic or substantive identity than the presidential party.

In addition to the relation between congressional parties and substantive content, congressional parties also serve to predict voting on the floor of the House and Senate better than any other factor. A recent study of voting in Congress from 1921 through 1964 concluded that "by any measure party remains the single most important factor in roll call voting." * The trend during this time period was toward weaker party unity on controversial issues, principally because of the growing ideological conservatism on the part of a number of southern Democrats. Nevertheless, party remained a relatively strong unifying force in Congress.

PARTY LEADERS

The functioning of congressional parties is shaped in large part by the individuals who hold critical institutional positions in those parties. This does not mean that other individuals are prevented from developing influence; it simply means that the most influential are those with formal titles.

The Positions of Leadership

In the House the principal leaders of the majority party in this century have been the Speaker and majority leader. In recent years the majority whip has also emerged as an important leader. The principal leader of the minority party has been the minority leader, sometimes joined by the minority whip.

In the Senate the principal leader of the majority party in this century has been the majority leader. The minority leader has generally been the chief leader of the minority party. Whips have become increasingly important in both parties.

Individuals selected for the five principal positions in the two houses (the majority leaders, the minority leaders, and the Speaker of the House) have been relatively senior members of their respective chambers, but they are not chosen on the basis of seniority. Table 5–2 summarizes the mean years of service in the House and Senate for the five principal leaders plus the whips in the four parties. This table makes it clear that the House Democrats consistently look to their more senior

---

* Julius Turner, *Party and Constituency: Pressures on Congress* (Baltimore: Johns Hopkins Press, 1970, revised ed.), Edward Schneier (ed.).

Table 5–2
Average Seniority of Principal House and Senate Leaders at Time of
Initial Selection, by Party, Twentieth Century.

			Mean Seniority			
	Speaker	(N)	Floor Leader	(N)	Whip	(N)
House Democrats	25.4	(8)	18.6	(15)	11.8	(12)
House Republicans	22.4	(5)	15.6	(9)	6.1	(10)
Senate Democrats	—		8.3	(10)	6.5	(14)
Senate Republicans	—		13.8	(12)	5.7	(11)

members to fill their vacant leadership positions, as do the House Republicans. Neither Senate party produces leaders who are as senior. The Senate Republican floor leaders have been more senior than the Senate Democratic floor leaders.

Except for the House Democrats no geographical region has dominated any of the four parties in Congress. In the case of the House Democrats southerners have been most frequently chosen.* Four of the eight Democratic Speakers from 1911 to the present have been southerners and two more have been from border states. Ten of the fifteen Democratic floor leaders from 1899 to the present have been southerners and two more have been from border states. Six of the twelve Democratic whips from 1921 to the present have been southerners and one more has been from a border state. The Senate Democratic party has also chosen a number of southern and border state men as their leaders, but not as many: four of the ten Democratic floor leaders from 1911 to the present were southerners and one more was from a border state; only four of the fourteen Democratic whips from 1913 to the present have been from the South and two more have been from border states.

Overall, 57 percent of the principal House Democratic leaders in this century have been southerners and 71 percent have been either southerners or from border states. But in the Senate only 33 percent have been southerners and only 46 percent have been either southerners or from border states.

Once selected, the leaders in all of the five principal positions tend to serve about the same length of time. Table 5–3 summarizes their service and shows the only exception to be the floor leadership in the House Republican party, which has more stability than the other offices.

---

* The South is defined as the eleven states of the Confederacy. Border states include Delaware, Maryland, West Virginia, Kentucky, Missouri, and Oklahoma.

Table 5–3
Average Length of Service in Principal Leadership Positions, by Party,
Twentieth Century.

	Speaker	(N)	Mean Service Floor Leader	(N)	Whip	(N)
House Democrats	6.3	(7)	5.3	(14)	4.6	(11)
House Republicans	5.6	(5)	8.3	(8)	5.2	(9)
Senate Democrats	—		5.6	(9)	4.5	(13)
Senate Republicans	—		5.2	(11)	4.6	(10)

The Party Loyalty of Leaders

If loyalty to party is defined in terms of the propensity to vote with
the majority of the party on the House or Senate floor then the principal party leaders are much more loyal than the average senator or
representative or any other subset of senators or representatives. Table
5–4 summarizes party loyalty in voting on the floor of the House and
Senate for all members of each party, for the chairmen or ranking
minority members of each party, and for the floor leader of each party
for the period between 1935 and 1970. As can be seen, party leaders
are considerably more loyal in both parties in both houses compared
either to all members or to the committee chairmen and ranking minority members as a group. It should also be noted that all categories in
both parties in the House are slightly more loyal than the same categories in the Senate, suggesting that party is a more important phenomenon in the House than in the Senate. Likewise, it is worth noting
that the gap between the loyalty of the leaders on the one hand and the
loyalty of the general membership and committee leaders on the other

Table 5–4
Party Loyalty in Floor Voting, 1935–1970.

Group	Mean Percentage of Votes with Majority of Own Party			
	House Democrats	House Republicans	Senate Democrats	Senate Republicans
All Party Members	82	84	77	80
Chairmen and Ranking Minority Members of Standing Committees	81	84	74	80
Floor Leaders	92	90	89	88

is greater for the Democrats than for the Republicans. This suggests that there is a greater ideological distance for the Democratic leaders to traverse in dealing with at least some significant part of their party (in this case, the conservative southerners).

The attitudes toward manifestations of loyalty vary somewhat between the two houses. In both houses general loyalty is expected. But in the Senate there is more tolerance of some overt behavior running contrary to generally understood party stands. For example, in 1973 the Senate Republican whip both voted and spoke against the president's position on the veto of the bill involving confirmation for the top officials in the Office of Management and Budget. Yet this occasioned no particular notice on the part of his party colleagues. In the same year, however, when the House Democratic whip voted against an anti-Cambodian bombing amendment and suggested on the floor to the manager of the bill that a point of order might be raised against the amendment there was considerable negative reaction on the part of his party colleagues, who had earlier been successful in getting the House Democratic caucus to endorse the amendment.*

Leadership Change †

The problem of succession from one leader to another is critical for any institution. Contests over succession can disrupt the institution. Smooth transitions can facilitate the functioning of the institution, although perhaps at the price of continuing outmoded policies or procedures. In the House and Senate, experience over the last several decades leads to a number of generalizations about change in leadership.

The most striking pattern that emerges is that succession is handled quite differently in the majority party from the way it is handled in the minority party. In the majority party, particularly in the case of a long standing majority, succession is likely to be smooth and divisive internal contests rare. The longer a party is in the majority the more likely it is to develop established patterns of leadership succession. For example, during the long period of dominance of the House by the Democrats from 1931 to the present (with only two two-year breaks) a pattern has

---

* See "House Democrats: Debate Over Leadership Role," *Congressional Quarterly Weekly Report* (August 4, 1973): 2135.

† This discussion draws heavily on Robert L. Peabody, "Party Leadership Change in the United States House of Representatives," in Peabody and Nelson W. Polsby (eds.), *New Perspectives on the House of Representatives* (Chicago: Rand McNally, 1969, 2nd ed.; and Peabody, "Senate Leadership Change: 1953–1970," (paper prepared for delivery at Stanford University, April 17–18, 1970).

emerged whereby, first, a sitting majority leader virtually automatically succeeds to the speakership when it becomes vacant and, second, the majority whip regularly wins election as majority leader when that job opens. Any contests in the majority party are most likely to take place for lesser leadership positions, not the top positions.

In the minority party, however, particularly in the House, internal fights of an intense character are likely to occur over leadership positions. These contests are likely to occur at all levels of leadership and are most likely to occur at the times of highest frustration for the minority—for example, after a major electoral disaster.

CONTEMPORARY PATTERNS OF LEADERSHIP

Throughout history many patterns of leadership have been used by both parties in the House and the Senate. Since roughly the 1880s the formal leaders of both parties in both houses have been consistently important in helping to determine the timing and character of legislation emerging from the House and Senate.

Examination of the recent leadership in the House and Senate reveals a high degree of stability in terms of institutional arrangements and the styles of the principal leaders even though some of the individuals have changed.

The *House Democrats* in the 1960s and early 1970s had a leadership pattern in which a three-man group (the Speaker, the majority leader, and the majority whip) formed the core. This group met daily to plan the general strategy and the specific tactics of action on the House floor. As bills were reported from committees for floor consideration, the three-man group would coopt a committee leader, usually the chairman, to work with them on tactical details of passing the committee's bill.

To aid the core group, the House Democrats used a whip organization consisting of a deputy whip and eighteen regional whips in addition to the chief whip. The Committee on Committees for the party, although not totally dominated by the core group, helped perform the leadership function of assigning Democrats to standing committees. Until 1975 this group consisted of the Democratic members of the Ways and Means Committee, with each member responsible for a particular state or region. Beginning in 1973 the Speaker, majority leader, and caucus chairman were added to the membership of the Committee. In addition, the Democratic caucus (comprised of all Democrats) also helped to perform some leadership functions.

The *House Republicans* had a more diffused pattern of leadership during the 1960s and early 1970s. At least five positions carried leadership status in the Republican party, even though it was much smaller than the Democratic party in the House: the minority leader, the chairman of the conference (the Republican version of the Democratic caucus), the minority whip, the chairman of the Policy Committee, and the chairman of the Research and Planning Committee.

The Republican leaders were also aided by a whip organization and by the members of the Policy Committee and the Research and Planning Committee. The Republicans also had a large committee on committees to perform the function of assigning Republicans to standing committees. This committee tended to be relatively independent of the principal individual leaders. The full conference also helped organize the party.

In addition, the norms and traditions of the Republican party in the House also gave unusually heavy weight to the senior Republican members of various standing committee delegations. Senior Democrats on standing committees were also important in their party but not as independent within the party as the senior Republicans.

The *Senate Democrats* operate with only a few leaders. The only consistently important individual in a Senate leadership position is the majority leader. During the 1960s and early 1970s the majority leader has been Mike Mansfield (D-Mont.), whose attitude towards leadership has been consistently low-key. In theory he is aided by a majority whip and the secretary of the party conference (the name for the total Democratic membership). There are also four deputy whips, a steering committee, and a policy committee. But the majority whip, secretary, and deputy whips perform mainly housekeeping chores; the majority leader himself chairs the Steering Committee and the Policy Committee. He is certainly constrained by the deliberations in those committees but, if he chooses, he can also be the most important figure in those deliberations. Although Mansfield did not choose to be dominant most of the time, the potential in the position clearly exists as was well illustrated by his predecessor in the 1950s, Lyndon Johnson (D-Tex.). Where Mansfield is tolerant of dissent, Johnson would often charge disloyalty; where Mansfield refused to apply even mild pressure, Johnson would skillfully "arm-twist" using the full range of resources; where Mansfield consistently is quiet and calm, Johnson would run through a range of moods and appeals including some dramatic and boisterous ones.

The *Senate Republicans* can limit the activities of the minority leader because, unlike the Democrats, they have party committees that he is not permitted to chair. Nevertheless, the minority leader is the single most important figure in the party. He is aided by a minority whip, the chairman of the conference, and the chairman and members of the Policy Committee. The Senate Republicans also have a committee on committees with a separate chairman but, as will be explained below, this committee does not have much to do independent of an automatic rule of seniority for making committee assignments in most cases.

LEADERSHIP FUNCTIONS

The leaders of all four congressional parties perform (or at least have the potential of performing) five major functions.

First, the leaders help organize the party to conduct business. Essentially this means that they participate in the selection of new leaders and the decisions concerning who will sit on which committees. This choice determines which individuals will be sitting in the most critical institutional positions when policy decisions are made.

In the House Democratic party the caucus elects the Speaker and the majority leader, and, until 1975, elected Ways and Means members. Usually, the Speaker can determine who the majority leader will be if he announces his preference publicly or lets it be widely known privately, although some Speakers have refrained from making their choice known. The Speaker could also usually endorse winning candidates for Ways and Means vacancies, although occasionally the caucus chose someone other than the Speaker's candidate. The Speaker and the majority leader appoint the whip. The Speaker and the majority leader can also influence committee assignments made by the Committee on Committees. This influence is used selectively, but it means that in at least a few policy areas the leaders can help pre-determine policy statements and actions emanating from a specific committee by helping see to it that the membership represents policy positions congenial to theirs.

In the House Republican party the conference elects the minority leader, the minority whip, and the chairman of the conference. The Committee on Committees is constituted entirely through the state delegations—with one member of the committee coming from every state that has at least one Republican in the House. The minority leader (and the other central leaders too) have minimal influence on the decisions of the Committee on Committees and on the choice of other leaders.

In both Senate parties the leadership seems disposed not to play a very active role in helping with the leader and committee choices in the party. Every individual senator seems to fend for himself and little central direction is evident in organizational terms in either party.

The second of the five functions that the leaders of all four congressional parties perform is the scheduling of business to come to the House and the Senate floors. In the House the Speaker and majority leader make these decisions, although they occasionally consult the minority leader to make sure that his sense of fairness is not violated. In the Senate the majority leader routinely consults the minority leader; if they agree they have great flexibility because the Senate usually proceeds in an ad hoc fashion under so-called unanimous consent, which is based on agreements among everyone present to proceed in a specified way (time of debate, day of debate, control of time, allowable amendments) regardless of any formal Senate rules. Naturally, the scheduling decisions made in both houses are not neutral and can be used to influence the chances of success or failure of specific pieces of legislation. For example, if the majority party leaders fear a close vote they will postpone floor consideration if they know that some of their reliable supporters have to be absent. Or they may move floor action to a day on which some known opponents have to be absent.

Third, the leaders are responsible for promoting attendance on the floor of the House and the Senate. Both of the parties in the House do this primarily through their whip organizations, which are responsible for informing all party members that a critical vote is at hand and that their presence on the floor is required. This is done through an established telephone network between staff members in the regional whips' offices and staff members in the offices of individual congressmen who are responsible for knowing the whereabouts of the "boss." In the Senate, neither party routinely uses their whip apparatus. Consequently, a senator who is interested in a particular piece of legislation will frequently do his own "whipping" to increase attendance.

Obviously, selectivity is exercised in this attempt to increase attendance. For example, the whip organization of one of the House parties may well not contact a known opponent of the leaders' position when a critical vote is imminent.

Fourth, the leaders are constantly engaged in the collection and distribution of information. Reliable information is a precious commodity in both houses. In the House the whip organizations in both parties serve as focal points for this function. They solicit members' attitudes on selected upcoming bills and disseminate the leaders' preferences and limited information on the content of proposed legislation to party members. In the Senate, however, individual senators particularly interested in a bill usually wind up doing their own "headcounts" and their own distribution of substantive information.

Fifth, the party leaders in both houses maintain a liaison with the White House on policy matters. This involves the leaders of the president's party more frequently than the leaders of the other party. Between the late 1930s and the late 1960s the leaders of the president's party met with him weekly. President Nixon had less frequent meetings with the Republican leaders in Congress. There may also be meetings on an emergency basis and the members of the opposition party may be invited from time to time for specific briefings and consultation. Presumably the leaders can serve as mediators between the president and the rank-and-file members, helping to facilitate the flow of policy-related information and preferences in both directions.

All five of these functions can be performed in such a way as to enhance the possibility of attaining specific desired policy statements and actions and reducing the possibility of producing undesired statements and actions. The leaders' central task is to persuade members to support their policy preferences on the floor of the House and the Senate. It should be noted, however, that the content of a leader's preferences is usually based on the stance of his party's delegation in the relevant standing committee for any given issue. That is, the leaders usually take their substantive cues from a committee delegation and then exercise their persuasive powers to gain ratification for that position, rather than attemping to push a personal position on their party in an authoritarian manner.

THE PRINCIPAL LEADERSHIP RESOURCES FOR AFFECTING LEGISLATIVE RESULTS

The party leaders in both houses have four principal resources at their disposal as they labor to influence the policy statements and actions emerging from the Senate and the House.

The first is their ability to use the rules of the House and the Senate. Leaders, out of desire and necessity, develop considerable expertise in manipulating the intricacies of the rules.

In the House the majority party leaders, particularly the Speaker, are in a very strong position to use the rules to further their policy ends. The minority leaders in the House have some obstructive powers, but the House rules generally put the majority party in a consistently dominant position. For example, the Speaker can be selective in placing legislation on the "suspension calendar," a device for expediting relatively non-controversial bills (bills brought to the floor on this calendar are debated for only forty minutes and require a two-thirds vote for passage). Many bills of low visibility would die if they were not moved through the House quickly in this fashion. This means that the Speaker is in a good position to build credits for the future, to reward past loyalty, or to punish past disloyalty by either granting or withholding a member's request to place a low visibility bill that is important to him on the suspension calendar.

In the Senate the leaders of both parties have influence over the use of the rules. The legislative process in the Senate is highly flexible because of the use of unanimous consent agreements. The leaders play a central role in arranging these agreements, thereby enhancing their ability to collect IOUs for the future and to reward or punish past behavior.

The second resource possessed by the leaders of both houses is their control over a number of forms of tangible preferment. Tangible preferments include: appointments to special and select committees, commissions (such as those overseeing service academies), and delegations to foreign meetings (such as the NATO parliamentarians); appointments to standing committees; help in pushing specific bills; and help aimed at re-election. Again the granting or withholding of such preferments is used selectively to shorten the odds that the leaders will succeed when they ask for specific policy actions.

The leaders' control over assignments to standing committees is not as evident as their control over other appointments but it can be significant. In the House, for example, the Democratic Committee on Committees will not appoint a Democrat to the Rules Committee without the approval of the Speaker. The Democratic leaders can also intervene selectively in the assignments to other committees. In the 1950s, for example, Speaker Rayburn saw to it that the Democratic membership on the Education and Labor Committee was reoriented from conservative to reliably liberal. In general, the Democratic Committee on Committees pays some attention to party loyalty in making assignments —those members more loyal to the party are more likely to receive their preferred assignments.*

The House Republican leaders have less influence over standing committee assignments. The Committee on Committees is selected and operated so that, typically, a few senior conservatives from the states with the largest Republican delegations effectively make the assignment decisions. This means that the Republican delegations on the most important committees are heavily weighted in the conservative direction.

In the Senate the leaders have only minor influence on committee assignments. This is particularly true in the Republican Party where the Committee on Committees makes initial assignments on the basis of seniority (that is, with only minor exceptions, if two individuals apply for the same opening the more senior man automatically gets it). The influence of the Republican leaders can be seen only occasionally when they might ask a more senior man to apply for an opening in order to keep an undesirable senator off the committee. The Democratic Steering Committee, which is the committee on committees, is not bound by

---

* For evidence on this point see Ripley, *Party Leaders in the House of Representatives:* 59–61.

seniority and the majority leader chairs the committee. But his degree of influence is related to his degree of aggressiveness.

The leaders of all four parties can facilitate or impede committee and floor consideration of specific bills.

An additional tangible preferment is campaign help, which leaders can channel to particularly helpful members. Both of the congressional Republican parties have several million dollars at their disposal to aid candidates, both incumbents and non-incumbents. This can be given on a selective basis, with maverick incumbents getting little or no aid. The Democratic congressional parties have much less money at their disposal and so the impact of the aid is considerably reduced. The leaders of all four parties can personally campaign for a few incumbents each year. Obviously it is very flattering for a rank-and-file congressman to have the Speaker or the majority leader speak personally in his or her district during a campaign. These appearances are rare and, like most scarce commodities, are highly valued by those who benefit.

The third resource the leaders can use to affect policy statements and actions is psychological preferment. This simply means that the leaders, particularly in the House, are in a position to give cues on how highly they value an individual member. These cues, once given, help establish a member's reputation. A member with a high reputation is likely to be more successful legislatively than a member who is not so highly regarded. House members know they need the respect and good will of their fellows to help make their careers successful in terms of achievement of legislative goals, and therefore are extremely sensitive to the leaders' cues. Skillful leaders can help sway member behavior by the content and timing of the cues and by selective publication of those cues to appropriate audiences. For example, if the Speaker stops a group of four congressmen and singles out one for praise on a floor speech that is a signal to the others about the esteem in which that individual is held. Likewise, if he pointedly ignores one member of the group that also conveys a message.

Senators also need respect and good will in the Senate if they are to be deemed successful legislators. On the other hand, senators can also command wider attention than that accorded to House members and many may not worry excessively about their perceived legislative effectiveness. They can also attain gratification by being public figures in their states or regions or even nationally. Almost any senator can command good newspaper space in his state and with a little extra effort can be quoted and pictured regionally or nationally. This opportunity is not open to most House members, which means that they are very sensitive to their standing in the House. Senators who want above all to be considered effective legislators are susceptible to psychological preferment manipulated by the leaders. Senator Mansfield has not used this tactic although his predecessor, Lyndon Johnson, was masterful at it.* The Republican leaders in the 1960s and 1970s were somewhere between Mansfield and Johnson in their level of activity.

The fourth resource that can be used by the leaders in seeking specific legislative action is their dominance over the communications processes internal to the House and Senate. The leaders are in a unique position to control what is learned by members about the schedule and rules affecting pending legislation and about the legislative intentions of the president, key members, and the leaders themselves. Particularly in the House, members of both parties routinely look to their party leaders for reliable information on such matters. They are not, however, heavily dependent on their party leaders for information on the substance of legislation; for that they rely on the standing committee members from their party. Even in the Senate a skillful leader like Lyndon Johnson can make the senators of his party (and even of the other party) come to him or his staff members for the most current and most reliable information.

The dominance over the communications process means that the leaders occupy a critical place. They learn as well as inform and can use their knowledge to enhance their chances for success by urging minor but critical amendments, for example, or by changing the schedule to accommodate a number of members who are in the leaders' camp on a given bill.

THE IMPACT OF THE LEADERS

The Leaders and Individual Members

The members of the House and Senate have definite expectations about the intrusion of the party leaders into their lives as legislators. House members are more likely to consider aggressive leadership legitimate than are senators. Senators acknowledge the legitimacy of their leaders stating party positions on at least some legislative matters, appealing for unity and loyalty on important bills, and distributing and collecting information on scheduling and substance. They do not, however, accept coercion as legitimate, nor do they think that the party leaders should interfere with the business of standing committees, aside from urging them to keep on schedule.† Most House members accept

---

* For a good discussion of Johnson as Majority Leader, see Rowland Evans and Robert Novak, *Lyndon B. Johnson: The Exercise of Power* (New York: New American Library, 1966).

† See Ripley, *Power in the Senate:* 104–106.

the same tasks as legitimate for the leaders to perform but they are more willing than senators to accept the coercive activities of leaders as legitimate.* This difference is rooted both in history and tradition (the simple fact that House leaders have usually been more aggressive than their Senate counterparts) and in the perceived necessities of managing a body of 435 people as opposed to a body of only 100 people.

The leaders understand that they must lead through a complicated process of interaction with the members. They can state preferences and apply a variety of pressures to get maximum support. But their job is persuasion—they do not have sanctions available that will always produce compliance. Leaders feel the need, however, to be restrained in the use of the sanctions they do possess because they realize the party membership can balk if it feels it is being subjected to unfair pressure. Members of Congress are keenly aware that they have been elected largely on the basis of their own resources and wits, and they inevitably feel a strong pull toward their constituencies. Likewise, members prize their own independence and resent what they consider to be unfair attempts at coercion to achieve unity for its own sake or even for a specific policy goal. When the pull of constituency or the dictates of conscience conflict with the demands of the party leaders, the member's decision can go either way. The most successful leaders acknowledge the existence of these cross-pressures and undertake a constant balancing act between demanding partisan unity and loyalty and deferring to constituency interests and the dictates of individual judgment.†

The Techniques of the Leaders. The party leaders of both houses have a number of specific techniques they can employ to gain the support of their members for specific legislative ends, although they must constantly decide how aggressive to be in using them. Among these techniques are the following:

1. Using personal contact to ask for such actions as favorable roll call votes, votes in committees, certain kinds of speeches on the floor, absence or presence on the floor.
2. Promulgating permanent or temporary changes in the rules, procedures, and practices of the House or Senate that will make favorable legislative outcomes easier to achieve.
3. Using influence over committee assignments to achieve a certain ideological balance on a committee.

---

* See Ripley, *Party Leaders in the House.*
† For an interesting interview in which the House Democratic Majority Leader talks, in part, about the job of leading see "O'Neill: Watergate May Help Free Republican Votes," *Congressional Quarterly Weekly Report* (May 19, 1973): 1208–1211.

4. Encouraging the development of unanimous positions by standing committee contingents before floor debate begins.

5. Announcing official party positions on pending legislation by a letter to all members, by a statement from a policy or steering committee, or by the adoption of an official party position in one of the caucuses or conferences.

6. Coopting key members into the leadership circle for the duration of a given legislative struggle.

7. Stimulating key intra-party groups such as state delegations to unify behind specific positions.

8. Influencing the distribution of tangible rewards such as federal patronage, federal projects and electoral aid.

9. Distributing information selectively to the members on substance and procedure.

10. Giving special concessions to a few key members of the opposition party when a winning coalition cannot be formed from within a single party.

11. Manipulating floor proceedings by scheduling critical business at the most propitious time, arranging for influential speakers, managing the pattern of voting, and helping arrange the optimum time and amendment limits for a particular bill.

*Conditions for Success.** Not all leaders are equally successful in achieving what they want as they seek to stimulate certain kinds of behavior from the members of their party. The leaders of the minority party are, by definition, dependent on some support from members of the majority party. Their hand is strengthened when the president is also of their party, but the problem of insufficient numbers remains. The leaders of the majority party, who presumably have the numbers on their side, must labor to maximize the unity of their members and prevent defections that could cause losses. In general, majority party leaders have greater chances of legislative success when their majority is large, when it is a relatively new majority, and when there is supportive activity coming from the president and the White House.

The leaders of both parties have increased chances for success on issues not terribly visible or salient to constituents. This leaves members freer to succumb to the blandishments of the leaders. Leaders are also more likely to prevail with specific requests at relatively invisible points in the legislative process. That is, if a member perceives that his position

---

* See Randall B. Ripley, *Majority Party Leadership in Congress* (Boston: Little, Brown, 1969): 184–187; and Lewis A. Froman, Jr. and Randall B. Ripley, "Conditions for Party Leadership: The Case of the House Democrats," *American Political Science Review* 59 (1965): 52–63.

might cause some negative reaction in his constituency, he would feel more secure honoring a leadership request on a final roll call on the floor. His action in the committee is likely to go unnoticed at home by either the press or public whereas his action in the floor is likely to be reported. Leaders are also more likely to gain converts on issues that are defined in procedural terms than on issues that are defined in substantive terms. For example, a motion to adjourn may really be a motion that will kill a bill. A person who may mildly favor the bill can still claim that position and yet vote with his party leaders in favor of adjournment and rationalize his action—if it is ever questioned—as "only procedural." Again the relative visibility of actions on procedurally-defined issues is lower than on the substantively-defined issues and this allows members to adhere to the requests of the leaders without worrying in detail about constituency reaction.

The Leaders and Standing Committees *

The party leaders are potentially the main centralizing forces in the legislative process, the standing committees the main decentralizing forces. Leaders and committees must necessarily interact in conducting the business of the two chambers. The exact nature of the interaction, however, can vary as can the relative importance of leaders and committees on critical items of substance.

In many ways leaders and committees are interdependent. As party leaders seek specific legislative ends they must rely on the standing committees for a number of things: the detailed substance of bills, the timetable within which bills are ready for floor consideration, the transmission of leaders' legislative preferences to the members of the committee during committee deliberations, and aid in the transmission of those preferences to all party members during floor consideration. Committee leaders must rely on the party leaders for scheduling business for the floor and working for its passage or defeat, for communicating important information about members' preferences to the committee, and for helping distribute committee opinions to non-committee members.

The Nature of Leader-Committee Interaction. There are three particularly important points of interaction between party leaders and committee leaders. The first involves assignments to committees. Who sits on a committee may, in many instances, determine what emerges from that

---

* For a more detailed version of what follows, with specific reference to the House, see my paper prepared for the House Select Committee on Committees, "Party Leaders and Standing Committees in the House of Representatives," (June 1973).

committee. The custom of seniority limits leaders' potential impact on committee assignments to sitting members who desire to change assignments or to new members. In the case of freshmen members and new assignments the leaders of both parties are generally disposed to exercise only minimal influence unless vital issues are at stake.

In changes made in 1971 and 1973, however, the House party leaders have moved into a position to prevent individuals from becoming chairmen or ranking minority members if they can persuade a majority of the party that such individuals are undesirable for those jobs. In 1971 the Republican conference agreed to allow the conference to vote individually by secret ballot on the representatives nominated by the Committee on Committees to be ranking minority members. If the Republicans should again become the majority party in the House the same procedure would presumably apply to chairmanships. No successful challenges to seniority appointments have been made under the new procedure.

In 1971 the Democratic caucus made a similar change. Committee on Committee recommendations come to the caucus one committee at a time and, if requested by ten members, nominations can be debated and voted on—not just for chairmanships but for any position on any committee. If a nomination is rejected then the Committee on Committees will submit another nomination. In 1971 an unsuccessful challenge was mounted against reappointment of the chairman of the Committee on the District of Columbia on the implied grounds that he did not reflect the majority Democratic opinion about committee business, that he was an arbitrary chairman, and that he pursued racist (anti-black) policies.

In 1973 the Democrats extended their procedure by making it necessary for chairmen to obtain a majority vote in the caucus. Twenty percent of the members can demand a secret ballot. In 1973 all chairmen were voted on by secret ballot and all won by very large margins. Beginning in 1975 Appropriations subcommittee chairmen were also required to win caucus approval.

In short, despite lack of real change in personnel through 1974, both parties in the House have the machinery for rejecting an unacceptable product of the seniority system in the top spot of any standing committee. The Republican conference members and Democratic caucus members could, of course, ignore the preferences of the formal party leaders either to retain or reject a chairman or ranking minority member. But it seems likely that members who have come to those positions through seniority will not be deposed if they have the support of the party leaders. And, if the party leaders should ever agree on the necessity of rejecting a nomination for a top position based on seniority, they would probably stand a reasonably good chance of carrying either the caucus or the conference with them.

A second major point of interaction between party leaders and the committee system involves the scheduling of floor activity that, of necessity, has implications for the scheduling of committee business. If the party leaders of the majority party have an overall program in mind (and this is particularly likely to be the case if their party also controls the White House) they are going to need to spread the program out over a Congress. They cannot afford to have all of the important legislation come to the floor in the last two months of a session or, worse yet, the last two months of a Congress. Thus the leaders consult with chairmen about the major items on the agenda both to get some reading on when reports might be expected and to make some requests either to speed up or, less frequently, slow down committee consideration and action.

Similarly, committee chairmen have their own agenda to consider. Therefore, they make timing requests of the leaders for floor consideration on specific dates.

A third point of interaction between party leaders and committees involves the substance of legislative proposals. Party leaders may well be too busy with scheduling matters for the floor and working for their passage (or defeat) to have preferences on the substantive details of legislation. If they are working together with representatives of the White House or individual executive departments or agencies, however, they may have detailed requests on some matters. And some leaders have strong personal interests that they pursue. For example, when Sam Rayburn (D-Tex.) was Speaker he followed the work of the Ways and Means Committee on trade (he wanted fewer restrictions) and the oil depletion allowance (he wanted it preserved unchanged) and did not hesitate to intervene if he felt it necessary.

Leaders in the last few decades have tended to keep their intervention in the work of standing committees to a minimum. They have been much more likely to allow the committee to produce its substantive product by whatever natural processes exist in the committee and then work with the senior members of the committee for the passage (or defeat or amendment) of the committee's handiwork.

A rule adopted in 1973 by the House Democratic caucus increases the likelihood of more substantive input by the leaders into the work of committees. This rule allows fifty or more members of the party to bring to the caucus any amendment proposed to a committee-reported bill if the Rules Committee is requesting a closed rule. If the proposed amendment is supported by a majority of the caucus then the Rules Committee Democrats will be instructed to write the rule for floor consideration so that that specific amendment could be considered on the floor. In effect, this will prevent closed rules on bills if a majority present at a Democratic caucus opposes such a rule. The leeway for leadership intervention is again present here if the Speaker and/or majority leader and/or majority whip should decide to side with the members who want to force floor consideration of a specific amendment not favored by the committee (including at least some of the Democrats on the committee).

The Impact of Leader-Committee Interaction. The nature of the interaction between leaders and standing committees is particularly critical to the performance by Congress of its lawmaking function. In general, the nature of the interaction can be viewed along a spectrum ranging from virtual committee autonomy at one end to leader activism at the other. In a situation of committee autonomy the central party leaders rarely intervene in such matters as committee assignments, the scheduling and timing of committee business, and the substance of matters before committees. In a situation in which leader activism is predominant there is a considerable amount of such intervention. There are, of course, a number of mixed patterns along the spectrum.

Some facets of lawmaking for domestic policy and the domestic aspects of foreign policy (for example, defense procurement, or "buy American" or "ship American" provisions in foreign aid legislation) are different than for the non-domestic aspects of foreign policy. What is the same, however, is that the committee autonomy pattern leaves the congressional party leaders out of an important substantive role in policy of either kind.

When domestic policy is at stake (and also the domestic aspects of foreign policy) the existence of committee autonomy promotes the dominance of what Douglass Cater has called "subgovernments." * These are small groups composed of a few key bureaucrats, interest group representatives, and senior members of subcommittees who, in effect, make policy by themselves with very little input by anyone else— whether rank-and-file members of the two chambers, the party leaders, or the president or institutional presidency. Leader activism, on the other hand, promotes increased influence not just for the leaders but also for the president and presidency when the leaders are in accord with presidential policies and for rank-and-file senators and repre-

---

* The term "subgovernments" to describe this phenomenon comes from Douglass Cater, *Power in Washington* (New York: Random House, 1964). The term "whirlpools" for the same phenomenon comes from Ernest S. Griffith, *Congress: Its Contemporary Role* (New York: New York University Press, 1961, 3rd ed.).

sentatives. This increased influence does not eliminate the influence of the subgovernments, but it puts some restraints on it. The subgovernments may or may not produce good or reasonable policy decisions but, in any event, they cannot be expected to consult more than a narrow range of interests in making their decisions. The increased influence for non-subgovernment members that is facilitated by leader activism allows for a broader range of interests to be articulated and consulted.

Another value that can best be served by the leadership activism pattern of interaction is coherence of the legislative program. This simply means that some order is apparent in the welter of proposals presented to Congress—both in terms of substance and in terms of timing. The leadership activism pattern leaves room for an activist president, but in no way does it place Congress in a subordinate position to the president. It simultaneously affords maximum influence for the party leaders and all members. In addition, it puts some restrictions on the influence of the members of the issue-specific subgovernments. If the program is set —both in substance and in timing—by these subgovernments, then little relationship will be seen between programs that are in fact competing for scarce resources or have other logical ties. In the leader activism pattern the centralizing forces can spell out those relationships so that the decisions can be made on the basis of more rather than less information and there is a chance for greater coherence of all legislative results considered together.

The major difference between the situation just described and the situation when non-domestic aspects of foreign policy are at stake is the enormous impact of the president and institutional presidency. Presidential influence over Congress is no longer as much of a problem for the president except on those occasions when he needs a treaty ratified or a new program approved. He may have more problems in relation to appropriations requests. Another major difference is that interest groups play only a very limited role. Thus the chief actors in this policy arena are the president and institutional presidency, the foreign policy bureaucracy, key committee members on the Senate Foreign Relations, House Foreign Affairs, and the two Appropriations Committees, the party leaders, and the individual members of the House and Senate.

An alliance between members of the foreign policy bureaucracy and senior committee members may have considerable influence on the routine aspects of foreign policy, particularly when a pattern of committee autonomy exists. Such an alliance may even limit presidential influence on such matters, although it seems as if the alliance is much less close between the foreign policy bureaucrats and committees and subcommittees than it is in many domestic areas (including the domestic aspects of foreign policy). The major "subgovernment" in foreign policy may, in fact, consist of the presidency and foreign policy bureaucracy with all congressional elements, including the key committee and sub-committee members as well as the party leaders, relegated to relatively minor roles.

In a pattern of leader activism the leaders increase their potential for influence in the foreign policy arena and can also enhance the potential for influence on the part of members of the two chambers not on the specific committees dealing with central foreign policy issues by serving as their spokesmen and by helping them aggregate their positions. It also seems likely that in the event of a major disagreement between a committee and the president, the committee itself will have a stronger hand if backed by at least some of the central party leaders—especially if the leaders are from both parties. Thus leader activism does not necessarily diminish the potential for influence on the part of committees, except perhaps in some of the routine matters that are left mostly to the interaction of committees and subcommittees and the foreign policy bureaucracy. The difference is that in domestic policy and the domestic aspects of foreign policy these routine matters, when aggregated, constitute the bulk of policy both in amount and importance. But in the foreign policy arena routine matters are not as important.

*   *   *

If Congress is assessed in terms of its potential for important and swift policy action, the party leaders necessarily play a critical role. On those occasions when Congress has been at its most active the party leaders have usually been aggressive—both in their own right and in responding to an aggressive president. When the leaders are the most constrained in their actions, either of their own volition or by virtue of matters over which they have little control, Congress is most likely to be proceeding on a "normal" course of handling most matters in a disaggregated and incremental fashion. Thus the performance of the leaders offers an index to the overall mood and performance of Congress. And, since the leaders can help shape the environment in which they work, the choices they make on how they use their resources, what techniques they employ, and how they perform their functions can help determine the nature of congressional influence on public policy.

6

OTHER INFLUENCES: FORMAL AND INFORMAL GROUPS AND CONGRESSIONAL STAFF

MEMBERS OF THE HOUSE AND SENATE RECEIVE A CONSTANT barrage of advice—both solicited and unsolicited—on which policies to support from their standing committee colleagues and from the party leaders. The committees and leaders are the most consistently important forces internal to Congress that shape public policy. There are, however, other forces inside Congress that also serve as important sources of advice and direction for individual members as they seek to cope with a staggering workload in a limited amount of time. State delegations, regional blocs, ideological groups, and staff members working both for individual members and for committees all perform this function. The relative sizes of the two houses dictate that state delegations and ideological groups have particular importance in the House and that staff members have particular importance in the Senate.

STATE DELEGATIONS AND REGIONAL BLOCS

Throughout the American political system the states have always been important objects of loyalty. The federal scheme of the Constitution springs in part from such loyalty. Our national parties are more properly thought of as confederations of fifty state parties. State loyalties

146

are also extremely important inside Congress, particularly in the House of Representatives (which, in a way, is ironic given that senators are explicitly thought to be the representatives of states). In the House, state loyalty is made operational through the functioning of the state delegations, usually divided on a partisan basis. These clusters of members can help each other by the sharing of useful and timely information and by aiding each other to maximize their ability to achieve desired ends such as attractive committee assignments and a "fair share" of federal program money and installations for their individual districts.

Sometimes state delegations meet on a bipartisan basis. Occasionally senators from the same state will be included, regardless of party. But these bipartisan, bicameral meetings are relatively rare and involve only questions relating to direct federal benefits for the state or region in which the state is included. Ordinarily, the state delegations that are important in the flow of information and benefits are the party delegations from the House alone. These delegations will be the focus of he following section.*

State Party Delegations in the House

Types of Delegations. State party delegations vary greatly in the frequency of their meetings, the extent to which they help socialize new members, the amount of interaction they have outside of meetings, the topics they discuss in their meetings, and whether they seek unity in voting on the floor of the House. In short, they vary greatly in cohesion.

State delegations can be grouped into four broad types.† The first type rarely meets, discusses only local issues (for example, new federal installations or the performance of federal programs in the state) at meetings, and explicitly does not seek unity in voting on the floor. The second type also meets rarely, but discusses national as well as local issues, and does seek floor unity. The third type meets often, discusses national and local issues, and seeks floor unity. The fourth type meets often, discusses only national issues, and does not seek floor unity. About half of the delegations in both parties seek unity and about half do not.

Two conditions seem to promote state delegation cohesion: stable membership and a relatively high proportion of members desiring to

---

* In addition to the material cited in footnotes 2–11 on state delegations see also Charles L. Clapp, *The Congressman* (Washington, D.C.: Brookings, 1963): 41–45; John H. Kessel, "The Washington Congressional Delegation," *Midwest Journal of Political Science* 8 (1964): 1–21; and Leo M. Snowiss, "Congressional Recruitment and Representation," *American Political Science Review* 60 (1966): 627–639.

† Ripley, *Party Leaders in the House of Representatives:* 169–175.

make their careers in the House.* Socioeconomic homogeneity of districts is not necessary for cohesion—defined in terms of interaction, information flow, and socialization—to be high. Such homogeneity, however, may be necessary for unified bloc voting to occur.

Delegations in the Communications Network. Most members of the House constantly seek information on the substance of the great number of matters they have to consider, on the procedure by which those matters are considered, and on the preferences and intentions of others both in the House and outside of it. Given the vast workload, the complexity of the rules, and the large number of policy actors, members value time-saving devices that can provide them with reliable information.

State party delegations are a means of providing a lot of information to members quickly. Members do in fact look to their state delegations for much advice concerning both procedure and substance, particularly on matters coming from the standing committees on which those other members sit.† A large delegation is likely to have members on many or most of the most important committees in the House and a representative from such a delegation is in a good position to minimize the amount of time he needs to spend in collecting information about bills emerging from the committee structure.

Delegations also communicate voting cues to members on the floor of the House. These cues may be worked out ahead of time in a meeting of the delegation when the preferred voting position for members is discussed and decided. The cues may also be transmitted at the last minute on the floor, perhaps by word of mouth or perhaps simply by members observing and imitating the vote of a key figure.

There are several motives for members to accept the cues. One is simply that they respect the opinion of the individual in the delegation to whom they turn for the cue in any given situation. A second is that if all of the members of a state party delegation vote the same way they protect themselves from criticism at home. They can offer each other a protective coloration by sticking together. Third, they are aware that they enhance their bargaining potential within the House if they main-

---

* Barbara Deckard, "State Party Delegations in the U.S. House of Representatives: A Comparative Study of Group Cohesion," *Journal of Politics* 34 (1972): 199–222.

† See Arthur G. Stevens, Jr., "Informal Groups and Decision-Making in the U.S. House of Representatives," (Ph.D. dissertation, University of Michigan, 1970); and Alan Fiellin, "The Function of Informal Groups in Legislative Institutions," *Journal of Politics* 24 (1962): 72–91. See also Fiellin, "The Group Life of a State Delegation in the House of Representatives," *Western Political Quarterly* 23 (1970): 305–320.

tain an alliance. If they can deliver a predictable number of votes, for example, on a given measure important to some other group or set of individuals in the House then they are in a position to ask for reciprocal action on something of particular importance to them (for example, an amendment to a public works bill adding a project in their state).

In addition to transmitting information on substance, procedure, and voting, state party delegations also serve as agents of socialization. In the discussions between more senior delegation members and more junior members the norms and traditions of life in the House are passed on, with any particular twists appropriate to the delegation involved. The delegations, especially those that are cohesive, also offer some relief from the normal frustrations of being a junior member of the House.* In general, members of delegations that interact a great deal both socially and substantively—delegations in recent years such as the Democrats from Illinois, Massachusetts, and Texas—seem to enjoy life in the House and are generally more highly House career-oriented than members of delegations with low cohesion, such as both the Democrats and Republicans from New York in recent years.

Delegations and the Distribution of Benefits. State delegations work to channel the benefits distributed to individual members of the House and to states, regions, and districts. For the individual representative one of the most important benefits is committee assignments. Delegations that have members serving on important committees strive to ensure that their seat on that committee is retained within the delegation whenever it becomes open. About two out of every five committee seats in the House are, in fact, reserved for members from specific states, regardless of turnover of individuals.† For example, New York Democrats always hold a seat on Banking and Currency, no doubt because of the importance of the financial community in New York City. The member from the Virginia congressional district that includes part of the greater Norfolk area has consistently held a seat on the Merchant Marine and Fisheries Committee because of the importance of shipping, fishing, and other maritime pursuits to his district. In practice, since World War II this tradition of inheritance has protected medium and small Democratic delegations' seats on committees and has not allowed a takeover by the large states. In the Republican case, however, the norm of same state occupancy of key seats works in favor of the large delegations. Regionally, the norm works to the advantage of southern Democratic delegations; there is no such regional bias in the Republican party.

---

* See Deckard, "State Party Delegations," 222.
† Charles S. Bullock III, "Influence of State Party Delegations on House Committee Assignments," *Midwest Journal of Political Science* 15 (1971): 525–546.

Delegations work to gain support for projects important to their states and regions. The bargaining power of a united delegation is considerable. For example, dependable support for the policy positions of the party leadership and Democratic presidents through the years on the part of Illinois Democrats is certainly related to the favored treatment Chicago has received in many federal programs during Democratic administrations.

Delegations also work for programmatic amendments that have broader impact. In 1964, for example, the North Carolina Democrats extracted a promise that a given federal official they disliked would not be employed in the proposed poverty program before they agreed to vote for the program on the House floor. Also in 1964, the California Democrats obtained a promise from the leaders that they would work to raise the amount of the pay increase for congressmen in a pending pay bill from $7,500 to $10,000.*

Delegations can use their important committee positions in bargaining both with other members and delegations and with the House party leaders. They also can use a high degree of unity in floor voting as a bargaining tool—a united delegation can deliver a sizable impact on a given House vote. Ample empirical evidence shows that delegations do in fact tend to vote together.† The fact of being from a given state (and party) accounts for some cohesion in roll call votes that cannot be explained by party combined separately with type of constituency, region, or ideology of members.°

The conclusion reached by a recent study is that the influence of state delegations is strong enough "to warrant attention to state party as a 'standard' predictor in the analysis of congressional voting behavior." ‡

Regional Party Delegations in the House

Although region is often used as a category for analyzing roll call votes in the House, this does not mean that regional groups actually interact very often. In general, such interaction is limited. Western Democrats from the mountain states have met with some regularity in

---

* For additional information about these and other examples see Lewis A. Froman and Randall B. Ripley, "Conditions for Party Leadership: The Case of the House Democrats," *American Political Science Review* 59 (1965): 62–63.

† David B. Truman, "The State Delegation and the Structure of Voting in the United States House of Representatives," *American Political Science Review* 50 (1956): 1023–1045; Truman, *The Congressional Party* (New York: Wiley, 1959): 249–269; Stevens, "Informal Groups and Decision-Making"; and Aage R. Clausen, "State Party Influence on Congressional Party Decisions," *Midwest Journal of Political Science* 16 (1972): 77–101.

° Stevens, "Informal Groups and Decision-Making," 135–136.

‡ Clausen, "State Party Influence on Congressional Policy Decisions," 100.

some Congresses to discuss matters of common interest: reclamation, grazing policy, timbering policy, mining policy.

A group of conservative southern Democrats has also met with some regularity since the end of World War II in order to generate both discussion and positions on a wide variety of legislation. This group, called the "Boll Weevils" by the press, has had a fluctuating and uncertain membership. In the 1960s about thirty to thirty-five members usually attended meetings. The Democratic leaders in the House basically have been unwilling to deal with the "Weevils," most of whom are seen as uncompromisingly conservative. Occasionally the leaders will attempt to mute the "Weevils'" thrust, however. In 1963, for example, the most conservative Democratic member of the Ways and Means Committee (who was not a member of the "Boll Weevils") met with the "Weevils" at the request of the party leaders and Chairman Wilbur Mills to convince them that a Republican recommittal motion represented phony economy. His initiative met with some success; enough of the group voted against the Republican motion to insure that the leaders' and president's position would win on the floor.

In 1973 there was some discussion of reinvigorating the southern conservative group by providing for regular meetings and also by opening the meetings to conservative southern Republicans, whose numbers had grown considerably. But to date (mid-1974) nothing has happened.

Another regional development occurring in 1973 involved the New England states. Using money supplied principally by a regional business organization, New Englanders established two Washington offices —the New England Congressional Caucus and an Economic Research Office. In theory, the Caucus office is to supply information and help frame agendas for action on the part of all of the senators and representatives from both parties in the region. The focus will be on the economic problems of New England—high unemployment, tariffs, fuel oil imports, and bankrupt regional railroads. And one "thrust will be to see that New England gets what's coming to it." It is too early to assess the impact of the new organization although it did hire a few staff members and get widespread support from House members of both parties. Senators seemed much more reluctant to become involved.*

State and Regional Delegations in the Senate

Senators from the same state and same party tend to vote together because they share both party ideology and face the same constituency

---

* John L. Moore, "Washington Pressures/Business Forms Economic Study Unit to Support Bipartisan New England Caucus," *National Journal* (February 17, 1973): 226–233. The quotation is from Representative Silvio Conte, Massachusetts Republican, and appears on p. 230.

needs and demands. Senators from the same state but different parties may vote very differently although they may well cooperate on pork barrel matters of interest to the state. They cooperate only sporadically with House members on the same kind of matters.

Region has also been used as an analytical category for studying roll call voting in the Senate. But actual interaction of regional groupings of senators, with the possible exception of southern Democrats until the last few years, has been sporadic. In general, it can be said that the Senate is small enough to do without many intermediate groups between individual senators and the standing committees.

OTHER GROUPS IN THE HOUSE

Two other groups, both ideologically rather than geographically based, have been important in the House in recent years in furnishing information to specific groups of members: the Democratic Study Group and the Wednesday Club.

The Democratic Study Group *

The Democratic Study Group began in 1957 as a loose alliance of liberal Democrats. It immediately set up a whip organization, which functioned sporadically until 1959 when the DSG was formally established. The group has developed into a sturdy institution with an elected chairman, a full-time staff, and an effective whip organization. Its membership has fluctuated between about 120 and 175. The DSG attempts to bring all liberal Democrats (including those from the South) into its membership.

The members themselves form task forces and issue reports on various subject matter areas. The group's staff prepares fact sheets on upcoming legislation designed to inform the members in a few pages of the salient facts about the legislation. The staff also puts out a variety of special studies and reports as well as a supplement to the weekly notice from the Democratic whip outling the forthcoming week's program for floor action. The supplement briefs DSG members on matters of particular concern to liberals.

The DSG whip organization performs much as the regular party whip

---

* On the Democratic Study Group, see Mark F. Ferber, "The Formation of the Democratic Study Group," in Nelson W. Polsby (ed.), *Congressional Behavior* (New York: Random House, 1971): 249–267; Kenneth Kofmehl, "The Institutionalization of a Voting Bloc," *Western Political Quarterly* 17 (1964): 256–272; Ripley, *Party Leaders in the House:* 176–177; Stevens, "Informal Groups and Decision-Making," 142–148; and "Democratic Study Group: A Winner on House Reforms," *Congressional Quarterly Weekly Report* (June 2, 1973): 1366–1371.

organizations perform. Its main task is to get a good DSG turnout on the floor when critical votes are being taken.

In the 1964 congressional campaign the DSG moved into a new area of endeavor when it gave financial aid to the campaigns of 105 liberal Democratic candidates, 79 of whom won. Total spending in 1964 was $38,250, with between $250 and $1,250 going to each individual selected to receive aid (these were both incumbents and non-incumbents). In 1970 DSG campaign spending had increased to $120,000 and the size of contributions for individuals had also increased both because more money was available and fewer candidates were aided. Support was provided that year by the DSG for 68 candidates (26 incumbents and 42 non-incumbents), 46 of whom won (24 incumbents and 22 non-incumbents).

DSG members vote together on the floor. A study by the DSG staff of voting in the Ninetieth Congress (1967–68) concluded that DSG members voted together 91 percent of the time in support of Democratic programs and policies. An academic study also reached the conclusion that DSG members voted quite cohesively.* This is hardly surprising since ideological agreement is the basis for self-selected membership. Because of its size and increasing skill in working in the House the DSG has come to be an important force on a variety of issues.

The Wednesday Club

Liberal Republicans, not a very numerous group in the House, formed the Wednesday Club in the Eighty-eighth Congress (1963–64). It began with fourteen members, later expanded to twenty-one, and was up to twenty-six members in the Ninetieth Congress (1967–68). It has a small full-time staff but, given its size, does not have the elaborate organization of the DSG. Mainly, the Club sponsors limited research projects by the staff on problems of common interest and meets weekly to exchange information about pending business in the various standing committees. The list of members has never been made available so that no studies of voting cohesion have been made. It would be reasonable to assume a high degree of cohesion, however, given the ideological similarity with which the members start. The Club differs from the DSG in an important sense: while the DSG represents a majority of the Democrats and cooperates with the formal party leaders, the Wednesday Club represents a relatively small minority of the Republicans in the House and frequently disagrees with the Republican leaders on a number of issues.

---

* Stevens, "Informal Groups and Decision-Making."

CONGRESSIONAL STAFFS

Staffing for Congress has grown slowly. Only since World War II has Congress shown consistent concern for developing professional staff—both for individual members and for the committees. Since that time the "congressional bureaucracy" has grown from a few hundred to about 8000 in number. These staff members are essential in managing the very heavy workload of Congress. Without them neither the individual members nor the committees could perform adequately. Even with them the congressional workload is still heavy.*

Personal Staff

Congress began to provide money for individual senators and representatives to hire personal staff members for their Washington offices in the late nineteenth century. Since that time there has been a steady increase in the funds allocated for this purpose.

The amount of money senators receive for their staffs varies according to the size of the state the senator represents. Those from states with populations of less than three million received $295,938 in 1971. Those from states with more than seventeen million people received $477,978 to hire their staffs. Allowances for states between three and seventeen million vary between these limits.

In 1972 the 100 Senators hired a total of more than 2000 staff members, about 300 of whom were employed in offices within the various states, the remainder in Washington. Senate leaders had a few additional staff members assigned to them.

In 1971 each House member received a staff allowance of at least $141,492 with which they could hire up to 15 staff members. Representatives from districts of more than 500,000 people received $148,896 and were permitted to hire up to 16 staff members. In practice House members tended not to hire the maximum number of staff; instead they hired fewer people and paid them more. A total of more than 4000 staff members served all the representatives in 1972. Eleven hundred of these staff people were housed in district offices all over the country, and the rest were in Washington offices. The party leaders in the House also had about 25 additional staff members to assist them.

The Job of Personal Staff Members. Personal staff members are asked to undertake a great variety of jobs. In general, three kinds of skills

---

* On the place of staff in the functioning of Congress see Warren H. Butler, "Administering Congress: The Role of Staff," *Public Administration Review* 26 (1966): 3–13.

are represented in the typical office: clerical-bureaucratic support skills, technical-professional legislative skills, and political skills. Clerical-bureaucratic work dominates what goes on in a member's office. The mail must be answered, constituent casework pursued, visitors received, files kept, and phones answered. The substance of proposed legislation and other legislative matters also need staff attention but since the same individuals are usually required to perform in all three areas, the demands of clerical-bureaucratic support work often leave little time for legislative problems. On the political front, members need some staff people who know the political situation in their state or district and who can advise and work for successful re-election campaigns. Preparing for re-election is virtually a continual process, particularly in the House. Members of both chambers also need staff members who know the political situation inside both Congress and segments of the bureaucracy so that the member can maximize his impact on policy issues important to him.

A study of congressional workloads in the mid-1960s provides evidence that the staff, at least for House members, is unable to provide much legislative help.* Table 6–1 summarizes the results of that study. Only 14 percent of staff time was spent directly on legislative matters. No comparable study exists for Senate staff, but the same situation is likely to obtain there.†

The Organization of Personal Staffs. Senators and representatives organize their offices in a variety of ways. Some have all of their top assistants report directly to them; others have a more hierarchically structured office. House offices tend to have a single top aide who combines skills in bureaucratic, legislative, and political areas. The others on the office staff are likely to be more exclusively concerned with bureaucratic-clerical matters.

Most Senate offices are organized functionally; duties are more clearly divided and defined than in House offices (largely because senators have much larger staffs). Typically, there are one or more professionals in charge of public relations, casework, legislation, political affairs, and office administration. The professionals are, of course, aided by a number of clerical employees.

One central purpose for any pattern of organization, either in the House or the Senate, is to handle routine matters expeditiously so that

---

* John S. Saloma III, *Congress and the New Politics* (Boston: Little, Brown 1969).
† On Senate office staffs, see Kenneth Kofmehl, *Professional Staffs of Congress* (West Lafayette, Ind.: Purdue University Press, 1962): chapter 11; and Ripley, *Power in the Senate* (New York: St. Martin's, 1969): chapter 8.

Table 6–1

Average Staff Work Week for the Office of a United States Representative.

Activity	Percent of Staff Time Spent
Legislative Support	14.2
With member in committee	
With lobbyists and special interest groups	
Writing speech drafts, floor remarks	
On legislative research, bill drafting	
Constituency Service	24.7
Constituency casework	
Visiting with constituents in Washington	
Correspondence	40.9
On pressure and opinion mail	
On opinion ballots	
On requests for information	
On letters of congratulation, condolence	
On other correspondence	
Education and Publicity	10.3
On press work, radio, television	
Mailing government publications	
Other	9.9
Total	100.00

Source: Adapted from John S. Saloma III, Congress and the New Politics, *(Boston: Little, Brown, 1969): 185.*

the members and their top staff aides have time to deal with more important matters involving the substance of policy. Sometimes, however, the pressure of the routine consumes virtually all of the time of the staff member and perhaps of the member too. The items in Table 6–1 under Constituency Service, Correspondance, and Education and Publicity dominate staff time.

The Legislative Impact of Personal Staff. Staff members in the offices of individual senators and representatives can and do have substantial legislative impact, despite the limited time available for legislative work. This is particularly true of the top assistants to senators. For the most part, the average senator is not the genuine legislative expert that many House members are, given their limited and specialized responsibilities. Senators are fewer in number than House members and have a larger number of committee and subcommittee assignments. As a result they must spread themselves much thinner in terms of substantive expertise. Also, senators usually have more external demands on their time in terms of requests for speeches, television and radio appearances, newspaper interviews, and other such activities that do not as often involve the average representative. The typical senator therefore needs help, especially in the areas about which he knows very little and has little time to learn. For this help, he frequently turns to his staff members.

Case literature provides a great deal of evidence of the legislative importance of senatorial aides. For example, in the passage of the Clean Air Act of 1963 three assistants to individual senators were critical figures in making the final compromises that went into the statute.* They, working with one committee staff member, reached agreements that received only cursory scrutiny from the senators who were involved before final action was taken. Another example is provided by the legislative assistant for Senator Harrison Williams (D-N.J.) in the development of the bargains and compromises that led to the passage of the Mass Transportation Act of 1964.†

A close study of Oklahoma Democrat Mike Monroney's staff concluded that it "is designed to play many of the roles of a United States senator with a minimum of personal intervention." ° One man in particular became a specialist on water resources and reclamation questions and was so effective that he was sometimes called "the third Senator from Oklahoma". Because of the confidence Monroney placed in him he was free to make many decisions about important matters on his own.

Staff members can increase their legislative impact if they are aggressive in advising the individual for whom they work and in challenging the views of that individual at least some of the time. They can also enhance their influence if they have a sense of exactly the proper time to release critical information or a point of view to a member. One Republican staff member in the Senate put it well: "At the point when a senator gets to a committee meeting, particularly the executive sessions, and at the point when he goes to the floor to listen to the last few chords of debate and cast a vote, there an assistant who is either well read or at least well prepared and is able to pick out the salient points and say which does what to whom, when and how can make a big difference in the final decision of the senator." ‡

Members become particularly reliant on personal staff for legislative assistance on new problems they have not faced before and on matters on which they have not become expert themselves. Junior

---

* See Randall B. Ripley, "Congress Supports Clean Air, 1963," in Frederic N. Cleaveland and associates, *Congress and Urban Problems* (Washington, D.C.: Brookings, 1969).

† See Royce Hanson, "Congress Catches the Subway: Urban Mass Transit Legislation, 1960–1964," in Cleaveland, *Congress and Urban Problems*.

° John F. Bibby and Roger H. Davidson, *On Capitol Hill* (New York: Holt, Rinehart and Winston, 1967): 94–112. For additional material on the behavior of specific staffs see Bibby and Davidson, *On Capitol Hill* (Hinsdale, Ill.: Dryden, 1972, 2nd ed.): 95–96, 111–114.

‡ Quoted in Ripley, *Power in the Senate:* 197.

members are more likely to rely heavily on personal staff for legislative help than senior members both because they are less experienced and expert personally and because they have less access to committee staff. Minority party members are also more likely to rely heavily on personal staff than majority party members because they have less access to committee staff.

Staff members for members from states with small populations (in the case of the Senate) or for members from states and districts geographically distant from Washington are most likely to be important legislatively. Senate staffs for members from large states are beseiged by an unusual amount of mail, casework, and personal visits that makes it difficult to free any time for legislative work. Staffs in either house whose member's state or district is relatively close to Washington have an inordinate amount of time eaten up by calls from constituents.

Committee Staff

In the mid-nineteenth century congressional committees gradually began to hire clerks to help them with their work, but formal professional staffs were slow to develop.* By the time of World War II only the two Appropriations Committees and the Joint Committee on Internal Revenue Taxation had well-developed professional staffs. A provision of the Legislative Reorganization Act passed in 1946 made clear the intention of Congress that professional staffs be developed for all committees—it provided for four professional staff members and six clerical staff members for each committee and allowed the size of committee staffs to expand beyond that number. In 1970 Congress increased the formal allotment of professional members to six.

Shortly after the 1946 act Senate committees had about 150 staff members and House committees had about 220. Those numbers have grown steadily since then. A count of staff members listed in the 1972 *Congressional Staff Directory* reveals that House committees and sub-

---

* On committee staff see Clapp, *The Congressman:* 256–264; James D. Cochrane, "Partisan Aspects of Congressional Committee Staffing," *Western Political Quarterly* 17 (1964): 338–348; *Congressional Quarterly's Guide to the Congress of the United States:* 160–164; George Goodwin, Jr., *The Little Legislatures* (Amherst: University of Massachusetts Press, 1970): 142–152; Kofmehl, *Professional Staffs of Congress;* John F. Manley, "Congresional Staff and Public Policy-Making: The Joint Committee on Internal Revenue Taxation," *Journal of Politics* 30 (1968): 1046–1067; Samuel C. Patterson, "The Professional Staffs of Congressional Committees," *Administrative Science Quarterly* 15 (1970): 22–37; David E. Price, "Professionals and 'Entrepreneurs': Staff Orientations and Policy-Making on Three Senate Committees," *Journal of Politics* 33 (1971): 316–336; and Ripley, *Power in the Senate:* 200–212.

committees employed 632 individuals and Senate committees and sub-committees employed 594 individuals.

Staffing of committees reflects the partisan nature of Congress itself. In virtually all committees, majority and minority party members have separate staff. The only formally non-partisan committee staff is that of the Senate Foreign Relations Committee. In fact, however, most committee staffs operate within a norm of non-partisanship on most matters.

Formal authority for selecting committee staff members rests with committee chairmen, and most chairmen exercise this authority to a considerable degree. They generally want a large portion of their staff to be personally loyal and responsible to them, and they exert considerable influence in the picking of staff. They may parcel out some appointing authority to other senior members of their party, usually subcommittee chairmen, or to the ranking minority member for selecting the few staff members designated as staff for the minority party.

Committee staff positions are generally well regarded on Capitol Hill and throughout the executive branch. Many committee staff members have had experience either in the executive branch or on the personal staff of one or more senators or representatives. There has been growing stability in the personnel on committee staffs. As is the case with the legislators they serve, seniority among committee staff members helps them develop influence in their jobs.

The Job of Committee Staff Members. Committee staff perform a variety of duties related to the work of the committee. For example, they may organize the hearings that the committee conducts. They may personally conduct research on topics relevant to committee investigations. They may draft bills and amendments, and prepare the language of committee reports. They may help legislators prepare for floor debate either by distributing materials to all members or by briefing the members of the committee who are primarily responsible for conducting the debate. They may participate in the preparation for meetings of conference committees and in the writing of conference reports. Committee staff members also serve as the committee's principal liaison agents with both the executive branch and interest groups.

Committee staff members also perform some tasks not related to the business of the committee.* The chairman of the committee may use part of the staff to assist him in his renomination and re-election campaigns. Committee staff may also serve as congressional staff members for the chairman, and the chairmen and ranking minority mem-

---

* Cochrane, "Partisan Aspects of Congressional Committee Staffing," 346–347.

bers may use their "men" as they perform their roles as members of Congress. Use of committee staff on extra-committee work is accepted by the staff members themselves because of the highly personal nature of their appointments, and by other committee members because of the partisan nature of staff appointments.

The job of committee staff members has been described in terms of four principal functions they perform: intelligence, integration, innovation, and influence.* In performing the intelligence function committee staff members collect and filter a great deal of information before passing it on to committee members.

Committee staffers perform an integration function in several senses. Most committee staffs are harmonious internally. They also generally work closely with staff members from the committee or committees in the other chamber that have the same jurisdiction. This helps bridge the bicameral gap. It also means that conference meetings usually go smoothly. Staff members also help promote integration between committees and the related pieces of the executive branch. They work closely with staff members in the bureaucracy and may well have served there before coming to Congress.

Some committee staff members innovate by seeking out new problems for attention or by proposing new solutions to problems already identified. The more highly bureaucratized (that is, specialized) a committee staff is the more likely are its members to be innovative in dealing with policy.†

Committee staff members are influential both because of the vital tasks they perform and because of the trust they build up in their relationships with members of the House and Senate.

In performing their tasks and functions, committee staff members interact with a number of individuals. Primarily they are responsible to their appointing authority—which, in the case of the majority party's staff, means that they are primarily loyal to the chairman of the committee or of the subcommittee, if the appointment power has been decentralized. The minority party's staff, usually very small, is loyal and responsible principally to the ranking minority member. Senior members of committees are, therefore, likely to have the most access to committee staffs. Junior members of committees tend to be distrustful of committee staffs and rely more heavily on their personal staffs for legislative help. In general, the typical member of Congress does not rely heavily on committee staff members. For example, a survey of 158

---

* See Patterson, "The Professional Staffs of Congressional Committees," 26–29.
† Eugene Eidenberg, "The Congressional Bureaucracy," (Ph.D. dissertation, Northwestern University, 1966).

House members in the Eighty-ninth Congress (1965–66) produced the findings that in three categories of legislative activity committee staffs were relatively unimportant.* These members said that only 11 percent of their legislative research was done by committee staff (in contrast to 30 percent done by themselves and 45 percent done by their own staff); that only 21 percent of their preparation for committee meetings and hearings was done by committee staff (compared to 61 percent done by themselves); finally, that only 9 percent of their preparation for floor debate was done by committee staff (compared to 28 percent by their own staff and 60 percent by themselves).

Committee staff members also work closely with both executive branch officials and lobbyists. When asked about the best contacts on Capitol Hill 25 percent of a sample of Washington lobbyists named committee staff members.† This was the single largest category—closely followed by 24 percent naming staffs of executive agencies and 23 percent naming members of Congress. When asked to name the second best contact another 29 percent named committee staffs, compared to 19 percent naming staffs of executive agencies and 15 percent naming members of Congress. When asked about the best and second-best sources of "unofficial information" 29 percent named committee staffs as the best source (compared to 20 percent naming members and 14 percent naming executive agency staffs) and 25 percent named committee staffs second (compared to 15 percent naming members and 16 percent naming executive agency staff members).

Committee staff members, like senators and representatives, operate within the constraints of relatively well-developed norms as they perform their jobs. Although the norms vary from committee to committee both for members and for staff members, six norms are widespread.° These norms include: limited advocacy (the staff person is expected to restrain himself in advocating his own policies, conclusions and proposals), loyalty to chairmen, deference to congressmen, anonymity, specialization (committee staff are expected to become experts in a particular subject), and limited partisanship (the majority of the work of most committees is non-partisan, and the general expectation is that the committee's work will be conducted with limited partisanship). No norm is inviolable, however; the limited partisanship norm is particularly likely to be ignored on occasion.

---

* Donald G. Tacheron and Morris K. Udall, *The Job of the Congressman* (Indianapolis: Bobbs-Merrill, 1966): 285.

† The findings in this paragraph were reported in Lester W. Milbrath, *The Washington Lobbyists* (New York: Rand McNally, 1963): 266, 268.

° See Patterson, "The Professional Staffs of Congressional Committees," pp. 29–31.

Committee staffs are organized in a variety of ways, but three patterns predominate.* One pattern has a single staff director who is in charge of both the professional staff and the clerical staff and who reports to the chairman. A second pattern has two staff directors (one for the professional staff and one for the clerical staff) who each report to the chairman. In the third pattern, a staff director for the clerical staff reports to the chairman; each of the professional staff members also report directly to the chairman.

Partisanship and Committee Staff Members. For policy-related committee staff positions chairmen usually hire individuals from their own party who share their general policy orientation. Ranking minority members appoint members who share their party and political orientation. As suggested above, partisanship is muted on many committees. Committees that regularly deal with divisive partisan issues, (for example, House Education and Labor) however, are likely to have staffs with definite partisan orientations, simply because the appointing authorities on those committees are likely to be strong partisans.

Even though hiring is on a partisan basis, retention of professional staff members may be non-partisan. For example, a large number of staff members survived the party turnovers in Congress in 1947 (from Democrat to Republican), 1949 (from Republican to Democrat), 1953 (from Democrat to Republican), and 1955 (from Republican to Democrat). Nor is there a necessary conflict between a partisan staff and a professional staff. Individuals whose hiring and tasks are imbued with partisanship may simultaneously be first-rate professionals. In general, congressional staffs have become increasingly professional although they may well have remained at about the same level of partisanship.

In recent years, Republican members of the House and Senate, seemingly condemned to perpetual minority status, have become increasingly concerned about the small numbers of committee staff members assigned to the minority. In 1962, for example, out of a total of 504 staff persons for all House Committees (both standing and select) only 43 were assigned to the minority; only 54 of 508 staff members for all Senate committees were assigned to the minority. The joint committees had only 2 out of 72 assigned to the minority.†

The 1970 Legislative Reorganization Act provided for at least three minority employees on most committees. The Republican capture of the White House in 1969 has resulted in an increase of more sympa-

---

* Ibid., 32–33.
† Cochrane, "Partisan Aspects of Congressional Committee Staffing," 341–342.

thetic employees in the executive branch for Republican congressmen to turn to, hence their concern for minority staffing has lessened.

The Legislative Impact of Committee Staff. Committee staff members, like personal staff members, may have considerable independent impact on the shape of legislation. This impact varies from committee to committee. One study of staff behavior on three different Senate committees (Finance, Labor and Public Welfare, and Commerce) concludes that two kinds of behavior can be observed among equally competent staff members on different committees.* "Policy entrepreneurs" dominated the Labor and Public Welfare and Commerce Committee staffs. These individuals were not shy about consulting both their own policy preferences and political considerations as they carried out their jobs. Much of the time they did not pretend to be neutral. On the other hand the staff of the Finance Committee was dominated by "professionals" who valued neutral expertise most highly and who downplayed both their own preferences and politics.

A study of the staff of the Joint Committee on Internal Revenue Taxation concluded that it is "powerful," but that its power is largely based on the adroitness with which the staff members take cues from the members of the committee itself.†

Committee staff members cannot initiate public policy without regard to the wishes of their nominal and actual superiors. On the other hand, they can have considerable impact, at least on some committees and on some specific bills. Staff members with more seniority are likely to have more independent substantive impact than staff members with less seniority. Likewise, those who are closest personally to the chairman of a subcommittee or committee are more likely to be important. Staff members on subcommittees are in a particularly favorable position to develop influence because they work with only a few members on a limited agenda. Those working on technical matters that are hard for the members themselves to understand are likely to be independently important.

The Place of Congressional Staff in the National Government

Congressional staffs are a permanent feature of the governmental landscape in Washington. And, given the demands on the time of the elected members of the House and Senate, they inevitably will develop some independent influence. There is considerable sentiment for continuing to expand the staffs of Congress as a major way of seeking

---

* Price, "Professional and 'Entrepreneurs'," 335.
† Manley, "Congressional Staff and Public Policy-making."

to offset the superior numbers and superior informational base of the executive branch. There has also been some opposition simply to continuing the expansion of numbers. Worries about such expansion have been expressed on several grounds.* First, large staffs have the potential of becoming uncontrollable bureaucracies. Second, as staffs get larger there is probably a greater likelihood that staffers will simply perform chores for individual members that have little or no relation to the legitimate business of the committee—that is, every committee member will want his "man" on the committee. Third, it is impossible for the size of congressional staffs ever to match the size of the executive bureaucracy with which they interact. Rather than simply expanding the size of congressional staffs, then, attention should be directed toward improving their training and skills and increasing the resources available to them.

Thoughtful members and staff members alike express concern about the development of independent influence on the part of staffers. Staff members are, of course, not elected but speak in the name of individuals who are. And their views are usually accepted as those of the elected officials by other participants in the political system, including representatives of the media. (This problem is, of course, even more prevalent in the executive branch where bureaucrats and presidential appointees in top positions often presume to speak in the name of the president.)

Perhaps the most serious threat is that professional staff members in Congress may join with civil servants in the executive branch and representatives of interest groups to dominate policy in a variety of specialized areas. None of these individuals directly represents any segment of the electorate. All may be highly professional and highly competent, but the complexity of modern government means that they may in fact carry out large portions of government business without any meaningful intervention from elected representatives—either the president or the members of the Senate and House. Bad policy may not necessarily result (nor would good policy necessarily result from a greater intervention on the part of the elected officials) but a growing bureaucratization of Congress may reduce its representative character.

---

* On the various normative concerns with congressional staffing see Arthur Macmahon, "Congressional Oversight of Administration: The Power of the Purse," in Theodore J. Lowi (ed.), *Legislative Politics U.S.A.* (Boston: Little, Brown, 1965, 2nd ed.): 185–196; and a number of working papers published by the House Select Committee on Committees in the summer of 1973: Kenneth Kofmehl, "Three Major Aspects of House Committee Staffing"; Walter Kravitz, "Improving Some Skills of Committee Staff"; Samuel C. Patterson, "Staffing House Committees"; James A. Robinson, "Statement on Committee Staffing"; and John S. Saloma III, "Proposals for Meeting Congressional Staff Needs."

Both the genius of Congress and its greatest weakness may be that it contains large numbers of amateurs and semi-professionals in the policy business who may ask questions and reach decisions that bureaucrats, operating on strict grounds of efficiency, would not reach. The bureaucratization of Congress could also result in an erosion of both its political character and its representative character. Such a result is certainly not foreordained but it is an inherent problem with large-scale professional staffing.

PART III

The External Environment for Congressional Policy-Making

7

CONGRESSIONAL
ELECTIONS

I N MANY WAYS MEMBERS OF CONGRESS ARE ALWAYS RUNNING
for re-election. As one House member put it: "You should say
'perennial' election rather than 'biennial.' It is with us every day." *

Although members perceive everything they do as affecting re-election, the same perceptions are not necessarily shared by the masses of
potential voters in their constituencies. Many of these individuals
will not vote; and of those who will a large proportion will have little
precise knowledge about the behavior of their senators or representatives. Many will not even recognize their names. There are, however, a
few voters in every district and state who do pay attention to the behavior of their representatives and senators and much of the time it is
these individuals to whom the members try to be responsive.

THE VOTERS

From its beginning, the House of Representatives was conceived to be
a popular body—representing "the people" and chosen by them. The
Senate did not formally become a popular body until the ratification of

---

* Quoted in Charles L. Clapp, *The Congressman: His Work as He Sees It*
(Washington, D.C.: Brookings, 1963): 330.

169

the seventeenth amendment to the Constitution in 1913. In practice, however, the Senate was well on its way to becoming a popular body before 1913.*

The opportunity for direct popular impact on both the House and Senate is thus present, but it is an opportunity that is never fully exercised by the electorate. Turnout for elections of representatives is less than 60 percent; for elections of senators it is rarely more than 60 percent (see Figures 7–1 and 7–2).

Low turnout has been interpreted in several different ways. Some suggest that it indicates satsifaction with the governmental system. Others argue that it is a sign of alienation from the system, that people are cynical and do not believe that their vote will make any difference. Still others argue that it is merely a sign of apathy, that a large number of people just do not much care about the political system and are neither supportive nor hostile.†

Figure 7–1 illustrates the relationship between turnout for presidential elections and turnout for congressional elections for the years 1924–1970. In presidential election years, almost as many people voted for representative as for president; the average dropoff between presidential voting and voting for representatives was slightly less than 4 percent for this period. In years when there was no presidential election to act as a stimulant to bring voters to the polls, the turnout rate for congressional elections was considerably lower. The average dropoff was about 12.5 percent for the period between 1924 and 1970. That is, of every 100 eligible voters, more than 12 who voted for a representative in a presidential year did not vote for that office two years later in the off-year election.

Voting participation in Senate elections follows the same pattern as House races. Figure 7–2 reports turnout in those elections from 1950

---

* This was true for two basic reasons: 1) state legislatures had only infrequently tried to bind their senators' voting and policy positions in the Senate, a practice that virtually disappeared after the Civil War, and 2) several events occurred that introduced popular control, albeit indirectly, prior to adoption of the seventeenth amendment. These included the active involvement of senatorial candidates in the campaigns of candidates for state legislatures (so that voting by the populace for state legislators was in effect a referendum on U.S. senatorial candidates). The development of the primary election system after 1888 also offered popular control. Finally, shortly before the seventeenth amendment was adopted, a system was invented and used in Oregon that provided for direct popular vote on senatorial candidates in connection with the regular election, even though formal electoral power remained in the state legislature.

On all of these developments and their impact see William H. Riker, "The Senate and American Federalism," *American Political Science Review* 49 (1955): 452-469.

† On some of these issues see E. E. Schattschneider, *The Semi-Sovereign People* (New York: Holt, Rinehart, and Winston, 1960).

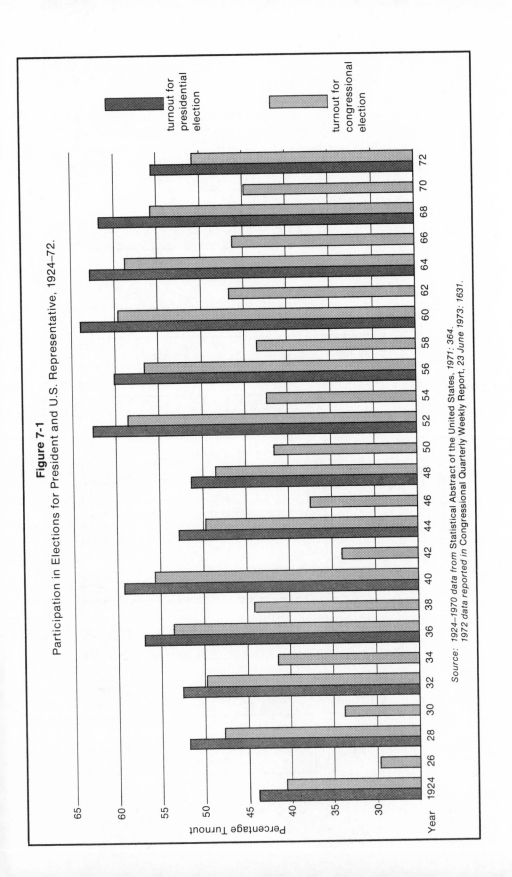

Figure 7-1

Participation in Elections for President and U.S. Representative, 1924–72.

Source: 1924–1970 data from Statistical Abstract of the United States, 1971: 364. 1972 data reported in Congressional Quarterly Weekly Report, 23 June 1973: 1631.

turnout for presidential election

turnout for congressional election

Percentage Turnout

Year

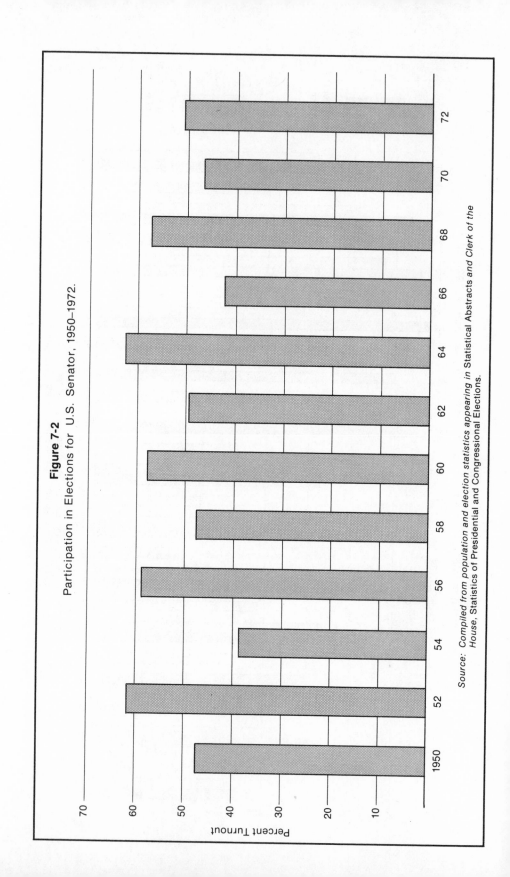

Figure 7-2

Participation in Elections for U.S. Senator, 1950–1972.

Source: Compiled from population and election statistics appearing in Statistical Abstracts and Clerk of the House, Statistics of Presidential and Congressional Elections.

through 1970. Turnout in presidential years was always higher than in non-presidential years.

One persistent factor related to the different levels of turnout is the public's awareness of different elections—presidential elections obviously have a much higher visibility than congressional elections. Other factors affecting turnout include the level of competition in the contests, the voter's sense of political efficacy, his sense of duty, the strength of his partisan preference, and his interest in the campaign.*

Those voters who turn out have mixed motives in making their choices for representative and senator. Voters can consider (not always consciously) their party identification, their opinion of the individual candidates, and their view of the issues as they relate to the candidates. Empirical evidence suggests, however, that the electorate collectively does not know much about the relationship between parties and issues, about which party controls Congress, and about policy stands taken by incumbent senators and representatives. Thus most voting for candidates for the Senate and the House is likely to be devoid of much specific policy content and is related instead either to party loyalties or to personal loyalties. One empirical study reaches the following conclusions:

> In the congressional election . . . the country votes overwhelmingly for party symbols, but the symbols have limited meaning in terms of legislative policy. . . . The electorate sees very little altogether of what goes on in the national legislature. Few judgments of legislative performance are associated with the parties, and much of the public is unaware even of which party has control of Congress.

> What the public's response to the parties lacks in programmatic support is not made up by its response to local congressional candidates. Although perceptions of individual candidates account for most of the votes cast by partisans against their parties, these perceptions are almost untouched by information about the policy stands of the men contesting the House seat. The increment of strength that some candidates, especially incumbents, acquire by being known to their constituents is almost entirely free of policy content.†

This absence of policy content in congressional elections in the mass sense enables members to exercise relatively independent judgment

---

* Angus Campbell, Philip E. Converse, Warren E. Miller, and Donald E. Stokes, *The American Voter* (New York: Wiley, 1964).

† Donald E. Stokes, and Warren E. Miller, "Party Government and the Saliency of Congress," in Angus Campbell and others, *Elections and the Political Order* (New York: Wiley, 1966): 209–210.

in weighing personal feelings about policy issues against the perceived needs or claims of constituencies. Congressmen do not need to feel terribly constrained to vote exactly as they think their districts would prefer, although some feel more independent than others.

The absence of policy content in mass voting also contributes to the incumbent members' chances for re-election. Basically, members are not judged at election time on the basis of their policy stands or performance. They are well aware that a very large part of the electorate in their districts does not know their policy stands and, even if it did, it would not vote solely on that basis.*

THE ELECTORAL DISTRICTS †

The apportionment of Senate seats and the provision of constituencies for senators present no problem: each state gets exactly two senators and all senators represent entire states. House seats, however, are more difficult to create. First, the number of seats must be *apportioned* among the fifty states on the basis of population. Then, within each state that has more than one representative, geographic areas must be delineated. This distribution of seats within a state, formally called *districting,* is also done on the basis of population. Apportionment is done by Congress itself (now using a virtually automatic formula based on the census figures that are collected every ten years). Districting is done by state governments. In recent years, federal courts have also become heavily involved in the redistricting process.

Apportionment can have some impact on the content of congressional decisions as regional strength changes. Districting within states is even more important, however, as skillful manipulation of district lines can alter the party and ideological complexion of both individual seats and entire state delegations. For example, in the 1972 elections for the House only 13 out of 378 incumbents who ran were defeated. Eight of these individuals were defeated primarily because of redistricting. Democratic strength was particularly hurt because 7 of the 8 were Democrats who lost districts whose electoral base had shifted to rapidly growing suburbs, dominated by Republican voters.

---

* See Clapp, *The Congressman:* 377 for a discussion of representatives' attitudes in 1959. See also Charles O. Jones, "The Role of the Campaign in Congressional Politics," in M. Kent Jennings and L. Harmon Zeigler (eds.), *The Electoral Process* (Englewood Cliffs, N.J.: Prentice-Hall, 1966).

† See Lewis A. Froman, Jr., *Congressmen and their Constituencies* (Chicago: Rand McNally, 1963): chapter 6, on the policy differences generated by the fact that senators come from whole states and representatives from districts. See also chapter 1 of this volume.

Reapportionment

Reapportionment has taken place every tenth year immediately after the census. This practice began following the 1790 census, and has occurred regularly with the exception of 1920. Different methods have been used but all of them have been based on population. The size of the House grew rapidly from 1790 until 1830 (increasing from 65 to 242 members). For the next several decades the size was stable, but growth resumed following the 1870 census, until the number of seats reached the present 435 in 1913.

The size of the House was not fixed permanently at 435 by Congress until 1929, because no agreement on an alternative number could be reached before that time. Then, as now, reapportionment touched fundamental political nerves. Prior to the 1920 census, all states had benefited from reapportionments by receiving an increased number of seats in the House. But following that census (and the impressive population shifts following World War I) many states were faced with a loss of seats for the first time. The result was a stalemating of reapportionment efforts until 1929 when President Hoover convened a special session of Congress and insisted on apportionment legislation. By that time it was evident that population distributions were not going to return to prewar patterns, and new urban areas were clamoring for greater representation; Congress relented, fixing permanently the number of seats at 435, and requiring that these seats be distributed among the states on the basis of population after each census. With the single exception of a temporary increase to 437 from 1959 to 1963 to accommodate the inclusion of Alaska and Hawaii in the Union, there have been no changes in the size of the House since 1913. Attempts to increase its size, usually initiated by states faced with the loss of seats because of reapportionment, have met with failure.

Redistricting

The districting of states has even more explosive potential than reapportionment, since the way in which district lines are drawn define constituencies and hence affect the chances of election success or failure for representatives of those constituencies. It is not uncommon to see districts redrawn after the censuses to the explicit benefit of the party in the majority in the state legislatures. Gerrymandering (named after Elbridge Gerry, a governor of Massachusetts in the early nineteenth century) is the name given to the manipulation of the shape of a district to benefit a specific party or candidate. It would be too idealistic to expect state legislators to strive for impartiality and resist the political influences that bear on them as they grapple with redistricting. These forces are strong and elemental: parties want to maximize the number of their seats in Congress, incumbent representatives want to be assured of re-election through the creation of "safe" districts, and potential candidates want to create districts for themselves in which they can win.

Until the 1960s state legislatures were free to manipulate district lines without regard to the distribution of population within a state, with the result that a single district could have as many as four times the number of people as another district in the same state. This practice was challenged in a 1946 court suit in Illinois.* When the case reached the Supreme Court, however, the majority declined to intervene, claiming that it was inappropriate for the Court to enter the "political thicket."

In a 1962 apportionment case † the Court reached an opposite conclusion: the majority ruled that legislative apportionment *was* a justiciable issue, and that if a violation of rights was involved then a judicial remedy was appropriate. Applying the equal protection of the laws clause of the fourteenth amendment, the Court ruled that districts for state legislatures must be equal in population. This decision led to a broader decision in a 1964 case,° the *Wesberry* case, when a six to three majority ruled that the Constitution (Article I, section 2—not the fourteenth amendment) required that House districts created by state legislatures must be equal in population. As Justice Black, writing for the majority, put it: "We hold that, construed in its historical context, the command of Article I, Section 2, that Representatives be chosen 'by the People of the several States' means that as nearly as is practicable one man's vote in a Congressional election is to be worth as much as another's." ‡ In short, the Court was endorsing the much used phrase "one man, one vote."

The unsuccessful dissenters in this case continued to claim that the courts had no business in a political area. Justice Harlan stated the minority position succinctly: "The claim for judicial relief in this case strikes at one of the fundamental doctrines of our system of government, the separation of powers. In upholding that claim, the Court attempts to effect reforms in a field which the Constitution, as plainly as can be, has committed exclusively to the political process." §

---

* *Colegrove* v. *Green* (328 U.S. 549).
† *Baker* v. *Carr* (369 U.S. 186).
° *Wesberry* v. *Sanders* (376 U.S. 1).
‡ *Wesberry* v. *Sanders* (376 U.S. 7–8).
§ *Wesberry* v. *Sanders* (376 U.S. 48).

The *Wesberry* case did not address the question of precisely how equal districts had to be in order to satisfy the requirements of the majority opinion. Federal courts involved in various redistricting suits following the *Wesberry* decision applied a variety of standards in determining what equality of size meant in practice. In 1969 the Supreme Court gave its own meaning to equality in the case of *Kirkpatrick* vs. *Preisler*.* Again by a six to three majority the Court held that equality meant absolute equality. Justice Brennan, writing for the majority, said "Equal representation for equal numbers of people is a principle designed to prevent debasement of voting power and diminution of access to elected Representatives. Toleration of even small deviations detracts from these purposes." †

Virtually every state has had to redistrict, sometimes more than once, as a result of these court decisions in the 1960s. Although requiring equality between districts, the courts have not, at least to date, involved themselves in prescribing the shape of districts. State legislatures still gerrymander in order to include or exclude blocs of voters, according to the prevailing dictates of political expediency. The latitude for manipulating the complexion of a state's representation in Congress has been decreased since the *Wesberry* decision, but it has by no means been eliminated.

Both before and after the Supreme Court's *Wesberry* decision the issue of reapportionment engendered much public debate, especially concerning the effects of having or not having reapportioned districts. Liberals in particular argued that the pre-*Wesberry* conditions favored rural areas over urban areas, and that as a result, congressional policy was conservatively biased. A study by *Congressional Quarterly* in 1962, however, showed that it was not urban but surburban areas that were underrepresented.° Andrew Hacker, in an empirical study of what an equally districted House might look like (undertaken before *Wesberry*), came to the conclusion that liberals were almost certainly not underrepresented in the House and might be even slightly overrepresented.‡ In fact, the redistricting that has occurred in accord with the *Wesberry* decision has produced a greater suburban representation in Congress, but neither political party nor any particular political ideology has benefited. In short, court action on redistricting may make good theoretical sense in a representative system but it has not basically affected the nature of Congress or its decisions. The central fact that

---

* *Kirkpatrick* v. *Preisler* (394 U.S. 526).
† *Kirkpatrick* v. *Preisler* (394 U.S. 531).
° *Congressional Quarterly Weekly Report*, 1962: 153–169.
‡ Andrew Hacker, *Congressional Districting* (Washington, D.C.: Brookings, 1964, revised ed.): 95–96.

members of the House come from fairly small districts, many of them relatively homogeneous, remains unchanged.

CAMPAIGNS

The question of why individuals choose to run for Congress has no single answer. Empirical research suggests that there are various motives. Some individuals value a political career and see the opportunity of election to Congress as furthering that career. Others think of politics more broadly than just elected office and may run for Congress simply as one more way of being politically active. Still others may not be interested in a political career and may not be consistently interested in politics per se but may run out of a rather vague sense of civic duty or because they are persuaded that it is an appropriate thing to do. If elected, many members who may not have thought seriously about the satisfaction that might come from a political career are increasingly attracted to seek re-election and remain in the House or Senate or at least in electoral politics for a long time. A few, even if they win, never really become very interested in the House or Senate or politics and voluntarily retire rather quickly. In short, members come to Congress (or lose races for Congress) for many different reasons and with many different self-images. Once in Congress, socializing pressures may impose more uniformity on what was at the outset a reasonably diverse lot of people.*

Nominations

Virtually all nominations for the House and Senate are made in primary elections held within the parties in the various states and districts. In a few districts and states the primaries merely serve to ratify the choice of the dominant political organization, but most primaries have at least the potential for being genuinely competitive. Likewise, in most districts and states the "party organization" is relatively unimportant in selecting nominees. As one commentator has put it, "Nominations are . . . . generally on a do-it-yourself basis." † The primaries that actually attract competition are, understandably, in states and districts where the nominee of the party has a reasonably good chance of winning.

Incumbents have very important advantages in nominating primar-

---

* See Jeff Fishel, *Party and Opposition* (New York: McKay, 1973): chapter 3; and Clapp, *The Congressman:* 31–34.

† H. Douglas Price, "The Electoral Arena," in David B. Truman (ed.), *The Congress and America's Future* (Englewood Cliffs, N.J.: Prentice-Hall, 1965): 41.

ies. These advantages are not guarantees of success, however—a number of incumbents are defeated in their party's primaries. In 1972, for example, two incumbent senators and seven incumbent represen- tatives were defeated in party primaries. Three of these seats were then lost to the other party in the general election.

In some districts and states the primary is, in effect, the most im- portant election because the general election is always won by the candidate of the same party. This is still true of a number of southern seats, which are reliably Democratic, although two-party competition has increased steadily in this region over the last several decades.

The primary system of nominating candidates for Congress under- scores the decentralized nature of American politics. National party lead- ers very rarely play any part whatsoever in seeking or supporting candidates for House and Senate seats. The men and women who run emerge in a variety of ways, but not because of the labors of national figures of virtually non-existent national parties.

General Elections

A candidate for Congress faces one central problem: how to make himself known to enough people and preferred over his opponent. Solving this problem is predicated on solving another vast problem: the acquisition of sufficient finances to achieve the goal. Incumbents have a natural advantage in solving the first problem and this helps, to some extent, reduce the magnitude of the second problem. Challengers of incumbents have a much more difficult time in the areas of both recog- nition and money.

The high rate of success among incumbents can be explained in both personal terms and in terms of the electorate. At the personal level the incumbent is known to a much larger proportion of his con- stituents than his opponent because of the media coverage he receives while in office. He receives a salary while campaigning. He can use his congressional staff to help in the campaign. He can use his franking privileges to mail materials to his constituents that will help establish both his name and a favorable image of himself. He can use that same privilege to conduct polls of his constituents' opinions. He has estab- lished links to contributors and campaign workers who have helped him in the past and for whom, presumably, he has provided favors, both tangible and intangible, while in office.*

The high rate of incumbents' electoral success can also be explained

* For some details on specific campaigns between incumbents and non-incum- bents for the House in 1962 in the San Francisco Bay area see David A. Leuthold, *Electioneering in a Democracy* (New York: Wiley, 1968).

by the relatively stable party identification of the voters. Since voting for Congress tends to be largely on the basis of party labels most districts elect members to Congress who share the most popular label. Thus party identification and voting stability are closely linked in the case of congressional elections. (They are much less closely tied in the case of presidential elections, in which there is room for the large-scale intervention of other factors such as personality.)

Like nominations, election campaigns are run largely on a do-it-yourself basis. Most members of the House and Senate do not receive extensive aid (financial or otherwise) from their political parties, even though those political parties have various state organizations, national committees, and congressional campaign committees that are presumably in business partially to provide such aid.* There are laws in many states that supposedly limit the amount of spending in congressional campaigns, but the effective limits tend to be what a candidate can raise.

Data on campaign expenditures are difficult to obtain. Virtually all of the reporting requirements have so many exceptions that only a fraction of the actual expenses are publicly reported. There are, how-ever, several fragments that allow some ranges to be established. In 1962, for example, the treasurer of the Democratic National Congressional Committee estimated that an average Democratic candidate for the House from a big city district would have to spend between $25,000 and $50,000, and that the average Democrat from a suburban or rural district would have to spend between $15,000 and $25,000.† By interviewing seventeen House incumbents of both parties Charles Jones estimated their actual expenses in the 1964 campaign as ranging between $5,000 and $100,000, with a mean expenditure of over $27,000. This figure included both the general election and primary election campaigns for some individuals; others had no primary opponents.° It should be noted, however, that expensive campaigns are not a new phenomenon. Although the data are partial, there is good evidence that campaigning has been a very costly activity at least for most of the twentieth century.

Senate campaign costs vary enormously with the population of the state. A serious campaign for a Senate seat in California or New York may well cost several million dollars. A campaign for a Senate seat in Wyoming or Delaware may cost no more than a campaign for a seat in the House. Senate primaries in populous states can also be enormously

---

* Clapp, *The Congressman:* 29, 352–53, 363.
† Ibid., 340.
° Charles O. Jones, *Every Second Year,* (Washington, D.C.: Brookings, 1976): 56.

expensive. In 1970, for example, the winning candidate in the New York Democratic primary for a Senate seat is estimated to have spent $1.8 million (he later lost the election). The losing candidate in the California Republican primary for a Senate seat is estimated to have spent $1.9 million.*

Overall estimates of spending on campaigns for House and Senate seats in 1970 ran as high as $100 to $150 million, less than $15 million of which was spent by official party committees.†

The high cost of gaining a House or Senate seat raises important questions. Can only rich men and women seek these offices? Are interested groups and individuals in a position to contribute so much of the needed money that they in fact "buy" public policy when they support a winning candidate heavily? There are no definitive answers to these questions, although the dangers implied by even qualified affirmative answers are certainly real. After the revelations of the Watergate affair and related matters, it seems that there will be new national laws on campaign spending. Public financing of campaigns and shortening the length of campaigns are also being discussed. There are no easy answers to the problem of how to finance campaigns so that candidates can make their appeals heard without being beholden to the specific interests and individuals that finance them. Even if one assumes totally honorable winners and undemanding campaign contributors there is reason to assume that some public decisions will at the minimum unconsciously give extra weight to the interests and opinions of the largest contributors. And, of course, not all large contributors are undemanding, and the definition of honor by members of the House and Senate varies from individual to individual.

ELECTION RESULTS

Congressional elections have two kinds of impacts: the *individual* impact of which candidates get to Washington and the *collective* impact of which party controls the House and Senate.

A Profile of the Members

The winners of seats in the House and Senate are by no means a cross section of the American population. By almost any measure they come from a social and economic elite. The same is true of the men and women they defeat.° The system of nominations and elections

---

* *Congressional Quarterly's Guide to the Congress of the United States* (Washington, D.C.: Congressional Quarterly, 1971): 477.

† Ibid., 475.

° Fishel, *Party and Opposition.*

Table 7–1

Educational Attainments of House and Senate Members and General Population, 1966.

Level of Education	House	Senate	General Population
No College	7%	4%	82%
Some college	14%	13%	10%
BA degree (or equivalent)	19%	14%	
Law degree	53%	59%	9%
Advanced degrees	7%	10%	
Total	100	100	101 [a]

[a] Does not sum to 100 because of rounding.

Source: The figures on House and Senate members came from Charles O. Jones, Every Second Year (Brookings, 1967). Those on the general population came from Department of Commerce, Bureau of the Census, Current Population Reports, Series P-20, no. 158, 19 December 1966.

used in this country produces a certain kind of member, defined in socioeconomic terms. Thus, in a narrow sense, Congress is never fully representative of the American people. This does not mean that only upper class interests prevail in the decisions of Congress but it does suggest that some of the less well-off classes in society may have little reason to identify with the decisions reached by Congress because they do not identify with the decision-makers.

Education. One striking characteristic of members of Congress is that they are highly educated. Table 7–1 summarizes the formal education of members of the House and Senate and the general population in 1966. It is clear that representatives and senators are equally well educated in formal terms and, in addition, they are vastly more educated than the general public.

Occupation. The majority of the members of the House and Senate are lawyers. Most of the non-lawyers come from a business or banking background. There are scatterings of teachers, journalists, farmers, and other occupations. Figure 7–3 summarizes the changing mix of professions in the House since 1789. Although the proportion of lawyers has declined since the 1850s, they still outnumber all other professions and occupations combined. The situation is similar in the Senate, where members of the legal profession abound.

Table 7–2 summarizes the occupations (as defined by the members

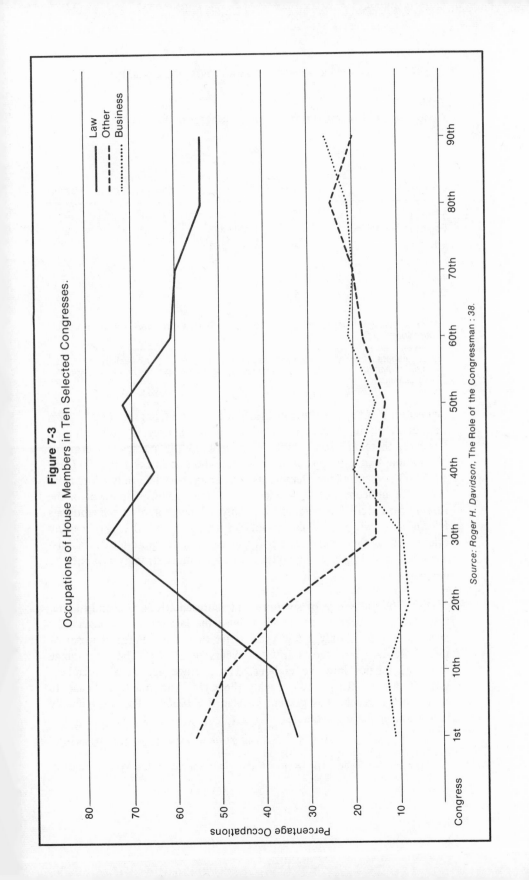

Figure 7-3

Occupations of House Members in Ten Selected Congresses.

Law
Other
Business

Percentage Occupations

80
70
60
50
40
30
20
10

Congress   1st   10th   20th   30th   40th   50th   60th   70th   80th   90th

Source: Roger H. Davidson, The Role of the Congressman: 38.

Table 7–2

Occupations of Members of the 92nd Congress, 1971–72.

| | House | | Senate | |
| | Percent of Total | | Percent of Total | |
Occupation	Membership [a]	Number	Membership [a]	Number
Law	54%	236	65%	65
Business or banking	33	145	27	27
Education	14	61	11	11
Agriculture	8	36	13	13
Journalism	7	30	7	7
Other	4	16	3	3

[a] The percentages sum to more than 100 because many members listed several occupations.

Source: Adopted from Congressional Quarterly Weekly Report, 15 January 1971: 129. "Other" includes labor leader, engineering, medicine, law enforcement, minister, and scientist.

themselves) of the members of the Ninety-second Congress (1971–72). The distribution of occupations in the two houses is quite similar; however, there are some differences between the parties in terms of occupation. For example, of all senators who served between 1947 and 1957, 63 percent of the Democrats were lawyers, while only 45 percent of the Republicans were lawyers. On the other hand, 40 percent of the Republicans were businessmen but only 17 percent of the Democrats fell in that category. This is not surprising, given the pro-business orientation of the Republican party in general. In most locales a businessman choosing to enter politics would be most strongly attracted to the Republican party.*

Age. The mean age of senators and representatives, presently about fifty-three, has been constant for at least the last several decades. The average senator is only a few years older than the average representative (fifty-six years versus fifty-two years in 1971). The ages range from the thirties into the eighties. The average age of all members was about forty-three until roughly the Civil War and then began to climb until it reached its present level in the 1930s.† This may chiefly reflect longer life expectancy.

* Donald R. Matthews, *U.S. Senators and Their World* (Chapel Hill: University of North Carolina Press, 1960): 36.
† Roger H. Davidson, *The Role of the Congressman* (New York: Pegasus, 1969): 38.

Table 7–3
Religious Affiliations of Members of the House and Senate and
the General Public

Religion	House	Senate	General Public
Protestant	73%	86%	72%
Catholic	23	12	21
Jewish	3	2	3
Other	1	0	3
Total [a]	100	100	99

[a] Does not sum to 100 because of rounding.

Source: *Based on data in* Congressional Quarterly Weekly Report, *15 January 1971: 126 for the House and Senate and on data in Donald R. Matthews,* U.S. Senators and Their World: *24, for the general public.*

Religion. Table 7–3 summarizes the religious affiliations of the members of the Ninety-second Congress (1971–72) and those of the general population. In general, Protestants are overrepresented, particularly in the Senate. Most of the Catholics and Jews are Democrats; virtually all Republican Senators and 85 percent of the Republican representatives are Protestant. By contrast only 65 percent of the Democrats in the House and 82 percent of the Democrats in the Senate were Protestant.

Race and Sex. Until recent years only very few women and nonwhites served in Congress. In the Ninety-second Congress there were twelve female representatives and one female senator. There were twelve black representatives (one was a woman) and one black senator. Twenty of the twenty-three blacks and/or women in the House were Democrats; the black and the female senators were both Republicans. Most of the black members came from predominantly black constituencies.

Political Experience. The average member of the House and Senate is a politically experienced individual who has previously held public office. For example, of the 179 senators who served between 1947 and 1957 only 10 percent of them had never held public office. Almost 80 percent of them had held public office for more than five years before coming to the Senate and 55 percent of them had held public office for more than ten years. Twenty-eight percent of them had been governors immediately before coming to the Senate and 28 percent came to the Senate directly from the House.

Representatives are also politically experienced when they come to the House. For example, a sample of members of the House in the Eighty-eighth Congress showed that three-quarters of them had held a state or local party position, almost half of them had served in a state legislature, and only 6 percent had no discernible political experience.*

Elections and Party Control

Virtually every congressional election in American history has provided a clear single majority party in the House and in the Senate. Before 1855 several different parties took their turn at organizing the House and Senate. Since 1855 only Republicans or Democrats have had majorities in either House.

Which party controls the House and Senate is important because of their differences on at least some major policy issues. Thus party control has implications for eventual policy decisions, even allowing for a great deal of slippage between party promises and performance and for a considerable amount of diversity within a party.

Figure 7–4 shows the relative strength of the majority party and largest minority party in the House between 1789 and 1853 in terms of the percentage of the total seats held (lesser minority parties are omitted). Figure 7–5 presents the same information on the Senate between 1789 and 1853. Figure 7–6 shows the relative strength of the Democrats and Republicans, again omitting small minority parties, from 1855 through 1971 in the House. Figure 7–7 presents information on the post-1855 period for the Senate. It is clear from these four graphs that there has been considerable competition overall for control of Congress.

The pre-1855 House was not a particularly competitive body. For 61 percent of the time between 1789 and 1855, there was a very large majority party that held 60 percent or more of the seats. This meant that the difference in the size of the majority and the majority parties was so large that the minority had little chance of defeating the wishes of the majority. For only 39 percent of the time between 1789 and 1855 was the size of the majority and minority parties less uneven, giving the minority a better chance to defeat majority party wishes.

In the House of the post-1855 period there has been a majority party holding 60 percent or more of the seats only 36 percent of the time. Because large (60 percent or more) majorities were less frequent than in the pre-1855 period, there was more opportunity for

---

* Ibid., 50.

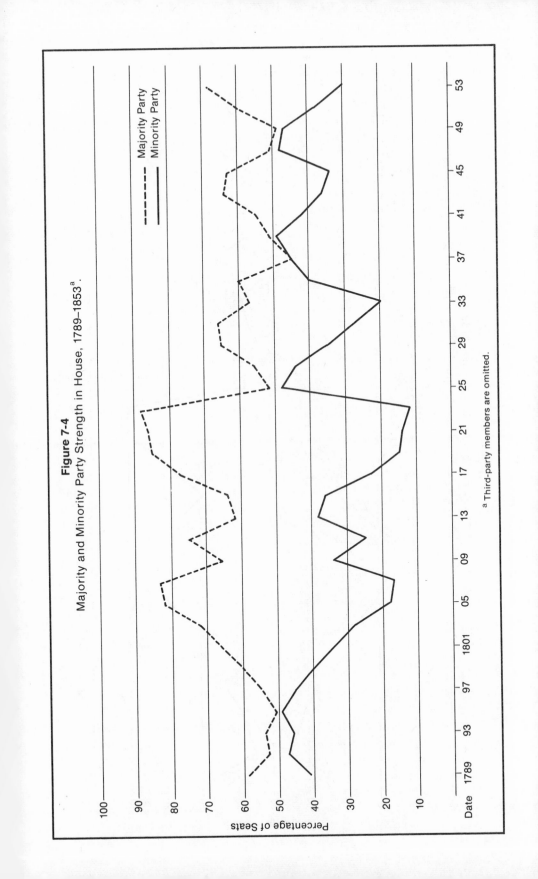

Figure 7-4

Majority and Minority Party Strength in House, 1789–1853[a].

Majority Party

Minority Party

Percentage of Seats

Date

[a] Third-party members are omitted.

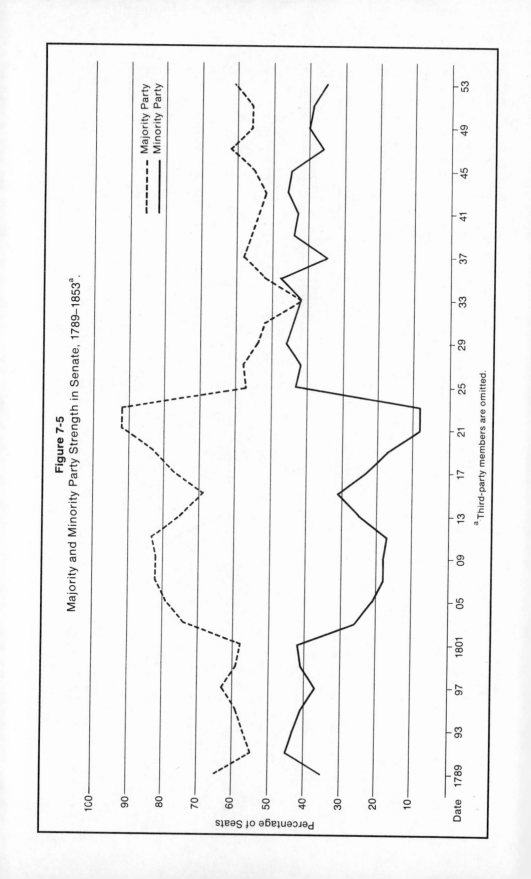

Figure 7-5

Majority and Minority Party Strength in Senate, 1789–1853[a].

Majority Party

Minority Party

Percentage of Seats

Date

[a]Third-party members are omitted.

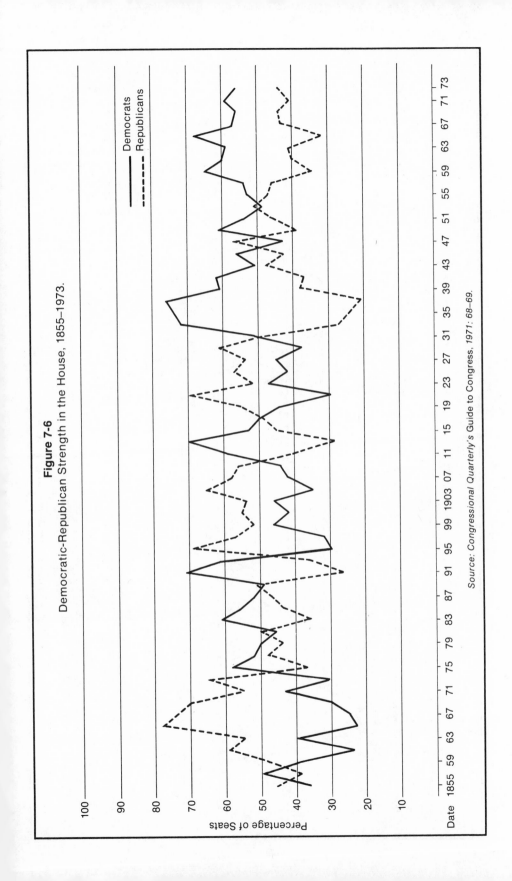

Figure 7-6

Democratic-Republican Strength in the House, 1855–1973.

Democrats ——
Republicans - - -

Percentage of Seats

100
90
80
70
60
50
40
30
20
10

Date 1855 59 63 67 71 75 79 83 87 91 95 99 1903 07 11 15 19 23 27 31 35 39 43 47 51 55 59 63 67 71 73

Source: Congressional Quarterly's Guide to Congress, 1971: 68–69.

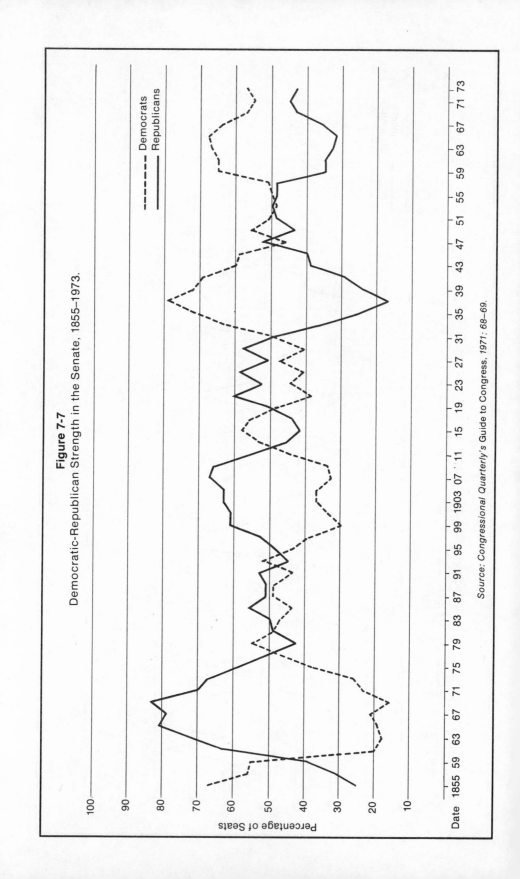

Figure 7-7

Democratic-Republican Strength in the Senate, 1855–1973.

- - - - - Democrats
———— Republicans

Percentage of Seats

100 90 80 70 60 50 40 30 20 10

Date 1855 59 63 67 71 75 79 83 87 91 95 99 1903 07 11 15 19 23 27 31 35 39 43 47 51 55 59 63 67 71 73

Source: Congressional Quarterly's Guide to Congress, 1971: 68–69.

competition between the majority and minority parties. For 64 percent of the time from 1855 to 1971 the minority party had a realistic chance of defeating the legislative wishes of the majority party because only a few defections from the majority party to the minority party were necessary to make the majority party lose.

In the Senate the level of party competition as measured by the percent of seats held by each party has been higher than in the House. In the pre-1855 Senate, the majority party held 60 percent or more of the seats 45 percent of the time. That figure was 44 percent in the post-1855 Senate. This represents less of a change than in the House, and indicates that competition was more nearly equal in both time periods. The minority party had a realistic chance of legislative success (that is, defeating the wishes of the majority party) more than half of the time.

Figures 7–6 and 7–7 also reveal that in both houses a dramatic change in the majority-minority party seat distribution occurred in 1925. The percentage of seats belonging to the majority party in the pre-1923 period was very large in both houses (between 51 percent and 88 percent for the House, and between 55 percent and 94 percent for the Senate). In the Congress convening in 1925 the percentage of seats belonging to the majority party dropped dramatically in both houses, and has not returned to pre-1925 levels. Thus a sharp increase in party competition occurred after the 1924 election and has been sustained since then.

Table 7–4
Inter-Party Competition for Congressional Seats, 1914–1960.

Years	Percentage of Fluidity [a]	Percentage of No-Change Districts [b]
1914–26	12.0	62.1
1932–40	10.6	69.9
1942–50	11.9	74.0
1952–60	7.8	78.2

[a] Fluidity measures the proportion of elections within the time periods indicated that resulted in a change of party control of the seat. Thus, if 1000 elections were held in a time period, and 100 resulted in a party change, the fluidity percentage would be 10.

[b] A no-change district is simply one in which the same party won every election within the time period (the first time period contains 7 elections, the others all contain 5).

Source: Adapted from Charles O. Jones, "Inter-party Competition for Congressional Seats," Western Political Quarterly 7 *(1964): 465.*

Table 7–5

Percentage Democratic House Members, by Region, Elected in
Selected Years between 1924 and 1972.

Region	Democratic Percentage of Seats Held by Republicans and Democrats Combined following Election of:				
	1924	1936	1948	1960	1972
South	98	98	98	93	69
Border States	60	95	88	84	77
New England	13	48	39	50	60
Mid-Atlantic	26	68	49	49	54
Midwest	16	78	44	41	38
Plains States	13	45	16	19	36
Rocky Mountain	21	100	75	73	42
Pacific Coast	11	82	36	51	58

The states contained in the various regions are as follows: South (Alabama, Arkansas, Florida, Georgia, Louisiana, Mississippi, North Carolina, South Carolina, Tennessee, Texas, and Virginia), Border States (Kentucky, Maryland, Missouri, Oklahoma, and West Virginia), New England (Connecticut, Maine, Massachusetts, New Hampshire, Rhode Island, and Vermont), Mid-Atlantic (Delaware, New Jersey, New York, and Pennsylvania), Midwest (Illinois, Indiana, Michigan, Ohio, and Wisconsin), Plains States (Iowa, Kansas, Minnesota, Nebraska, North Dakota, and South Dakota), Rocky Mountain (Arizona, Colorado, Idaho, Montana, Nevada, New Mexico, Utah, and Wyoming), and Pacific Coast (Alaska, California, Hawaii, Oregon, and Washington).

Third party members are omitted; the percentages are calculated on the combined Democratic and Republican seats.

Source: Adapted from Milton C. Cummings, Jr., Congressmen and the Electorate (New York: Free Press, 1966): 221.

Even though competition for control of the House has increased, competition for individual seats in the House has decreased. Table 7–4 summarizes this decline between 1914 and 1960. As the declining percentage of fluidity indicates, the percentage of elections resulting in a party change is decreasing. Reciprocally, the percentage of districts that do not undergo party change has increased.

Although there has been no substantial change in the level of party competition in the Senate, contests for individual Senate seats have been getting closer as larger numbers of states have become competitive rather than dominated by one party.*

Despite decreased turnover of House seats, the long-term trend has been toward reduced sectional dominance by one party or the other. Even though the transfer of seats between parties is rare, the few changes that have occurred have tended to spread both parties more

* See H. Douglas Price, "The Electoral Arena," 42–45.

evenly across the country. Table 7–5 summarizes the regional distribution of House seats at twelve-year intervals from 1924 to the present. Particularly striking is the decline of Democratic strength in the South. By 1973 neither party completely dominated any region.

Turnover, Safe Seats, and the Advantages of Incumbency

Members of the House and Senate who already hold seats and seek to retain them usually do so. Charles Clapp reported, on the basis of his roundtable discussions and interviews in 1959, that members of the House "agree that as incumbents they possess extraordinary advantages over their opponents. There is a tendency to believe that, aside from isolated instances where an overriding issue is present, there is little excuse for defeat. At the beginning of a new Congress legislators often discuss the defeat of former colleagues in terms of failure to make full use of the many perquisites of incumbency." * One estimate of the impact of incumbency for House members is that simply holding the seat adds somewhere between 2 percent and 5 percent to the incumbents' vote—an amount usually sufficient to insure victory.† The margin of the advantage, according to the same analysis, has increased in recent congressional elections.

Table 7–6
Success of Incumbents Seeking Re-election to House Seats, 1954–1970.

Year	Number Seeking Re-election	% Who Won	% Who Lost
1954	401	94.5	5.5
1956	403	96.5	3.5
1958	390	91.0	9.0
1960	400	93.8	6.2
1962	385	96.1	3.9
1964	386	89.1	10.9
1966	405	89.4	10.6
1968	401	98.8	1.2
1970	389	97.2	2.8

Source: The data on 1954 through 1960 came from Charles O. Jones, "The Role of the Campaign in Congressional Politics," in M. Kent Jennings and L. Harmon Zeigler (eds.) The Electoral Process (Englewood Cliffs, N.J.: Prentice-Hall, 1966): 24. Data from 1960 through 1970 were compiled from Congressional Quarterly materials.

* Clapp, *The Congressman:* 331.
  † Robert S. Erikson, "The Advantage of Incumbency in Congressional Elections," *Polity* 3 (1971): 395–405; and Robert S. Erikson, "A Reply to Tidmarch," *Polity* 4 (1972): 527–529.

Table 7–7
Success of Incumbent's Party in Retaining House Seats
Vacated by Incumbent, 1954–1970.

Year	Number of Seats	% Won by Candidate of Incumbent Party	% Won by Challenger
1954	34	85.3	14.7
1956	32	81.3	18.7
1958	46	67.4	32.6
1960	37	70.3	29.7
1962	29 [a]	79.3	20.7
1964	49	77.6	22.4
1966	12 [b]	41.7	58.3
1968	27 [c]	77.8	22.2
1970	38 [d]	65.8	34.2

[a] Excludes twenty-three seats where there was no incumbent due to vacancies or the creation of new districts.
[b] Excludes eighteen seats where there was no incumbent due to vacancies or the creation of new districts.
[c] Excludes seven seats where there was no incumbent due to vacancies or the creation of new districts.
[d] Excludes seven seats where there was no incumbent due to creation of new districts or vacancies, plus one seat where two incumbents challenged each other.

Source: The data on 1954 through 1960 came from Charles O. Jones, "The Role of the Campaign in Congressional Politics," in M. Kent Jennings and L. Harmon Zeigler (eds.) The Electoral Process (Englewood Cliffs, N.J.: Prentice-Hall, 1966): 26. Data from 1960 through 1970 were compiled from Congressional Quarterly materials.

Table 7–6 reports the success of incumbents seeking re-election to their House seats in the nine congressional elections between 1954 and 1970. In some elections (for example, 1968) virtually every incumbent won. Only in the 1964 election did fewer than 90 percent of the incumbents seeking re-election win, and that was a year of an enormous Democratic victory.

Even when one of the parties makes a major gain in the House, as did the Democrats in 1958 and 1964 and the Republicans in 1966, only a very small number of incumbents lose. In the nine elections between 1954 and 1970, an average of 91 percent of all incumbents chose to run for re-election in any given campaign. When the average percentage of incumbents running is multiplied by the average percentage of those who win it becomes apparent that over 85 percent of the average House contains the same members as the previous House.

Even when an incumbent decides not to run, his seat is usually retained by a member of his party. Table 7–7 summarizes the success of the incumbent's party from 1954 through 1970 in retaining seats that

Table 7–8
Success of Incumbents Seeking Re-election to Senate Seats,
1954–1970.

Year	Number Seeking Re-election	% Who Won	% Who Lost
1954	31	80.6	19.4
1956	31	87.1	22.9
1958	28	64.3	35.7
1960	29	93.1	6.9
1962	34	85.3	14.7
1964	32	87.5	12.5
1966	29	96.6	3.4
1968	24	83.3	16.7
1970	30	80.0	20.0

Source: Compiled from Congressional Quarterly *materials. This includes special elections.*

the incumbent had left through death, retirement, or primary defeat. Obviously the challenging party has a better chance in these elections than in those in which they must face an incumbent, but usually only 20 percent to 30 percent of these seats change party. And since it is rare that as many as 10 percent of the incumbents do not seek re-election these victories by the challenging party account for only a few changes: somewhere between five and fifteen seats every two years during the 1954–70 period.

In Senate elections there is more variation: incumbents certainly have an advantage, but it is not as uniformly strong as is that of House incumbents. Table 7–8 summarizes data on senatorial elections from 1954 through 1970. In these nine elections an average of 84.2 percent of the incumbents running were successful. This table supports the earlier assertion that states are getting more competitive at the same time that districts are getting safer.

The few seats vacated by incumbent senators for whatever reason also tended to remain with the party of the incumbent. For the nine elections between 1954 and 1970, fifty-seven seats were contested in which there was no incumbent. The party of the previous incumbent won thirty-seven (about 65 percent) of these contests.

Congressional Elections in the South and Congressional Seniority

Since the mid-1930s the South has been a highly visible section of the country in congressional politics. One reason is that it has routinely supplied a large portion of the virtually continuous Democratic majorities of the House and Senate. The region has also supplied most of the conservative Democratic mavericks who have defied the stances of presidents and congressional leaders of their party on a wide range of issues.

There is a popular belief that southern Democrats dominate Congress because they have safer seats than do northern Democrats, and as a result can amass more seniority and the choicest committee chairmanships. This is untrue in the House, where southerners and northerners have almost equal seniority patterns. It is true, however, that senior southerners in the House tend to be younger than senior northerners and they may be, therefore, somewhat more vigorous—but that is a purely speculative conclusion.*

In the Senate the southern Democrats do hold more important institutional positions (especially committee chairmanships) because of their greater seniority. In 1971, for example, the seventeen southern Democrats averaged 16.6 years in the Senate; the thirty-eight northern Democrats averaged 10.2 years. Eight of the nine most senior Democrats were from the South. It should be added, however, that two of these men died in 1971 and 1972 and the next five most senior senators were all northerners. In short, the differences in seniority between southern and northern Democrats are likely to decrease, especially as Republicans capture some southern seats (they already had seven of the twenty-two "Confederate" seats in 1973).

Voting for Congress and Voting for President

The basic phenomenon to observe in the relationship between voting for president and voting for representatives and senators is that in presidential years there is a close articulation of the voting whereas in "off-years" (that is, non-presidential years) the candidates of the party of the president tend to be at a disadvantage. In presidential years when a state or district votes heavily for a presidential candidate, the Senate and House candidates of his party from that state or district are also very likely to win.†

---

* See Raymond E. Wolfinger and Joan Heifetz Hollinger, "Safe Seats, Seniority, and Power in Congress," in Raymond E. Wolfinger (ed.), *Readings on Congress* (Englewood Cliffs, N.J.: Prentice-Hall, 1971).

† On this phenomenon, see V. O. Key, *Politics, Parties and Pressure Groups* (New York: Crowell, 1964, 5th ed.): chapter 20; Angus Campbell and others, *Elections and the Political Order:* chapter 3; and Barbara Hinckley, "Interpreting House Midterm Elections: Toward a Measurement of the In-Party's 'Expected' Loss of Seats," *American Political Science Review* 61 (1967): 694–700.

The momentum built up by a winning presidential candidate that helps carry in some additional senators and representatives from his party (the so-called "coattail" effect) usually has subsided two years later in the off-year elections, enabling the minority party to make something of a comeback. Often this comeback is interpreted as dissatisfaction with the president and his policies, but in fact it is a natural phenomenon that is a good measure of underlying party strength and party identification in the country at the time. Presidential year congressional results are abnormal in the sense that the basic attitudes toward who ought to be in Congress get distorted by the presidential voting. Off-year results should not be interpreted as a policy referendum (either positive or negative) but rather as a return of the party balance to "normal" for the period. Thus, for example, after a particularly large presidential victory it is most natural for the president's party to lose seats in both houses in the succeeding congressional election. After a very narrow presidential victory the loss should not be nearly as great.*

A second phenomenon in voting for Congress and the president is also present: winning presidential candidates lead the candidates of their party for Senate and House elections in terms of percentage of the vote more often than the reverse occurs. What is surprising, however, is that the reverse occurs a significant proportion of the time. For example, between 1924 and 1964 the winning presidential candidate led his party's House nominees in 60 percent of the individual districts (2606 of 4318 individual instances spread over the forty years) but the House nominee polled a higher percentage of the two-party vote than the winning presidential candidate in 40 percent of the cases. Predictably, those House nominees who won by the largest percent of the vote led the president more often than he led them. Those who won by relatively small margins or lost were more often led by the president. Figure 7–8 portrays this relationship. Thus "coattails" are extended in both directions in presidential years: more often they run from a winning president to the candidates of his party for the House (and presumably the Senate), but in some districts, where there is an unusually strong and well-established candidate for House or Senate his "coattails" might well help the presidential candidate. It seems reasonable to assert that the basic strength of the Democratic party in congressional elections helped carry both Presidents Truman and Kennedy to victories in 1948 and 1960, respectively.†

---

* See Hinckley, "Interpreting Midterm Elections," 699.

† On the entire subject of the articulation between voting for the president and voting for House members in presidential years, see Milton C. Cummings, Jr., *Congressmen and the Electorate* (New York: Free Press, 1966).

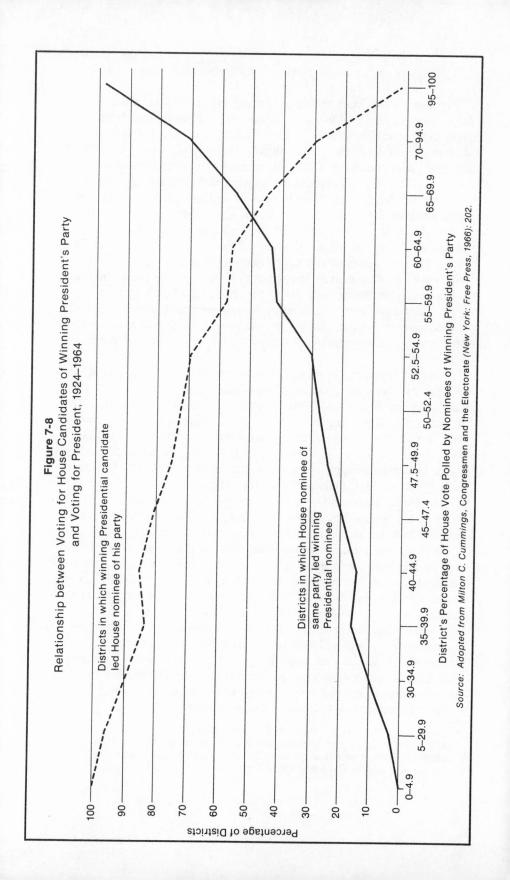

Figure 7-8

Relationship between Voting for House Candidates of Winning President's Party and Voting for President, 1924–1964

Districts in which winning Presidential candidate led House nominee of his party

Districts in which House nominee of same party led winning Presidential nominee

District's Percentage of House Vote Polled by Nominees of Winning President's Party

Percentage of Districts

0–4.9   5–29.9   30–34.9   35–39.9   40–44.9   45–47.4   47.5–49.9   50–52.4   52.5–54.9   55–59.9   60–64.9   65–69.9   70–94.9   95–100

0   10   20   30   40   50   60   70   80   90   100

Source: Adopted from Milton C. Cummings, Congressmen and the Electorate (New York: Free Press, 1966): 202.

THE IMPLICATIONS OF ELECTIONS
FOR CONGRESSIONAL BEHAVIOR

The aspects of congressional elections recounted in this chapter have a profound effect on the way in which Congress as an institution works. In many ways the electoral system pushes in the direction of a stable, conservative body in which the most controversial issues are avoided, the agenda remains static, and proposed solutions to problems are rarely fresh. Only certain kinds of individuals tend to be electable to Congress, whose members share a kind of socioeconomic homogeneity. This fact probably helps limit the perspective and imagination of members. The low turnout for congressional elections helps result in at least a partially stagnant congressional agenda; no new voices in the electorate are loud enough to add items to the agenda. The high rate of electoral success on the part of incumbents also promotes stability of agenda and solutions. Few freshmen members are sent to Congress every two years and, given the restraints put on them, they have minimal chances to make policy inputs in their early years, particularly in the House. The district system of election also adds to the conservatism of the House because of the creation of a large number of relatively homogeneous districts, themselves conservative.

The high cost of campaigns helps reinforce the attractiveness of "playing it safe" in Congress. If members do not offend important constituents with unusual stands or new ideas, serious threats in either the primary or general election may be avoided. Thus they may run relatively inexpensive campaigns. Since incumbents of both parties share this interest it seems reasonable to assert that they may seek to protect each other from controversial issues. They may not share either party labels or beliefs but all have a common stake in returning to Washington as cheaply as possible. This fact also helps freeze the agenda so that only highly familiar items are on it.

Finally, for much significant policy change to occur, a change in the partisan control of Congress is often necessary. Yet the great advantages of incumbents, coupled with the stable voting habits of those who elect senators and representatives, have made such party turnovers very rare for the last four decades.

On the other hand, there are some features of the electoral system that promote responsiveness, a broadened agenda, and innovativeness. Two features that promote this activist and innovative stance are the existence of a strong two-party system and single-member districts. This means that every Congress meets with a single majority party in at least nominal control of the House and Senate (only very rarely have different parties controlled the two chambers). Thus a real majority is potentially present in every Congress. When the nominal majority is also a new majority—that is, when the electorate has put a different party in control—a situation is created in which the likelihood of aggressiveness on the part of that majority is relatively high *because* it is likely to have come into majority status after a number of frustrating years in minority status.

Apathy and ignorance on the part of the electorate are features of the electoral scene that can cut two ways. They may allow members to be lethargic, uninnovative, and responsive to only a few selected interests. But they also allow members the freedom to be creative, innovative and responsive to some larger vision of the pressing needs of public policy. Given adequate leadership and possessing adequate skills in manipulating the internal machinery of Congress, a majority, usually partisan, can emerge and can help create new directions in the solution of national problems.

8

CONGRESS,
INTEREST GROUPS,
AND CONSTITUENTS

GIVEN THE CONCERN—BOTH APPARENT AND REAL—OF MEMBERS
of Congress with representation and the fact that there are various
groups eager for a place on the public agenda it becomes important
to ask which competitors (that is, constituents or special interests) receive the most attention. In general, it can be said that special interests—particularly as they articulate their requests through organized
groups—claim much attention from the members. They do not necessarily dominate the resolution of issues but they help set the agenda
on which Congress acts.

However, constituencies and constituents also claim some congressional attention, sometimes working with special interest groups and
sometimes simply because they have access to a member who is concerned about their stated needs. One alternative almost never available for the constituencies to use in communicating with their members
in Washington is local political parties. These parties often pay attention to the offices of senator and representative only for purposes of
nominating candidates. Once elected, a member almost never hears
from his state or local parties. Thus both the member and those seeking to influence him must use other channels. This fact also enhances
the potential impact of special interest groups.

MEMBERS AND INTEREST GROUPS

Interest groups enter the policy-making process through their lobbying activities. These activities, however, are more subtle than popular opinion usually portrays. In fact, the myth of the power and effectiveness of lobbies is not borne out by analysis of lobbies' actual behavior. To reach a balanced conclusion about the effectiveness of lobbying, one needs to consider the nature of the interaction that occurs between lobbyists and legislator, the setting in which that interaction occurs (particularly the systemic bias that characterizes the interaction), the variety of lobbying participants, the patterns and techniques that characterize lobbying, and finally the range of impact that lobbying can have.

The Setting for Interaction

Whom do interest groups represent? At the most general level the interest group system in the United States has a distinct bias favoring upper class and predominantly business interests. E. E. Schattschneider, a leading scholar of interest groups, has estimated that 90 percent of the adult population cannot get into the "pressure system," (his label for the phenomenon of organized groups pursuing special or private interests in the political arena).* Most of the active organized groups that lobby in the government represent very narrow segments of the polity with highly focused interests. The few groups that represent more general interests tend to have memberships that encompass only a small portion of their theoretically potential constituencies. And there are very rarely any interest groups that are effective lobbyists for the "public interest." So, in short, the lobbying arena is loaded in favor of special interests. An example contrast between the two types of groups is useful: a group for the chemical companies (Manufacturing Chemists Association) has only 180 member companies and a staff of 74 people. The 180 constitute a very large proportion of eligible members. On the other hand, Common Cause, which asserts it represents the public interest and thus, presumably, everyone, has 110,000 individual members and a staff of 35.

There are two parties involved in every lobbying activity—the lobbyist and the legislator—and they interact, usually to their mutual benefit. The relationship that is often portrayed of vulture-like lobbyists preying on helpless legislators is distorted. Lobbyists, to be sure, seek favors and assistance for their particular interests. But they are

---

* E. E. Schattschneider, *The Semisovereign People* (New York: Holt, Rinehart, and Winston, 1960).

required to register and publicly identify themselves as lobbyists so their identity and affiliations are not secret. Also, legislators seek out lobbyists for the information on substance, on bureaucratic intent, and (less often) on constituency preferences that they can provide. The exchange of mere information for influential favors may at first seem an uneven trade, for legislators are in a position to do so much more than the lobbyist in terms of magnitude of favors granted. But the congressional system values the acquisition of a great deal of accurate information and this necessity balances out the exchange of favors for knowledge. At any rate, interest groups continue to flourish and their major offering continues to be information.

The interest groups are not always the initiators of action. Legislators will often take the lead in promoting a certain kind of action and will be joined later by lobbyists. For example, in 1973 when Congress debated at length the issue of whether to approve an oil pipeline across Alaska a senator from that state was the first individual to conceive of the possibility and necessity, from his point of view, of suspending some of the provisions of the National Environmental Policy Act to facilitate construction of the pipeline. Only after he had gathered about one-third or more of the senators as supporters of his amendment did the lobbyists for both the oil companies and the administration become active in its behalf.

Members in general view themselves as being free to act on the basis of their own judgment despite lobbying from interest groups. They feel pressure but also think they can withstand it. Occasionally they say there is no lobbying activity even on an important bill.* They often attribute influence on the part of lobbies in relation to other members, since most members do not willingly damage their self-image of independence. In general, it probably is accurate to say that lobbies rarely dominate a vote but there are at least usually a few members particularly concerned with enhancing their relation with one or more lobbies.

Generally, very few members question the legitimacy of interest groups and lobbying. In fact, a large proportion work actively to facilitate the interests of specific groups. Only a few think it necessary to state that their position is to resist the requests of groups.† And, of course,

---

* Charles L. Clapp, *The Congressman* (Washington: Brookings, 1963): 163, 182.
†Roger H. Davidson, in *The Role of the Congressman* (New York: Pegasus, 1969) reports on the attitudes of eighty-seven members of the House toward interest groups in the Eighty-eighth Congress (1963–64). He categorizes the members as facilitators, resistors, and neutrals. Facilitators are those members with a friendly attitude toward group activity and considerable knowledge about it. Resistors are those with a hostile attitude toward group activity and considerable knowledge about it. Neutrals are those who either had no strong

even these members may in fact sometimes be helpful to a lobby supporting ideas they favor.

Types of Interest Groups and Lobbyists

There are many different types of interest groups—ranging from the large and well-financed to the miniscule and impoverished. There are also many types of lobbyists—ranging from full-time professionals to part-time amateurs.

Under the rubric "interest group" the large national associations (composed of both individual and organizational members) come to mind first—groups such as the National Association of Manufacturers, the U.S. Chamber of Commerce, and the American Federation of Labor-Congress of Industrial Organizations. There are also a number of industries that have their own national groups that engage in lobbying activities, for example, the American Petroleum Institute, the Manufacturing Chemists Association, and the National Coal Association. Some individual corporations, to some extent, constitute interest groups by themselves. When aerospace companies for example, compete for major contracts, they actively lobby on their own behalf.

Interest groups do not represent only industry, commerce, and labor. There are groups that represent smaller units of government: the National Association of Counties, The National League of Cities, and the U.S. Conference of Mayors, for example. A number of states, counties, and cities maintain their own representatives in Washington too.* Some national groups represent professions and act as interest groups when they become involved in the legislative process. The American Medical Association and American Bar Association fall in this category. Some professional or semi-professional groups specifically represent employees of other governmental units. For example, there is a National Association of State Aviation Officials, a National Association of

---

attitude about groups or who had very little knowledge. Of his sample Davidson classed 29 percent as facilitators, 21 percent as resistors, and 49 percent as neutrals. Republican members were much more inclined to be facilitators (38 percent) than Democrats (24 percent) and much less inclined to be resistors (6 percent) than Democrats (31 percent). As Democrats became more senior they also became less likely to be facilitators and more likely to be resistors. Senior Republicans were more likely to be facilitators. Members from marginal districts tended to be resistors. Republicans from safe districts tended to be facilitators.

As with most studies of self-perceived roles there is no empirical evidence about whether these differing attitudes resulted in differing patterns of behavior.

* See John L. Moore "Washington Pressures/State-Local Lobbying Grows Despite Drive to Decentralize Government," *National Journal* (February 24, 1973): 262–270.

Table 8–1
Number and Type of Lobbying Organizations Registered during
the 91st Congress.

Type of Group	Number of Registrations
Business Groups	223
Citizens Groups	96
Employee and Labor Groups	18
Farm Groups	6
Foreign Groups	8
Foundations	3
Individuals	5
Military and Veterans Groups	3
Professional Groups	11
Total	373

Source: Congressional Quarterly Almanac *1970: 1208.*

Public Health Officials, and an Airport Operators Council (most airports are owned by a municipality).

Table 8–1 summarizes the number and type of lobbying organizations registered with the Clerk of the House to lobby in Congress during the Ninety-first Congress (1969–70). This breakdown of groups indicates both the variety of lobbying groups and the predominance of business interests.

Interest groups often ally with one another for specific legislative battles. These alliances may be more or less permanent in some instances. For example, even before they merged their staffs in late 1969 the National League of Cities and the Conference of Mayors cooperated on virtually all issues. Other alliances may be formed over a single issue and may, in fact, unite groups that have fought each other in the past and may do so in the future. For example, during the controversy over the SST in the early 1970s environmentalist groups such as the Sierra Club, Friends of the Earth, and the League of Conservation Voters opposed the efforts of the aerospace companies such as Boeing to gain congressional approval of the project. However, in 1973 the environmentalists were joined by a number of aerospace companies such as Boeing, Rohr Industries, and LTV in working for passage of a highway bill that allowed highway trust fund money to be used for mass transit. The environmentalists favored the bill as a way to reduce the polluting effects of the automobile and the environmental and aesthetic damage resulting from what they considered excessive road-building. The companies favored the bill because the aerospace industry was in considerable economic trouble and a number of firms had turned to the manufacture of mass transit equipment such as subway cars in an effort to survive.*

In the effort to get support for the passage of the Alaska pipeline bill a consortium of interested companies was formed behind the leadership of the Alyeska Pipeline Service Company. These included the three oil companies that were the principal owners of the oil on the North Slope of Alaska. Cooperating with these companies were representatives of the Alaska State government, the Department of the Interior and the AFL-CIO, particularly the Maritime Unions who were eager for jobs in the shipping business that the pipeline would create.†

When the Nixon administration suspended or terminated most housing programs aimed at helping low income families in early 1973 a National Ad Hoc Housing Coalition was quickly formed behind the leadership of the National Association of Housing and Redevelopment Officials. Although much of the work of the coalition was performed principally by NAHRO, the alliance was symbolically important because of the more than one hundred interest groups represented.

The largest interest groups maintain substantial Washington offices with a number of full-time lobbyists. Some even have their own buildings, usually located close to government offices. Small groups maintain a minimal Washington office—a staff of one professional lobbyist, one secretary, and a mimeograph machine is typical of a number of operations. Some groups and companies prefer not to maintain an office of their own but, instead, hire a "Washington lawyer" to represent their interests. These individuals specialize in lobbying and do very little legal work in the narrow sense. Some law firms in Washington are wholly devoted to this kind of work; others have some individuals specializing in it while others pursue more usual legal work. Some "Washington lawyers" are former government figures themselves (ex-senators and ex-secretaries of departments, for example). One of this breed of lobbyist may have a number of clients whose interests literally range from soup to nuts.

Others who serve as full-time lobbyists for an association, corpora-

---

* "Busting the Highway Trust: An Unlikely Alliance," *Congressional Quarterly Weekly Report* (March 24, 1973): 643–644.

†Richard Corrigan and Claude E. Barfield "Energy Report/Pipeline Lobby Uses Its Political Muscle to Bypass Environmental Law," *National Journal* (August 11, 1973): 1172–1178.

tion, or union are retired military officers, ex-employees of the bureaucracy, and former congressional staff members. Perhaps the most prized catch for an interest group is an ex-senator or ex-representative. These men are particularly valuable because of their personal and professional contacts on Capitol Hill. They probably also have a number of potentially useful contacts in the executive branch. There are few of this type of lobbyist—only nine former members of Congress or their law firms registered to lobby in 1970, for example. More common are retired high-ranking public officials other than members of Congress —sixty-six were listed as registered lobbyists in 1970.*

Patterns and Techniques of Lobbying Activity

There are several general features that characterize almost all lobbying activity. First, it should be stressed that the lobbyists' major task is mobilization of those who already believe rather than conversion of the infidels.† Lobbyists do not, by and large, concentrate on changing congressmen's minds. Rather they seek out persons whom they have identified as supporters and work to reinforce their views, providing them ammunition to use in pursuing the cause in which they both believe. Interest groups can accomplish nothing without creating and maintaining good relations with at least a few members of Congress.

Second, Washington lobbyists have a broader job than simply soliciting tangible actions—legislation, appointments, investigations—from members of the House and Senate. The lobbyist's principal goals are to use Congress to influence the administrative branch, to get information, or to achieve favorable publicity for an organization.° The typical request from the lobbyist to the legislator seeks help for personal, business, or professional problems; Lewis Dexter calls the handling of such requests by legislators "casework." ‡ Most of these casework requests are not something the legislator can directly solve; usually the best he can do is to intercede with a bureau in the executive branch.§ Such intercession can take many forms—ranging from one perfunctory telephone call by a congressional staff member that results in nothing to

---

* *Congressional Quarterly Almanac 1970:* 1208–1213.
† See Raymond A. Bauer, Ithiel de Sola Pool, and Lewis A. Dexter, *American Business and Public Policy* (New York: Atherton, 1963); and Randall B. Ripley, "Congress Champions Aid to Airports, 1958–59," and "Congress and Clean Air: The Issue of Enforcement, 1963" in Frederic N. Cleaveland and associates, *Congress and Urban Problems* (Washington, D.C.: Brookings, 1969).
° Lewis A. Dexter, *How Organizations Are Represented in Washington* (Indianapolis: Bobbs-Merrill, 1969): 80.
‡ Ibid., 81.
§ Ibid., 84.

repeated personal requests from a member that are likely to result in the desired bureaucratic response.

Lobbying itself—that is, asking for explicit congressional action rather than information or indirect intervention in the bureaucracy—occurs principally when there is the occasion and some likelihood that Congress can and will act, when the interested lobbies have enough resources (mostly manpower) to spend on the enterprise, and when the bad effects of lobbying (indignant opponents, for example) are not likely to outweigh the good effects.* Unless an interest group takes these factors into account it is probably wasting its resources and perhaps harming its own cause.

The specific techniques that lobbyists employ as they pursue favors and information in Congress are numerous.† They make personal contacts with members of the House and Senate and staff members who work for individual representatives and senators and committees. These communications can be made in person or by phone. Personal efforts may well involve a social aspect—such as the lobbyist taking the staff member out for lunch or a drink. Lobbyists can also work indirectly through other individuals thought to be important to or influential with specific congressmen—key constituents (for example, an important publisher or campaign contributor), representatives of allied interest groups, key bureaucrats, or, most important, other members of the House and Senate. These latter are the most persuasive "lobbyists" of all.

Lobbyists provide useful information to members and can often package this information in directly usable ways—as, for example, by preparing a speech for the member to deliver that espouses the interest group's viewpoint, thereby saving the time of the member and his staff. Lobbyists also testify before congressional committees that are holding hearings on bills. They prepare their testimony and distribute it widely in written form both before and after delivering it. They also respond to questioning, often in colloquies that are prearranged with sympathetic members of the committee. Their prepared testimony and the oral interchanges are also printed in the record of the hearings issued by the committee.

Lobbyists and their employers often attempt to influence critical assignments to committees that handle legislation of importance to

---

* Ibid., 56.
† For discussions of these techniques see Clapp: chapter 4; Harmon Zeigler, *Interest Groups in American Society* (Englewood Cliffs, N.J.: Prentice-Hall, 1964); Dexter, *How Organizations Are Represented in Washington;* David B. Truman *The Governmental Process* (New York: Knopf, 1951); and Lester W. Milbrath, *The Washington Lobbyists* (Chicago: Rand McNally, 1963).

them. They may make representations to the members of the relevant committee on committees about which members, or at least which type of member, would be satisfactory. They may work to get specific committees to conduct hearings they think would highlight information favorable to their positions.

Lobbyists try to stimulate mail supporting their position. This can be done on a selective basis (for example, from a few corporation presidents or union leaders) or it can be a mass campaign (for example, from as many members of a union or a chamber of commerce as possible). In general, the selective mailing is likely to attract more attention from the senators and representatives than the mass mailing. Mass mailings are generally obviously that and usually require minimal effort on the part of the individual mailer. Thus members often ignore or at least downplay them.

Interest groups may be particularly useful to members of Congress at election time by helping provide the large amount of funds necessary either to gain or retain a seat. In the 1972 congressional elections, for example, four different political action groups representing the milk industry contributed over $1.3 million to candidates for the House and Senate; the political arm of the American Medical Association contributed over $850,000; a banking group contributed almost $200,000; the political agency of the National Association of Manufacturers contributed over $440,000; the political arm of the AFL-CIO contributed almost $1.2 million; and the United Auto Workers contributed over $500,000.

One of the last milk contributions is particularly interesting. Near the end of the campaign the milk industry gave $462,000 to unidentified congressional campaigns through the House and Senate Republican and Democratic Campaign Committees. They simply trusted the party officials to give the money to the friends of the milk interests. A spokesman for the group said that the allocations were made on the basis of offering support for "friends of dairy farmers and supporters of agricultural legislation. We try to keep our friends in office and elect those who are our friends." Spokesmen for the congressional campaign committees say the money was given without explicit instructions on who should receive it. All parties in this arrangement indicated satisfaction that the "proper" individuals had benefited. Subsequent disclosures have showed the milk industry to have been heavy financial backers of Richard Nixon's 1972 presidential campaign and allegations were made that those contributions facilitated favorable action by Nixon and the Department of Agriculture in considering a substantial increase in the support price for milk. Leading members of both parties

(Nixon being the most prominent Republican and Johnson, Humphrey, and Mills being the most prominent Democrats) have received major campaign help from the milk interests for a number of years.*

The provision of money for campaigns is the most important election-time service rendered by the interest groups. They can also be helpful by conducting voter registration drives and by providing campaign workers and campaign literature.

It should be noted that not all interest groups are equally skillful in using the techniques identified above. Even the most effective lobbyists can be rebuffed or make mistakes. Among the commonest errors committed by lobbyists are the misidentification of potential friends, sympathizers, and opponents; inattention to important stages in the legislative process; and the use of tactics that aggravate potential supporters. Interest groups—particularly the large ones—can also be rendered impotent by conflicts within their own membership.† For example, different individual unions may take opposing views, thus making it impossible for the AFL-CIO to take a strong position. An inept lobbyist can alienate even a natural ally. Groups are at their most effective when their representatives are, in fact, "reenforcing, providing ammunition for, and serving their sympathizers in the Congress." °

Conditions for Interest Group Influence

Although interest groups do not dominate congressional decision-making or policy responses emanating from Congress, a number of conditions enhance their potential impact.

If the groups on one side of a controversy are unified and coordinated on the major issues they want to push or if they can cover up any disagreements, they will enhance their chances of success. When a single group, or a few groups acting in concert can demonstrate the primacy of their interest in a particular area, it gains both visibility and effectiveness. For example, the walnut growers are represented by a single highly organized group. They are likely to get what they want legislatively. By contrast, chicken farmers are dispersed over the entire nation and have no effective single group to speak for them. Therefore they have difficulty in achieving their legislative ends.‡

---

* "Milk Group Gave $462,000 Just Before the Election," *Congressional Quarterly Weekly Report* (March 17, 1973): 568–588. The spending figures in the preceding paragraph are all calculated from data reported in this article.

† For examples of interest group mistakes see Ripley, "Congress Champions Aid to Airports, 1958–59," and "Congress and Clean Air: The Issue of Enforcement, 1963"; also the story on the Alaska pipeline in the *National Journal* (August 11, 1973), cited above in a footnote on p. 206.

° Dexter, *How Organization Are Represented in Washington:* 72.

‡ On these two groups in the Eighty-sixth Congress (1959–60) see Clem Miller, *Member of the House* (New York: Scribner's, 1962): 137–140.

If there are key members of the House and Senate (for example, a subcommittee chairman) who actively believe in the interest group's position the chances of success are greatly enhanced. The same is true when a lobbying effort is made in a field where the power of Congress vis-à-vis the executive branch is unusually strong. Former Assistant Secretary of the Treasury Stanley S. Surrey makes this point in relation to tax legislation:

The Congress regards the shaping of a revenue bill as very much its prerogative. It will seek the views of the executive. . . . But control over the legislation itself, both as to broad policies and as to details, rests with the Congress. Hence a congressman, and especially a member of the tax committees, is in a position to make the tax laws bend in favor of a particular individual or group despite strong objection from the executive branch. Under such a governmental system the importance to the tax structure of the institutional factors that influence a congressman's decision is obvious.*

The visibility of the issues for which groups lobby is another very important factor affecting their impact. On issues regarded as routine by Congress without much wide public visibility, interest groups become entrenched in the decision-making system in Congress and the executive branch; subgovernments prosper. In these relatively invisible areas interest groups are likely to have maximum impact. Their impact is also likely to be high when they seek single, discrete amendments to bills as opposed to advocating a large legislative package. As the visibility of issues increases and public attention to issue areas grows the impact of interest groups tends to diminish.

Another factor that works in favor of an interest group is support for or, at least, no opposition to its aims from the relevant executive branch agency in its representations to Congress.

Groups sometimes state views on matters remote from their primary interests. But an interest group is likely to have greatest impact on issues that coincide with the interests the group purports to represent. Thus the AFL-CIO may be very influential in advising on matters concerning the working conditions of factory workers, but they receive less attention from legislators when they advocate a higher tariff for tung nut imports or when they make a broad pronouncement on foreign policy.

Interest groups will usually have a greater impact on amendments rather than entire pieces of legislation. This is because amendments are generally technical and thus less widely understood and salient.

---

* Stanley S. Surrey, "How Special Tax Provisions Get Enacted," in Randall B. Ripley (ed.), *Public Policies and Their Politics* (New York: Norton, 1966): 53.

Thus conflict can usually be limited. As the field of conflict widens, more participants enter the fray and any single participant is likely to be less influential. The fewer the participants, the greater their influence.*

The Defensive Nature of Lobbying

Much lobbying is defensive—that is, aimed at preventing changes in the existing situation. In many policy areas there are well-established patterns of special privilege and entrenched interests that will resist any change not to their benefit. Given the complexity of the decision process in Congress and the executive branch, those taking a negative position, rather than those urging something new to be done, have an advantage.†

A good example of defensive lobbying is provided by a recent debate over federal strip-mining legislation. Late in 1972 the House, by a large majority, passed a bill regarded tough on the mining industry. The Senate Interior and Insular Affairs Committee reported a weaker bill that never reached the Senate floor. The mining interest groups preferred the Senate bill to the House bill, although they really preferred no bill at all. The environmental groups favored the House bill. In 1973 Congress again began to consider strip-mining legislation. The Senate committee appeared likely to report a bill giving primary responsibility to state authorities—a provision favored by the mining interests and the Nixon administration and opposed by the environmentalists. In the House committee pro-regulatory forces introduced amendments making the bill even stronger than the 1972 House bill. In the face of this development the mining groups changed their stance to favor the 1972 bill that they had formerly opposed. Their only hope to prevent a bill was to create enough dissension in the committee that either no bill would emerge or a bill unacceptable to the whole House would emerge. They felt the 1972 House bill had maximum disruptive potential. If this strategy failed they could still anticipate a hard fight in the conference committee if the Senate passed a weaker bill.°

Defensive lobbying efforts were particularly successful in 1972 in defeating a number of major initiatives on a wide range of issues. The party split between Congress and the White House enhanced the position of the groups opposing new (especially Democratic) measures,

---

* See Schattschneider, *The Semisovereign People,* for an elaboration of this notion.
† See Dexter, *How Organizations Are Represented:* 62; and Truman, *The Governmental Process:* 391–392.
° Robert Gillette, "Strip-Mining: House, Senate Gird for Renewed Debate," *Science* (August 10, 1973): 524–527.

and the interest groups were aided in their efforts in many instances by the opposition of the Nixon administration. Their successes included the defeat of bills calling for no-fault automobile insurance, extended minimum wage coverage and a higher minimum wage figure, the establishment of a consumer protection agency, the opening of the highway trust fund for mass transit purposes (this succeeded in 1973), the exemption of small businesses from a new occupational safety law, strip-mining regulation, and gun control.* It should be noted that successful defensive lobbying in one year does not necessarily remove an item from the congressional agenda for future years. Legislation in a given area may eventually be forthcoming, but skillful defensive lobbying can postpone it and probably produce some amendments that weaken a measure when it finally passes.

The Impact of Interest Groups on Congressional Decision-Making: An Assessment

In the final analysis, the impact of interest groups "depends more on the harmony of values between the groups and the legislators than it does on the ability of a group to wield its 'power' either through skillful techniques or presumed electoral influence." † For example, the Welfare Rights Organization facing a predominantly conservative Congress will make much less headway on issues important to it than it will under a predominantly liberal Congress.

What are the implications of interest groups' activity for representative government? A measure of skepticism and distrust is not entirely misplaced. Much national public policy reflects the special interests represented by the various groups. And competing groups may all get part of their preferences written into statutes, even if that results in "irrational" public policy—that is, policies that contain built-in contradictions and simultaneously aim at opposing ends.° Unchecked, interest groups present some dangers. They participate in cozy little sub-government arrangements that essentially make policy in many areas without benefit or hindrance from other sources. They provide a large amount of issue-related information to legislators that naturally tends to be biased. Their very existence usually works for the maintenance of the status quo; they play an important role in keeping the agenda of Congress looking pretty much the same from year to year. They buttress Congress's preference for familiar, nonthreatening solutions to familiar issues.

---

* "Opponents of Major Legislation Score Success," *Congressional Quarterly Almanac* (1972): 1074–1080.
† Zeigler, *Interest Groups in American Society:* 274.
° Truman, *The Governmental Process:* 393.

Any system of government that is truly representative must allow interest groups to have their say, although participants must realize that the groups do not necessarily represent all legitimate interests. And there are checks on untrammeled influence on the part of interest groups. Congressmen may receive information that is biased, but they often are exposed to adverse views from competing lobbyists. It may not be possible to eliminate the coziness of subgovernment arrangements in many policy areas, but the entry of new people into a subgovernment helps new ideas to emerge. In addition, a watchful press can be very important in checking the activities of interest groups both in their subgovernments and as they lobby in Congress. The extensive role of the milk producers in financing both presidential and congressional campaigns, for example, was revealed by enterprising journalists. Journalists have also been aggressive in reporting on tax advantages engineered by and for special interests. Those stung by such revelations often brand the journalists as irresponsible "muckrakers," but the revelations may cause the lobbyists to abandon or curtail at least the most questionable of their practices.

Congress itself has made a presumably comprehensive attempt to regulate lobbying in Title III of the Legislative Reorganization Act of 1946. In fact, this act is based on the assumption that simple collection and publication of information about the identification of lobbyists and spending for lobbying activities will be sufficient to keep the activities within reasonable (although undefined) bounds. There is no particular evidence supporting the accuracy of this assumption. In addition, the act requires the filing of data only when a group is engaged in spending *principally* for the purpose of influencing legislation. This means that many groups that may spend considerable sums and hire a number of representatives for legislative purposes but can interpret their principal activities to be for other purposes do not file the required reports. In short, the information collected is only partial, is simply presented in raw form, and seems to have little effect on lobbying (although it should also be added that the drafters of this statute had no particularly clear desired effect at the time of its enactment).

MEMBERS AND CONSTITUENTS

In addition to dealing with groups, some of which purport to represent constituent interests, members of the House and Senate must also deal directly with constituents. Members view their constituents in a variety of ways. They sometimes see them through the filter of interest groups. For example, a House member might think of his district having 5,000 members of the United Auto Workers, 10,000 members of railway unions, 3,000 members of civil service unions, 1,000 members of the National Farmers Organization, 2,000 members of the American Farm Bureau Federation, 7 corporate members of the National Association of Manufacturers, 4,000 members of the Sons of Italy, 3,000 members of the National Rifle Association, and 2,000 members of the Sierra Club. Or he might see them as being affiliated with the major economic institutions of the district: 15,000 employees of the Burlington Northern, 5,000 employees of John Deere, 2,000 employees of Swift and Company, 14,000 employees of the federal government, and 5,000 employees of the state government.

Members might also think in terms of the general socioeconomic characteristic of their districts: highly urban or highly rural, large or small ethnic and black populations, well-educated or poorly educated, well-paid or poorly paid, predominantly Protestant or predominantly Catholic, highly identified with the Republican party or the Democratic party. They may not realize that they are using analytical categories but in fact they instinctively do so. Interviews with members include statements such as the following: "My people are mostly poor Czechs and Germans." "I've got a lot of blacks and poor white Appalachians." "Most of my folks own their own farms or own their own businesses in small towns. They have all lived in those counties a long time."

They might also think of at least a few of their constituents as individuals: the editor of the district's largest newspaper, the party county chairmen, the managers of the largest plants, the presidents of the largest unions, and other such local notables are likely to be known as individuals by a member.

Regardless of the filter he uses, the member of Congress is sure to be thinking of his constituents in one way or another almost all of the time. "This bill has important benefits for the folks back home and I have to work for its passage." "How will my vote on this controversial roll call be received at home?" "What are the responses from the questionnaire I sent home last week looking like?" "Will I have time to get home this month for some speaking and unofficial campaigning?" Constituency is important to members for a variety of reasons, but the most elemental, of course, is that it is constituents who elect and re-elect members to Congress. In this section we will look at the interaction between the congressman and his constituency and at the impact that constituency can have on congressional behavior.

Interaction between Constituents and Members

Members of the House and Senate have a number of methods of communicating with their constituents. They can appear on radio and television shows (in the Eighty-ninth Congress the average House member made eight radio appearances and four television appearances per month *). They can send newsletters to their constituents and can solicit opinions through mailed questionnaires. Other means by which the member informs his constituents include: promoting newspaper coverage of his activities; writing reports or columns for newspapers; sending committee reports and government publications; establishing film and record libraries on government activities and programs; speaking at public functions such as service club meetings and high school graduations; acting personally as a host for visitors from the constituency; and responding to constituent mail. There are other communications that don't contain information about legislation but which help the member to enhance his image: for example, most members write letters of congratulation and condolence and send such useful items as free seeds and booklets on baby care to constituents.†

Members receive information from their constituents through a number of sources, including: letters, telegrams, phone calls, personal visits to members and their staffs, and appearances before committees. The mail, however, is the most important vehicle for transmitting constituents' opinions to members. Organized letter-writing campaigns from constituencies, often generated by an interest group, are considered less important by congressmen than letters from individual constituents. An organized campaign is usually recognizable by the set phraseology or standard form of the letters.°

On a number of important issues there is little mail from constituents to their representatives. Constituents are generally uninformed about the procedural and substantive details of congressional life, their level of issue-specific information varies from issue to issue. In fact, well-formed constituent opinion does not exist on most matters; even that opinion transmitted to members of Congress is likely to be somewhat vague and poorly expressed. This means that much of the time the member does not have any empirical indications of constituency opinion to guide his behavior.

Even when constituent opinion is expressed, two distortions accompany it. First, it tends to come from individuals who already agree with the position of their representative or senator. Second, members tend to interpret what they hear as being supportive of views they already hold. This is relatively easy since many communications from

---

* John S. Saloma III, *Congress and the New Politics* (Boston: Little, Brown, 1969): 174–175. See also Donald G. Tacheron and Morris K. Udall, *The Job of the Congressman* (Indianapolis: Bobbs-Merrill, 1966): 280–288.
† See Clapp, *The Congressman:* chapter 2 on all of these activities.
° See Lewis A. Dexter, "What Do Congressmen Hear?" in Nelson W. Polsby (ed.), *Congressional Behavior* (New York: Random House, 1971).

constituents are unclear and ambiguous. In short, members tend not to be heavily influenced by constituency opinion, except that which agrees with what they already feel or believe. Thus a member generally represents his image of his district or state, and that image is largely of his own shaping and creation.*

Some members of Congress let the expressed opinions of a few individual constituents speak for the opinion of the entire constituency. These are people the congressman trusts and considers to be representative. Although they may transmit no opinion other than their own, the important point is that the congressman values those opinions, accepts them as representative, and probably interprets them as endorsements of positions he already holds.† The identity of these individuals varies widely from case to case. They may include prominent industrialists, editors, union leaders, local politicans, or rather obscure people who just happen to be old friends and confidants.

Congressional Workloads and Constituency Service

There is conflicting evidence on how much of their time congressmen allocate to constituency services. Roundtable discussions with members of the House in 1959 led Charles Clapp to assert that legislators spent most of their time dealing with constituency-related aspects of their jobs:

> A congressman is administrator, educator, and errand boy, as well as legislator. In each of these roles he is mindful of his constituents. He organizes his office with them, rather than his legislative responsibilities, in mind. Though he considers his work in behalf of individuals as less fundamental to his job than work on legislation, he nonetheless gives it precedence. He both derives satisfaction from it and is dismayed by it. It often is an onerous chore, but it meets a real need, brings him valuable information, and is the activity most likely to 'pay off' at the polls. He resents the time it takes, but he will not slight it.°

More systematic surveys have found that members claim legislative work to be more time-consuming than constituency service. In Roger Davidson's study, only 16 percent of the legislators listed constituency service as their primary activity (although 59 percent listed it as their secondary activity); 77 percent claimed legislative work to be their

---

* Lewis A. Dexter, *The Sociology and Politics of Congress* (Chicago: Rand McNally, 1969): chapter 8.

† For a discussion of this phenomenon at the state level, see George R. Boynton and others, "The Missing Links in Legislative Politics: Attentive Constituents," *Journal of Politics* 31 (1969): 700–721.

° Clapp, *The Congressman:* 103; see also 50–53.

primary activity. Constituency service was less important to senior members than to junior members because senior members felt less need to strive for electoral safety (which they had already achieved) but junior members were still building it.*

An elaborate survey of workloads in the Eighty-ninth Congress showed that the average member spent only 28 percent of his time on constituency service; legislative work consumed 65 percent of his time.†

If the work of the representative or senator is divided between legislative work and constituency support, the job of congressional staff is much less divided—staff work is principally devoted to constituency service. A survey of congressional staff in the Eighty-ninth Congress showed the average office spent 25 percent of its time in direct constituency service, 41 percent of its time answering the mail, 10 percent of its time on education and publicity, and only 14 percent of its time on legislative support.°

Constituency Impact on Member Behavior

Constituency impact on the behavior of members of the House and Senate falls into two broad categories. First, there are a few issues on which enough constituents are so concerned that a major wrong move by a member could cost him his seat. If in the 1940s or 1950s a southern member had come out in favor of strong civil rights legislation he almost surely would have been defeated. If a member from a strongly unionized district came out in favor of the Taft-Hartley Act in 1947 he might have been defeated in 1948. If a member from a middle-class suburban area came out in favor of massive busing to achieve school integration with an adjacent metropolitan area even now he might be defeated. If a member from a sparsely populated western state vigorously espoused the cause of gun control he might well lose his seat. But this kind of issue is relatively rare. On most issues the member has a great deal of freedom to maneuver because most of his constituents are uninformed or unconcerned about the issue.

Thus the second kind of constituency impact occurs principally in the mind of the senator or representative himself. He thinks that representing constituents is important and therefore attempts, usually by intuition rather than by gathering data, to reflect the opinion of the constituency on a given issue or to hypothesize what the constituency would favor if it was asked to voice an opinion. In making these calculations a number of subtle processes occur. Most members seek infor-

---

* Davidson, *The Role of the Congressman:* 99; Clapp, *The Congressman:* 52.
† Saloma, *Congress and the New Politics:* 184.
° Ibid., 185.

mation that confirms them in their previously held beliefs. They can distort information they receive or simply rely, almost unconsciously, on a previously held image of constituency opinion. But this still does not mean that constituency opinion is not a very real phenomenon in the minds of members. It is a factor that concerns them constantly.

And, of course, members are aware of the voting habits of their constituents—both for Congress and in general. Typical statements from members might include the following: "Registration in my district is two to one Democratic but a smart Republican can still carry it." "The district is competitive. My constituents always split their tickets and elect some candidates from both parties." "My people don't much like political parties. You are better off not harping on party."

As members internalize all of these various understandings and pressures, both perceived and real, they tend to lean toward one of two poles in terms of how they articulate the effect of constituency on their behavior. At the one pole are members who perceive themselves to be "delegates"—that is, individuals who are simply instructed in one way or another by their constituents how to behave and how to vote and who willingly do it. At the other pole are members who perceive themselves to be "trustees"—that is, they consider constituency opinion and make-up as they understand it but they take final responsibility for reaching decisions, on the grounds that they hold the welfare of their constituency in trust and should do what is best for the constituency regardless of the constituents' own perceptions or misperceptions.* Most members generally operate on the basis of some middle position and the categories of "delegate" and "trustee" are not very useful empirically except to indicate that members have a wide range of choice both about what they perceive and how those perceptions influence them. There is nothing fixed about the outcome of this transaction; what is fixed is that members are concerned with representing constituencies well according to their own individual lights.

Unfortunately, students of Congress have not found definitive ways of measuring the impact of constituency using the general considerations above. Rather they have focused on making inferences about the impact of constituency—both in terms of opinion and in terms of socioeconomic and partisan categories—by examining roll call votes. There are some limits to the use of roll calls in this way but, if the issues selected are fair tests of congressional behavior, roll calls can provide evidence about variations in the impact of constituency.

Constituency attitudes vary in impact from issue to issue and can be reflected in members' behavior on roll call votes in several ways.

---

* On representational votes see Roger H. Davidson, *The Role of the Congressman,* chapter 4.

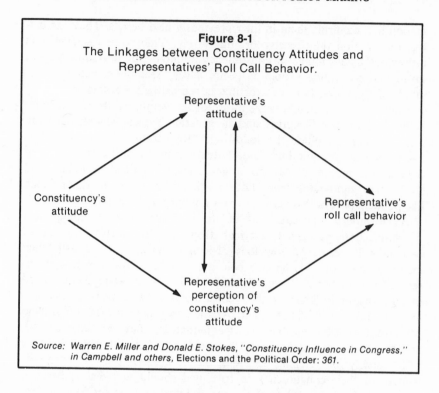

Figure 8-1

The Linkages between Constituency Attitudes and Representatives' Roll Call Behavior.

Source: Warren E. Miller and Donald E. Stokes, "Constituency Influence in Congress," in Campbell and others, Elections and the Political Order: 361.

Figure 8–1 provides an overall scheme. The critical variables are the member's own attitude, the way he perceives the constituency's attitude, and his willingness to deviate from that perception in his behavior. After investigating roll call votes in three issue areas—civil rights, social welfare, and foreign involvement—Warren Miller and Donald Stokes concluded that the local constituency does have a measure of control over member behavior. The pattern of constituency-representative relations varied from issue to issue: in the civil rights issue domain the correspondence between roll call behavior and constituency attitudes was greatest (and quite high), in the area of foreign affairs it was least (and quite low), and if fell into a middle ground in the area of social welfare.*

Another way to explore the impact of constituents is to aggregate their characteristics by district and then examine the difference that variations in these characteristics seem to make in the behavior of the members. A number of such studies have been done—always with roll

* Warren E. Miller and Donald E. Stokes, "Constituency Influence in Congress," in Angus Campbell and others, *Elections and the Political Order* (New York: Wiley, 1966).

Table 8–2

Comparison Between Democratic and Republican Districts, by Region, 92nd Congress (1971–72)

	Democratic Districts			Republican Districts		
	All (N = 255)	*Northern and Western* (N = 176)	*Southern* (N = 79)	*All* (N = 180)	*Northern and Western* (N = 153)	*Southern* (N = 27)
% Urban	75	81	61	70	70	68
% Non-White	18	15	23	7	5	17
% Owner-Occupied Housing Units	59	57	65	68	69	65

Percent owner-occupied housing units is used as a measure of both wealth and social class. A family able to buy a house—even if it is not particularly imposing—is likely to be relatively well-off financially and think of itself as solidly in the middle class whereas a family that rents is more likely to be less well-off financially and is also less likely to have a middle class image of itself. The other measures in the table are self-explanatory.

Source: Calculated from Congressional District Data Sheets prepared by the Census Bureau.

call voting as the measure of member behavior—and some conflicting findings have emerged.* But there are areas of agreement.

First, certain kinds of constituencies tend to elect Democratic members and others tend to elect Republican members. In general, districts represented by Democrats are poorer and more urban than districts represented by Republicans. They also have a larger proportion of non-white population. There is an important regional variation that should be noted, however: southern Republican districts are more urban than southern Democratic districts. They remain "whiter" than Democratic districts but there is virtually no difference in the percent of owner-occupied housing units. Table 8–2 summarizes data from the Ninety-second Congress (1971–72) to support these generalizations.

Table 8–3 portrays some differences in the *distribution* (*averages*

---

* See, for example, Thomas A. Flinn and Harold L. Wolman, "Constituency and Roll Call Voting: the Case of the Southern Democratic Congressmen," *Midwest Journal of Political Science* 10 (1966): 192–199; Lewis A. Froman, *Congressmen and their Constituencies* (Chicago: Rand McNally, 1963); Julius Turner and Edward V. Schneier, Jr., *Party and Constituency: Pressures in Congress* (Baltimore: Johns Hopkins, 1970); W. Wayne Shannon, *Party, Constituency and Congressional Voting* (Baton Rouge: Louisiana State University Press, 1968); Duncan MacRae, Jr., *Dimensions of Congressional Voting* (Berkeley: University of California Press, 1958); and Aage R. Clausen, *How Congressmen Decide* (New York: St. Martin's, 1973).

Table 8–3

Selected Constituency Characteristics, by Party for
The House of Representatives, 88th Congress.

Type of Constituency Characteristic	% of All Democratic Seats (N = 256)	% of All Republican Seats (N = 178)
Median Income in District		
Under $4000	25	2
$4000–6999	70	76
$7000 and over	6	21
Percent Owner-Occupied Housing Units in District		
Under 50.0	20	3
50–69.0	62	55
70.0 and over	19	43
Percent Non-White Population in District		
Under 10.0	51	91
10–19.9	14	8
20.0 and over	34	1
Urbanness of District		
Urban	38	20
Suburban	12	21
Rural	50	60

Source: Data on the first three characteristics are calculated from the Congressional District Data Book for the 88th Congress. The urban-suburban-rural classification comes from Congressional Quarterly Almanac 1963: 1170–83.

are reported in Table 8–2) of constituency characteristics among all Democratic and Republican representatives in the Eighty-eighth Congress (1963–64). This shows that Democrats were more likely to come from poorer, more urban districts with a relatively large non-white population and Republicans were more likely to come from richer, more suburban districts with a relatively small non-white population. It also shows, however, that there is not an absolute cleavage between the parties: there are Republicans from districts with basically Democratic characteristics and there are Democrats from districts with basically Republican characteristics.

A second conclusion of most studies is that constituency characteristics are wedded to ideological differences among congressmen. Democrats and Republicans generally differ in their views, particularly on domestic policy, with the Democrats being generally more liberal and the Republicans generally more conservative. Within the parties, however, differences between the districts represented by individuals are not always systematically predictive of which party members will be the more liberal or more conservative or more or less loyal to the party.* A few variables are more predictive of ideological differences than others. For example, among urban southern Democrats (N=36) in the Eighty-eighth Congress the percent urban population in the district was highly correlated with party unity, support for a larger Federal role, and support for President John Kennedy's programs. That is, among this subset of congressmen those from the more urban districts were the more liberal, loyal Democrats. Among rural southern Democrats (N=42) the percentage of black population in the district was negatively correlated with party unity, support for a larger federal role, and support for the president's programs. That is, the rural southern Democrat with the greatest proportion of blacks in his district tended to be the most conservative and least loyal to his party's legislative positions.† The whites in the districts with the largest number of blacks have reacted to that "threat" in part with conservative politics.

Finally, when constituency characteristics are weighed against the influence of party affiliation, party generally emerges as the stronger force. One classic study specifically found party differences to be more explanatory than differences in urbanness or ethnic or racial composition of districts.°

A recent study presented more differentiated findings. When the impact of party and constituency were compared on five policy dimensions, constituency was found to be relatively potent on questions of international involvement and civil liberties but party was found to be more important on questions of agricultural assistance, social welfare, and government management.‡

* * *

Neither interest groups nor constituents set the agenda for Congress. Likewise, neither of them determine policy outcomes. But they both help set the bounds within which Congress operates. Their presence is tangible and real in a variety of ways. Congressional awareness of these groups is particularly important. Their preferences, as perceived by the members of Congress, help shape the policy statements and actions emanating from Congress. Members want to be representative. Different members define the task of representation differently but no definition completely eliminates the influence of interest groups and constituents.

---

* Ripley, *Party Leaders in the House of Representatives:* 157–158, 211–212.
† See Flinn and Wolman for these data and a discussion of them.
° Turner and Schneier, *Party and Constituency.*
‡ Clausen, *How Congressmen Decide.*

9

CONGRESS,
THE PRESIDENT,
AND THE PRESIDENCY *

IN MANY WAYS THE PRESIDENT AND CONGRESS ARE NOT EQUAL. Nowhere is this more apparent than in the framing of policy. A single individual with considerable formal power can inevitably declare a position and follow through on it more skillfully and rapidly than a multi-headed body like Congress. An example from 1973 is worth describing at some length to make this point.

In 1973 the Democratic majority in Congress was anxious to prepare its own program of wage and price controls rather than simply extending their delegation of that power to the president for another year, the course favored by President Nixon. Yet, despite overwhelming party sentiment for such congressional initiative, Congress ultimately passed, with a great many Democratic votes, the exact extension desired by the president.

The reasons for the Democratic failure on this issue are several and are particularly apparent in the House. The central problem was that the Democrats could not agree on a single strategy. In the Banking and Currency Committee, which first considered the bill, different points of

* Some of the material in this chapter has been adapted from Randall B. Ripley, *Kennedy and Congress* (Morristown, N.J.: General Learning Press, 1972) and *Majority Party Leadership in Congress* (Boston: Little, Brown, 1969).

view among the Democratic members were never resolved; instead a variety of amendments were added to the bill. A number of relatively stringent provisions on prices were added by liberal Democrats even though there was considerable feeling that they went too far for the whole House to accept. In the Rules Committee, which next had to consider the bill, it was found necessary to send the bill to the floor with a provision against points of order, a provision that offended many House members, including Democrats. By the time the bill finally reached the floor, it was an unpassable product, despite the numerous special allowances, regulations, and exceptions designed to satisfy particular interests and gain their support.

The Democratic leaders in the House tried to produce some order out of the chaos. According to Majority Leader Thomas P. O'Neill, "The speaker called in members of the Banking and Currency Committee and the House leaders on three different occasions, to try to iron things out." The leadership effort in the Banking Committee failed and this left the leaders without a defensible position on the House floor. They openly sought a winning formula during the floor debate as a large number of amendments, many of them dealing with the date a price freeze would take effect, were debated and voted on. But their quest for compromise, which might have been successful had it been done quietly and in advance, only added to the image of confusion and ineptness because of its hurried and visible nature.

Adding to the Democrats' woes was an unusually effective effort in support of the president by a great variety of lobbies, including those for the Chamber of Commerce, retailers, food chains, realtors, bankers, farmers, and cattlemen. Only some labor unions gave much effective support to the Democrats.

Ultimately, the House decided that it could not legislate in this complex area and had no choice but to acquiesce to the president's wishes, even though the majority did not agree with his position. Several members underscored the basic problem in post-debacle comments. Morris Udall, an Arizona Democrat, said "It's the difference between an organization headed by one powerful man and a many-headed organization." Sam Gibbons, a Florida Democrat, said, "I don't think this expresses our support for Nixon's handling of the economy but Congress can't administer the country. We are 535 people with no administrative authority at all. Some people do Congress a disservice by overstating the amount of authority we have." *

---

* This discussion of the House action on wage and price controls is based on "House Backs Nixon on Economic Controls Extension," *Congressional Quarterly Weekly Report* (April 21, 1973): 938–941; and Daniel J. Balz, "Economic Report/Mismanagement, Lobbying Imperil Democrats' Attempts to Impose Tough Controls," *National Journal* (April 28, 1973): 611–615. The quotations

But once the congressional disadvantage in initiation is acknowledged, then the president and Congress face similar kinds of tensions as they ponder how to deal with each other. Both must decide on the level of activism they will adopt as their basic legislative stance, and to what extent they will cooperate with some other branch. Some presidents and some Congresses are relatively restrained in the legislative tasks they set for themselves and in the energy they display in working toward the achievement of those tasks. Other presidents and Congresses set goals and expend much energy in the pursuit of them. And, of course, the minority parties in Congress might take very different stances from each other.

The decision about relative activism or relative restraint is much more conscious and explicit for the president than it is for Congress, simply because one person can decide something with greater clarity than 535 people. But leaders of different Congresses also express different attitudes toward the legislative task; their statements offer a fairly accurate guide to the level of activism likely to be espoused by the Congress. For example, in the Eighty-ninth Congress (1965–1966) the leaders of the majority party made it clear that they were eager to have Congress cooperate with President Johnson in working on a very full legislative agenda. But those same leaders in the Ninetieth Congress (1967–1968) were equally clear in their position that Congress should proceed at a more deliberate pace thus helping the government and the nation digest the new programs that had been created in the preceding Congress.

THE PRESIDENTIAL SIDE

Presidential access to Congress depends on a number of variables, the most important of which are the president's view of his legislative role, his skill at implementing his vision of the role both personally and through the institutional presidency, the willingness and ability of the leaders of the president's party to transmit and obtain his legislative wishes from the standing committees and the rank-and-file members on the floor, and the president's direct access to the leaders of his party, the other party, the committees, and the rank-and-file members. In short, presidential will, style, and institutions are all important elements affecting the outcome of the policy process, but they are balanced against a variety of congressional wills, styles, and institutions.

---

from Udall and Gibbons come from the first article. The quotation from O'Neill is taken from "O'Neill: Watergate May Help Free Republican Votes," *Congressional Quarterly Weekly Report* (May 19, 1973): 1210.

Presidents' backgrounds help explain some of the variations in personal relationships between them and the members of Congress. Presidents who have served for a long time in Congress and who have risen to positions of leadership in the House or Senate seem more likely both to enjoy working with members of Congress on a personal basis and to have a good "feel" for how to deal with members in the most efficacious way. Thus, for example, before the Vietnam escalation soured his relations with Congress Lyndon Johnson, a formidable leader in the Senate before becoming president, was praised by many as an authentic genius in interacting with key members of the House and Senate so as to get desired results. His performance in 1964 and 1965 contrasts with those of his predecessor, John Kennedy, and his successor, Richard Nixon. Kennedy and Nixon had served in both the House and Senate but neither had risen to leadership positions and neither seemed to enjoy legislative life very much. Both were reluctant to deal personally with members after they became President and neither possessed a great deal of skill at it. In his last year in office Nixon's relations with most members of Congress simply ceased.

President Ford did not have the flair or reputation for leadership in Congress during his long service in the House that Johnson did during his period of Senate leadership. Nevertheless, he was clearly a career congressman until he was nominated to be vice-president by Nixon after Spiro Agnew resigned in the autumn of 1973. He began his presidency indicating that he expected close and cordial relations with individual members of Congress even though he knew there would be policy disagreements. In his first address to Congress, just three days after becoming president following Nixon's resignation, he expressed admiration both for Congress as an institution and for congressmen as individuals. Given the values inculcated by twenty-five years of service in the House, Ford should feel little discomfort in dealing with members of Congress.

Presidential Techniques for Dealing with Congress

If a president decides on an aggressive approach to Congress on legislative matters he has a number of techniques at his command.

First, he can set much of the agenda for Congress by making a series of specific proposals. Presidents have always submitted some preferences. In the last few decades the "program of the president" has emerged as the largest part of the legislative agenda for Congress, even in those cases in which Congress and the White House are controlled by different parties. Since the early 1930s all presidents have routinely assumed they would submit a large program to Congress.

The only partial exception occurred in 1953 when President Eisenhower was unsure of the wisdom of doing so. But his advisers, especially those in the Bureau of the Budget (the forerunner of the office of Management and Budget), convinced him that he must submit a large program and he did so in 1954.

Presidential proposals are contained in the annual state of the union message (or multiple messages, as President Nixon used in 1973), the annual budget message, the annual economic message, and a great variety of special messages. The use of this technique is now virtually automatic and represents the minimum effort any president is likely to make. Congress has become dependent on these messages. In 1969, for example, the Democratic leaders of the House and Senate became publicly restless when President Nixon was, in their view, slow in putting forth a program. In effect, they complained that Congress could not really function until the president had set the most important parts of the agenda.

Second, the president can seek to garner popular support for his proposals by making public statements in support of them. Presumably, if popular support develops it will be transmitted in one way or another to the members of Congress and increase their willingness to support the proposals. All presidents make appeals to the public but vary a great deal in the frequency with which they use this method. Franklin Roosevelt, for example, sought popular support for a great variety of programs, especially through the medium of his "fireside chats" on radio. Presidents Truman and Eisenhower were considerably more restrained than Roosevelt. John Kennedy was selective in his addresses to the people, focusing on a few issues like medical care for the aged and economic policy. Lyndon Johnson returned to a more Rooseveltian posture, speaking often and with great force on a wide variety of issues, notably aid to education and civil rights early in his presidency and in defense of his policies in Southeast Asia late in his presidency. President Nixon did not make public statements on every issue but concentrated on a few, such as Southeast Asia policy, revenue-sharing, and economy in government.

Presidents can also seek to magnify their public appeal by having other respected and well-known citizens openly endorse their views. On critical matters of foreign policy, for example, recent presidents have sought and received the public support of living ex-presidents. Business leaders, labor leaders, and other such individuals are also approached by presidents for their public support. A president often finds it particularly useful to seek endorsement for a proposal from a well-known national figure from the opposition party. President Kennedy and Johnson used this technique often in trying to build support for foreign aid proposals, for example.

Third, the president can take a hand in allocating projects and patronage to encourage Congress to back his proposals. The executive branch has many resources at its disposal: jobs, post offices, courthouses, dams, federal contracts, and other tangible rewards. Because of civil service laws the president's power over the dispensation of federal jobs (the "spoils system") has been reduced. But he and his departmental secretaries still have about 6,700 positions at their disposal. These include about 3,500 top jobs throughout the executive branch exempt from civil service, White House employees, 140 ambassadors to foreign countries, 523 federal judgeships, 93 U.S. attorneys, 94 U.S. marshals, and about 2,100 part-time positions on commissions and boards. Even if the last category is deleted the president is or can be the effective appointing authority for 4,600 highly desirable positions.*

Fourth, the president can give personal attention to members of the House and Senate. By inviting members to meals at the White House, having them conspicuously present at bill signing ceremonies, calling them on the phone, writing complimentary letters that are released for publication, sending them autographed pictures, and boosting their egos in a number of other ways a president can enhance his chances of legislative success. President Johnson was particularly skillful in using this technique, especially in the first years of his incumbency.

Fifth, a president can get personally involved in the inevitable compromise and bargaining process that takes place once a presidential proposal has arrived on Capitol Hill. By making critical compromises at just the right time the president can help to insure the success of most of the initiative. Presidents Kennedy and Johnson used this technique extensively especially in courting the support of Senate Minority Leader Everett Dirksen on matters such as civil rights, foreign aid, the nuclear test ban treaty, and support for United Nations bonds.

Sixth, a president can give direct campaign help to particularly helpful members of the House and Senate from his own party by campaigning for them personally or by channeling campaign funds to them. He can give indirect campaign help to members of the opposition party by refraining from any activity on behalf of their opponents.

Institutional Support for Presidential Relations with Congress

The president is a powerful individual in dealing with Congress. But he lacks the time to pursue his congressional relations single-

---

* These figures come from *National Journal* (April 6, 1974): 503.

handedly, and the volume of work and the scope of subjects prevents him from having a personal grasp of all that is going on. Over the years, two parts of the institutional presidency—the White House and the Office of Management and Budget—have become important presidential agents in seeking congressional support for the president's program.

The White House Liaison Operation. A central part of the relations between the presidency and Congress involves extensive personal contact. The liaison office in the White House is basically in business to provide such contact. The liaison staff spends a great deal of time in communication with members and staff members of the House and Senate. In early 1974 the White House had seven full-time liaison personnel (not counting clerical support). The chief of White House liaison also directed a network of about seventy-five department and agency liaison people scattered throughout the bureaucracy.

Presidents Franklin Roosevelt and Harry Truman both used assistants in the White House in dealing with Congress but neither routinized much of the job. Under President Eisenhower, however, the liaison staff was expanded: more individuals were added and duties were divided. Different individuals were responsible for the Senate and for various regional groupings in the House. The whole operation was overseen by a close and trusted adviser to the president, Bryce Harlow.

President Kennedy appointed Lawrence O'Brien as his chief liaison officer. O'Brien expanded and centralized the operation inherited from Harlow. The basic innovation was to require the legislative liaison offices in all departments and agencies to report on Monday to O'Brien's office on their activities completed during the past week and projected for the coming week. O'Brien's staff digested these reports and briefed Kennedy before his weekly Tuesday breakfast with the Democratic leaders of the House and Senate. Thus the president was kept informed, and liaison activities were coordinated so that not too many messages were being sent to the Hill simultaneously and so that there would be no contradictory message sent, although there was some confusion in the early months of the operation. This arrangement also allowed the president to give the leaders of his party the sense of helping control the flow of information to the House and Senate.*

Presidents Johnson and Nixon both kept the essentials of the Kennedy-O'Brien operation, although, of course, the personnel changed. The major change during Nixon's first term was a great increase in size of

---

* For more details on White House liaison, especially in the Kennedy years, see Abraham Holtzman, *Legislative Liaison* (Chicago: Rand McNally, 1970).

the White House staff, to double what Eisenhower, Kennedy, and Johnson had had.

At the beginning of 1973 the Nixon liaison operation underwent several additional changes.* The liaison staff in the White House was given responsibility for dealing with interest groups as well as for dealing with Congress. This underscored formally the White House strategy of trying to orchestrate interest group campaigns in ways favorable to its own policy ends. A greater degree of control over departmental liaison personnel and operations was also asserted by the president and the White House liaison staff by making these individuals presidential appointees who would be supervised directly by the White House. This change was intended to increase the coordination of executive branch lobbying and counteract the centrifugal forces in the bureaucracy that sometimes set departmental objectives that differ from presidential objectives. Nixon planned to increase the frequency of his meetings with the Republican leaders of Congress. He also planned to invite the Democratic leaders for more ad hoc meetings. During early 1973 these meetings did, in fact, increase. But the breaking of the Watergate scandal in mid-1973 and the aftermath that led eventually to Nixon's resignation resulted in reduced contact during his last year in office. At the beginning of President Ford's administration it seemed very likely that personal contact between the president and congressional leaders would again increase substantially.

The Office of Management and Budget. OMB was created in 1970 as the successor to the Bureau of the Budget, which had been created in the Treasury Department in 1921 and was moved to the newly organized Executive Office of the President in 1939. OMB plays a number of management and substantive roles for the president. In relating to Congress it is in constant contact on the details not only of the budget and appropriations bills but also on the details of a broad range of substantive legislative questions.

Any agency that wants to submit proposed legislation to Congress must first clear it with OMB.† If OMB decides that the proposal of the agency is "not in accord with the program of the president" then the agency cannot formally submit its proposal, although a member of Congress in favor of the proposal may still submit it on his own.

---

* Dom Bonafede, "White House Report/Administration Realigns Hill Liaison to Gain Tighter Grip on Federal Policy," *National Journal* (January 13, 1973): 35–43.
† See Richard E. Neustadt, "Presidency and Legislation: The Growth of Central Clearance," *American Political Science Review* 48 (1954): 641–671.

OMB also gets heavily involved, along with the White House and relevant agencies, in generating the ideas that eventually are packaged annually as the program of the president.* In many ways virtually all of the professional staff members of OMB get involved in the development of the legislative program. The total OMB (BOB) staff was about stable in size between 450 and 525 under Eisenhower, Kennedy, and Johnson but grew considerably under Nixon. It was nearing 700 in fiscal year 1972.

Constraints on Presidential Legislative Activity

Despite the power and resources he commands and despite his substantial institutional support, the president still faces a number of practical limits as he seeks to influence the course of legislation in Congress. He is limited, for example, by the complexity of the government in which he must operate. The size of the enterprise alone is awesome. The president presides over roughly two and a half to three million civilian employees, another three million people in the armed services, eleven major departments, more than forty independent agencies and regulatory commissions, and an elaborate set of institutions collectively called the presidency. He also has to interact with two other elaborate sets of institutions, namely, Congress and the judiciary.

The president is the most visible individual in a large and complex government. Given the problems posed by the vastness of the government, the range of issue areas being dealt with, and the monitoring of information, the president faces constant difficulties as he attempts to overcome the ever-present problems of communication and bureaucratic inertia within the government.

Furthermore, a president cannot be too imperious in setting forth his program. He must request and persuade; he cannot demand and command. A president and his advisers who get the reputation for being too demanding must be prepared to suffer a negative reaction. For example, President Nixon and his closest White House advisers had poor relations with Congress much of the time. Congress felt it was being pushed around and/or ignored as Nixon tried to accomplish his policy goals. Thus when the Watergate scandal broke, congressional opinion was that now Congress could and would recoup both lost prestige and power. The Watergate affair provided the opportunity for Congress to reassert itself, but such a move would have occurred even without Watergate, for many members of Congress indicated that President Nixon and the White House staff had gone too far in trying to

* See Richard E. Neustadt, "Presidency and Legislation: Planning the President's Program," *American Political Science Review* 49 (1955): 980–1021.

legislate without Congress. Senate Majority Leader Mike Mansfield described the situation:

> It's my belief that before Watergate broke, the Congress was really on the ropes; that our influence was diminishing and that the influence of the men around the President was increasing.
>
> However, they pushed too far with their espousement of executive privilege, claiming it was applicable to all 2.8 million government employees; too far in the area of impoundment; too far in vetoing legislation and too far in lack of consultation with the Congress.
>
> So when the Watergate thing really broke open, I would assume it had a part in pushing ahead a movement that was already under way.

Senate Minority Leader Hugh Scott also expressed his displeasure with the way in which the White House had consulted with him and other members of the Republican leadership in Congress. "They never invite me for the take-offs, but they damned well want me there for the crash landings."

Still another Republican senator, one thought of as a supporter of Nixon programs, complained that top White House staff members such as John Ehrlichman and H. R. Haldeman "had the attitude that Congress was more fun and games than reality. So when Watergate broke, there was less room for maneuver by the White House because of the alienation process which had preceded it." *

The Watergate scandal and related problems of the Nixon administration certainly made members of Congress more aware of a desire to limit the presidency. But the basic fact of the president being in a position of asking rather than commanding has always been true. Had Watergate not intervened it is probably accurate to argue that the reaction to Nixon's presidential style would not have been as extreme and he probably could have achieved some of the centralization and some of the bypassing of Congress he desired. But Watergate underscored limits already present, and transformed some of them from potential to actual. The practical limits on the presidency grew because of Watergate, but they were not invented at that time. (What was, perhaps, "invented" because of Watergate was a willingness on the part of liberal Democratic intellectuals to criticize the power of the presidency in principle—a criticism rarely made by them for the preceding forty years.) From the congressional point of view the presidency had become bloated and arrogant under Nixon. Several moves were

---

* The quotations from Mansfield, Scott, and the unnamed Republican senator come from Andrew J. Glass, "Congress Report/Watergate Diminishes Nixon's Leverage, Forces Series of Legislative Compromises," *National Journal* (July 21, 1973): 1049–1056.

made to add language to legislation reducing the White House and Office of Management and Budget expenditures, staff sizes, and number of high-paying jobs. None of these measures became law but one of the first thing President Ford did upon assuming office was to make some changes in these two staffs that went a long way toward meeting congressional criticism. Had the Nixon administration somehow managed to finish its term such restrictions might well have been put into statutory form.

The president and the institutional presidency are virtually excluded from many policy areas because of the close-knit relationships within the numerous low-profile subgovernments. The more routinized a policy area becomes, the less the possibility that the president will have much impact on it. Less routine matters generally break out of these subgovernments and a wider range of participants becomes involved. Only then is there much opportunity for presidential access and leverage. But any president is likely to have minimal impact on such items as allocation of sugar quotas to foreign nations, the details of defense procurement, or the interpretation and application of patent policy.

Policies and programs tend to change very slowly and by small increments or decrements. In the very complex world of American public policy both the necessity for compromise among many actors and the technical nature of many policies make marginal change from an existing situation the most likely (but not an inevitable) outcome of any policy debate. The incremental nature of policy change means that under normal conditions the president cannot hope to alter dramatically a large number of policies simultaneously and quickly. He usually must choose to stress only a few areas and, even then, efforts to achieve dramatic change will meet with resistance. Of course, innovative congressmen meet this same resistance when they attempt to initiate substantial policy change.

The policy process can be divided into two recurring subprocesses and a series of stages in which identifiable participants wield varying amounts of influence. Table 9–1 summarizes these subprocesses and stages. The emergence of American governmental policy can thus be traced. Not all policies literally go through all stages, and sometimes the order varies—but, in general, both formulation (the first subprocess: the development of a preferred choice) and legitimation (the second subprocess: the ratification, amendment, or rejection of that choice) are each characterized by five stages:

1. *Information collection* is the stage in which information is sought on the scope of a problem that has been identified for government action and on possible approaches to dealing with that problem.

Table 9–1
The Policy Process in the Federal Government

Subprocess	Stage
Formulation	Information collection
	Information dissemination
	Alternative development and selection
	Advocacy
	Decision on preferred policy choice
Legitimation	Information collection
	Information dissemination
	Alternative development and selection
	Advocacy
	Decision on policy for implementation

2. *Information dissemination* is the stage in which the information collected on the problem and its possible solutions is passed along to those with more decision-making power.
3. At the stage of *alternative development and selection*, solutions are the specific focus.
4. During the stage of *advocacy* the partisans of solutions still thought to be viable make their respective cases where they think they will do the most good.
5. The final stage is one of *decision*—on a preferred policy choice in the case of formulation and on a policy to be implemented in the case of legitimation.

The influence of the president, Congress, and other participants varies at different stages in each subprocess. The president and Congress both are most visible in the advocacy of policy. Simply because Congress has no recognized single spokesman, the president may be a more effective advocate than Congress. The collection and dissemination of the information that limits the range of alternatives is dominated by the bureaucracy and neither the president nor Congress is as effective as the bureaucracy at this stage. They are both very influential in the making of decisions about preferred policy and mechanisms for implementation, but it is the bureaucracy and sometimes interest groups that are most influential in the making of decisions in the day-to-day administration of programs created by Congress. Naturally, at any stage of the policy process, the president's influence in relation to Congress will depend on his own feelings about a policy area and his skill in communicating with congressional leaders.

THE CONGRESSIONAL SIDE

The constraints the president faces when dealing with Congress are offset by constraints on Congress. The absence of a unified legislative program to counterbalance the annual program of the president is the major limitation. Because Congress is a multi-headed organization, it cannot organize and develop a unified program, although in the past the party caucuses have sometimes performed this function. Further, there is no single spokesman for Congress on controversial issues. Congressmen are likely to espouse quite different views on the same issue, often regardless of party lines. Moreover, even when there are forceful policy statements by leading members of Congress there is no assurance that the press will always transmit these views to the public whereas press coverage for presidential policy is much more assured.

The Critical Role of the Majority Party and Its Leaders

In chapter 1 the relationship between the presidency and the party leaders in Congress was identified as essential to the policy-making role of Congress. Particularly crucial is the relationship between the majority party and its leaders on the one hand and the president and presidency on the other. Even if the majority party suffers from internal dissension it still has the potential for dominating congressional performance. And although the leaders cannot dictate outcomes in Congress, they play a mediating role between the presidency and the rank-and-file members of Congress and, occasionally, the standing committees, thus setting the tone for congressional response to presidential wishes.

The Types of Relationship between Presidents and Majority Parties and Their Leaders

The Presidential Majority. In a presidential majority the president and the majorities of both houses are of the same party; the president, viewing himself as the single most significant legislative leader, actively attempts to have Congress enact his legislative preferences into law.

Leader-president relations in a presidential majority in twentieth century Congresses have been characterized by a trend of increasing cooperation on the part of congressional leaders. The more recent leaders in the presidential majority situation, faced with an active and demanding legislator in the White House, have come to see themselves almost unquestioningly as lieutenants of their president. Their fellow senators and representatives, the press, and the interested part of the general public have also begun to see the role of loyal lieutenant as the natural one for a congressional leader of the president's party.

The cooperative relationship that develops in a presidential majority underscores the importance of bargaining in a productive Congress. A presidential majority usually produces considerable legislation that follows the outlines of what the president wants. But that legislation may contain many modifications and concessions designed to avoid potential roadblocks in Congress. The president makes some of these concessions personally and authorizes others to be made on his behalf by White House officials and congressional leaders both on the floor and in committee. When compromise cannot be reached or is not sought, failure may result. Three examples scattered throughout this century illustrate how differing presidential majorities have functioned.

In the Sixty-third Congress (1913–1915) President Woodrow Wilson worked with able Democratic leaders and solid Democratic majorities in both houses. A major legislative agenda was set by Wilson and he and the leaders were successful in achieving a great part of it. Together they passed a new tariff, the Federal Reserve Act, the Clayton Antitrust Act, and the Federal Trade Commission Act. Other successes included: a ship registration and insurance bill, a war revenue bill, a bill to regulate cotton exchanges, and a bill providing a government railroad in Alaska. Wilson was also successful in gaining the repeal of the tolls exemption for American coastwise ships using the Panama Canal, even though the House leader opposed this measure and some of the Senate leaders were lukewarm. Only a few major disappointments marred the record of the Sixty-third Congress from the Democratic point of view: a ship purchase bill was buried in the Senate and two conservation measures and a Philippines autonomy bill never came to a vote.

But even with this highly successful legislative record a number of concessions and changes had to be made and bargains had to be struck to ensure final passage. For example, in the House Wilson promised progressives that a future antitrust bill would contain a provision outlawing interlocking back directorates in order to gain their support for the more conservative Federal Reserve bill. In working on a tariff bill Wilson bargained on details with the chairman of the Ways and Means Committee in the House, who was also the majority leader. In order to get the bill through the Senate Wilson submitted to the progressive Democrats' demand that the maximum surtax on large incomes contained in the House bill be doubled. Only in working for the ship purchase bill did Wilson reveal a streak of imperiousness and unwillingness to compromise, with the result that he failed to get any kind of bill at all.

In the Seventy-third Congress (1933–34) President Franklin Roosevelt worked with very large Democratic majorities and pliant Democratic leaders in the House and Senate. The sickening spectacle of the Depression made both the country and the Congress eager for a dynamic president bent on righting an upturned economy. In this two-year period Congress enacted a great volume of major laws. Major administration-leadership successes were scored in the areas of farm, welfare, banking, securities, conservation, industrial aid, public works, and trade legislation. The president and his congressional leaders also received some setbacks: the passage of civil service pay restoration over a presidential veto; the delay or defeat of bills concerned with pure food and drugs, labor disputes, the administration of oil resources, unemployment insurance, and old-age pensions; and the refusal to add desired amendments to laws already passed on agriculture and banking.

Even a dynamic president like Roosevelt in a crisis situation such as the Depression had to make important concessions in order to gain his ends. For example, the tax provisions of the industrial recovery bill were liberalized to appease congressional Democrats concerned about proposed rates for lower tax brackets. In order to pass the economy bill (which proposed major cuts in government spending, including salaries of employees) in 1933 Roosevelt had to agree to a compromise that restored about $100 million (a lot of money in 1933, even for the government!) of desired cuts.

In the Eighty-eighth Congress (1963–64) both Presidents Kennedy and Johnson worked with sizeable Democratic majorities and sympathetic Democratic leaders in pursuit of a number of legislative goals. The major legislation passed by the Eighty-eighth Congress provided a tax cut, an agency and program designed to fight poverty, increased civil rights guarantees, aid to hospitals, manpower training programs, a national wilderness system, aid for mass transit in urban areas, and a land conservation fund. From the Democratic perspective major failures were in the area of medical care for the aged and special aid for Appalachia.

In the effort to pass the anti-poverty bill the president agreed that a specific official considered too liberal by the North Carolina Democrats in the House would not be appointed to a position in the program. This was the price for their support on the floor. In laboring for a tax cut President Kennedy promised the chairman of the Ways and Means Committee that he would seek to tighten controls on federal spending in return for cooperation on the measure. President Johnson had to promise the chairman of the Senate Finance Committee specific economies in the federal budget in order to get his support on the same bill. In seeking approval of the mass transit bill, spokesmen for the President agreed to a "buy American" provision, a 25 percent cut in the cost of the program, and a specific amendment proposed by some labor unions. Thus the President simultaneously sought to appease Republicans, conservatives in both parties, and liberals principally in his own party.

Thus Wilson, Roosevelt, Kennedy, and Johnson all had reasonable legislative success. Critical to this success were the good relations with their respective party leaders who maintained presidential-congressional contact. They also took part in the bargaining process personally, as well as directing the involvement of subordinates.

The Congressional Majority. In a congressional majority the president and the majorities in both houses share the same party, but the president is willing to let Congress take more of a lead in legislative matters. He does not consider himself the most significant legislative leader. Although he may still make some recommendations to Congress, the volume is smaller and the advocacy is less vigorous than in presidential majorities. The congressional leaders themselves can state legislative preferences that are in part different from, or at least independent of, those of the president and they can expect to get action on them. They can also anticipate more control over the details of scheduling and tactics.

Much of the time in a congressional majority the basic relationship between the president and the majority party leaders is one of unsupported initiation. Each will state some preferences but neither will rally to support the preferences of the other.*

This relationship underscores the necessity of presidential-congressional cooperation in order to achieve policy of major importance. Same party control of Congress and the White House alone is not sufficient to insure a very imposing legislative product. In a congressional majority the majority party leaders don't take the president very seriously as a legislative figure. Even when he becomes active legislatively nothing very much may happen. And, typically, the leaders are

---

* There are four possible variations to this relationship of unsupported initiation. First, initiation can come from the president but be ignored by Congress. Second, both the president and the congressional leaders can initiate on the same issues, without ever supporting (or opposing directly) each other's initiatives. This variation is, of course, closely related to a relationship of opposition. Third, both the president and the congressional leaders can be inactive and allow initiation to come from other sources. Fourth, the congressional leaders can initiate and the president can remain largely inactive.

not in a position to generate much action on their own either. Again, examples taken from three congressional majorities in this century lend support to these generalizations.

In the Sixty-seventh Congress (1921–23) President Warren Harding and the Republicans controlled both houses by large margins. Harding obtained much of what he and the leaders of his party had agreed on concerning an emergency tariff, a permanent tariff revision, a revenue act, a packers and stockyards act, and a grant-in-aid program for road building. The farm bloc in Congress was successful in initiating and passing a number of bills, many of which were opposed by Harding and the regular Republican congressional leaders. These measures included an act to protect farm co-ops from antitrust laws and an agricultural credits act.

Harding had several major confrontations with Congress and was defeated in most of them. He did not get the pro-business tax legislation he wanted. His position favoring the reduction of surtax rates on high incomes was ignored. His proposal for a ship subsidy did not pass. His foreign debt refunding bill finally passed, but considerably altered. He won one battle, barely, when the Senate upheld his veto of a veterans' bonus.

In some of his dealings with Congress Harding simply acquiesced to what Congress wanted. In some he made proposals but got little support from his party's leaders. In others he was opposed by them. Only sporadically did he really try to mobilize the resources of his office to achieve what he wanted, and then he usually failed. The congressional leaders did not routinely look to him for leadership—in fact, they were surprised when it came—but they could not put together a legislative program of their own either.

In the Sixty-ninth Congress (1925–27) Calvin Coolidge was president and had moderately large majorities in both houses. Even more emphatically than Harding, Coolidge showed little desire to be a legislative leader. The legislative product of the Sixty-ninth Congress, mutually pleasing to the president and the Republican congressional leaders, was not large. The Senate passed a World Court bill. Administration forces were also successful in getting legislation on cooperative marketing, tax reduction, additional assistant secretaries for aviation in three federal departments, foreign debts, banking, control of radio, and railway labor disputes.

Several legislative developments displeased the Republican leaders and Coolidge. In the area of agricultural legislation both houses passed the McNary-Haugen bill, which proposed governmental purchase of some U.S. crops at the world market price plus whatever the tariff would bring. The government would then sell the crops abroad and assess a small fee on the participating farmers if it lost money. The purpose was to keep domestic crop prices relatively constant. A Coolidge veto stood without being tested. However, the major administration farm bill, designed to quiet demands for McNary-Haugen, was defeated. Coolidge suffered the humiliation of having his nominee for Attorney General rejected by the Senate. A filibuster at the end of the second session left a number of important bills dangling without final action. These bills included: a deficiency appropriations bill, a public buildings bill, a bill on Muscle Shoals (a large government-owned dam and factory on the Tennessee River that later became a key part of the Tennessee Valley Authority, created during Franklin Roosevelt's presidency), an alien property bill, and a postal rate bill.

Coolidge typically let Congress initiate what it wanted, but not much was forthcoming. Only on matters of economy did he exhort Congress forcefully. The danger of such lethargy for the president was that when a controversial matter did arise—such as McNary-Haugen, which Coolidge opposed vigorously—he could not offer his leaders in Congress much support, and his past performance had not given them any feeling of responsibility to him and the administration.

In the Eighty-third Congress (1953–54) Dwight Eisenhower was president and both houses were narrowly Republican. Eisenhower was more active than either Harding or Coolidge but had a number of doubts about how aggressive he should be as a legislative leader. His popularity was such that it would have supported activism but he voluntarily exercised self-restraint.

The Eighty-third Congress did not produce a large volume of major legislation. It moved slowly and its performance generally satisfied neither the president nor the congressional leaders sympathetic to presidential policies.

Congress allowed the president a free hand in his reorganization plans for the executive branch. It passed legislation restoring control of tidelands and the oil underneath to the states. It passed tax bills satisfactory to the president. The Senate defeated, by one vote, a version of the Bricker amendment to tie the hands of the president in making treaties and executive agreements. Congress also passed bills establishing the St. Lawrence Seaway, liberalizing social security benefits and unemployment compensation, and extending the reciprocal trade agreements program.

Other measures sought by the president and at least formally supported by the leaders were not passed. These included: a bill increasing the debt limit, a bill increasing postal rates, statehood for Hawaii, amendments to the Taft-Hartley Act, health insurance, and aid to education. Congressional revisions of immigration bills, mutual security bills, and the reciprocal trade bills were displeasing to the administration. The president was forced to use his veto power often, even with a Congress of his own party. He vetoed fifty-two bills, including a federal pay raise bill, and no vetoes were overridden.

Eisenhower and the Republican leaders usually avoided direct clashes with one another. Only occasionally did they work together closely and enthusiastically. On some matters the leaders responded to the president's initiative apathetically, and the president then either turned directly to relevant committee personnel or gave up. In general, Eisenhower's sporadic leadership and the leaders' sporadic loyalty contributed to a legislative product that was not highly pleasing to any of them.

The Truncated Majority. A truncated majority is defined simply: the majority of at least one house of Congress is controlled by the party in opposition to the president.

In a truncated majority congressional leaders usually cooperate with the president on matters of foreign policy, but oppose him on domestic matters. Congressional leaders may announce their own legislative program, but to succeed with it, they must command the votes to override a potential veto, and must also be able to appeal to public opinion or at least have a president who is ineffective in mobilizing public opinion.

Frustrations seem inevitable for a truncated majority because once the leaders have announced a legislative program, that program immediately is divided among the various standing committees. Consequently, it is neither seen as a whole nor thought of as a single program. The president's program is also split in this way, but he has the advantages of being able to call the program to the attention of the public by periodically submitting lists of "must" legislation and reminding the public of the nature and scope of his program. Reminders of this nature by congressional leaders are not often made and receive minimum attention when they are.

In general, not much legislation is produced in truncated majorities, particularly on domestic matters. What domestic legislation does pass is likely to be bland and inconsequential. If, somehow, controversial and far-reaching matters in the domestic area do get passed by a truncated majority they will continue to be intensely debated in the future, for truncated majorities rarely settle major issues of public policy in the domestic area for very long periods of time. Foreign policy legislation passed by truncated majorities can still be important. Examples taken from three truncated majorities in this century underscore the above general points.

In the Sixty-second Congress (1911–1913) William Howard Taft, a Republican, was president but the House was controlled by a solid Democratic majority. The Senate was nominally Republican but, in fact, the critical votes on many issues were in the hands of insurgent progressive Republicans. Without their support the regular Republicans fell short of a majority as did, of course, the Democrats.

Taft concentrated on obtaining approval of reciprocal trade with Canada and reforms in antitrust laws. He obtained his first objective, failed in his second, and was forced to veto a number of bills he disagreed with.

The legislative output of the Sixty-second Congress was small. Passed and signed by the president were: a bill ratifying a Canadian reciprocity treaty, a bill forbidding the shipment of liquor into states that prohibited its sale, a bill creating a place for the Labor Department in the cabinet, a bill granting free passage to American coastwise ships using the Panama Canal, and a bill providing for an eight-hour day on work done under government contract. Arizona and New Mexico were admitted as states after Taft had vetoed one bill on the subject.

Taft vetoed Democratic tariff bills, including ones on wool, cotton, metal, and the free list. Congress overrode none of the vetoes. He also vetoed an immigration bill because of a literacy test provision.

The Democrats, in addition to their largely successful attempt to embarrass Taft, also used their control of the House to hold a number of investigations and hearings focused on the money trust, the American Sugar Refining Company, campaign expenditures, the tariff, and the currency.

In the Eightieth Congress (1947–48) Harry Truman, a Democrat, faced a Congress controlled by moderate-sized Republican majorities. Truman had succeeded to the presidency in April 1945.

The president and Republican leaders did cooperate in the area of foreign policy. The Marshall Plan, Greek-Turkish aid, and the consolidation of the different armed services into the Defense Department were the leading achievements.

The president won some relatively minor and temporary victories on domestic policies, including a few changes in farm policy, highway aid, and the school lunch program. On matters such as civil rights, social security, universal military training, old age and survivors insurance, aid to education labor laws, and federal health insurance, his recommendations were ignored or defeated.

The Republicans in Congress were basically successful in the following areas: labor (with the Taft-Hartley Act completely rewriting the basic labor-management relations legislation and another act that covered portal-to-portal pay), reciprocal trade agreements, rent control, and tax reduction. Truman persuaded the Senate to pass major housing and aid to education bills but the House refused to go along.

In general, then, both parties to the conflict got something but a large number of major policy areas in which proposals were made saw no legislation passed. In the 1948 presidential campaign Truman explicitly ran against the record of what he called the "do-nothing Eightieth Congress," not a totally fair characterization but one that proved to be politically effective.

In the Eighty-sixth Congress (1959–60) Eisenhower faced a House and Senate overwhelmingly Democratic. His primary initiative was to fight for economy. Democratic leaders developed a number of their own domestic proposals.

The major legislative products of the Eighty-sixth Congress were a labor bill that was unsatisfactory to the Democrats and a civil rights bill that contained little substance. Bills that were desired by the Democratic leaders but that failed either in Congress or because of a veto included: a large-scale housing bill, a substantial increase in federal aid to airports, aid for depressed areas, federally insured medical care for the aged, an increase in the minimum wage, and federal aid for school construction. Eisenhower took a basically negative stance in the Eighty-sixth Congress: he asked for little and except for two vetoes that were overridden he got what he wanted. His few positive recommendations received little attention. In addition, he suffered the humiliation of having one of his cabinet nominees rejected by the Senate.

PRESIDENTIAL IMPACT ON CONGRESSIONAL POLICY-MAKING: AN ASSESSMENT

A customary way of measuring presidential impact is through the use of various "boxscores." The most common measure is simply the percentage of presidential requests passed by Congress. This measure is, of course, approximate. Many presidential requests may be passed in form but altered dramatically in substance by the congressional amending process. Even more important, the percentage of requests granted does not comment on the content of those requests and whether they represent intelligent responses to national needs. Despite these shortcomings, however, the simple percentage of presidential requests enacted, as calculated by *Congressional Quarterly* for the period since 1954, provides some interesting descriptive information on the gross impact of specific presidents on specific Congresses.

Figure 9–1 summarizes the percentage of requests enacted for the four presidents who have served since 1954. The only periods during

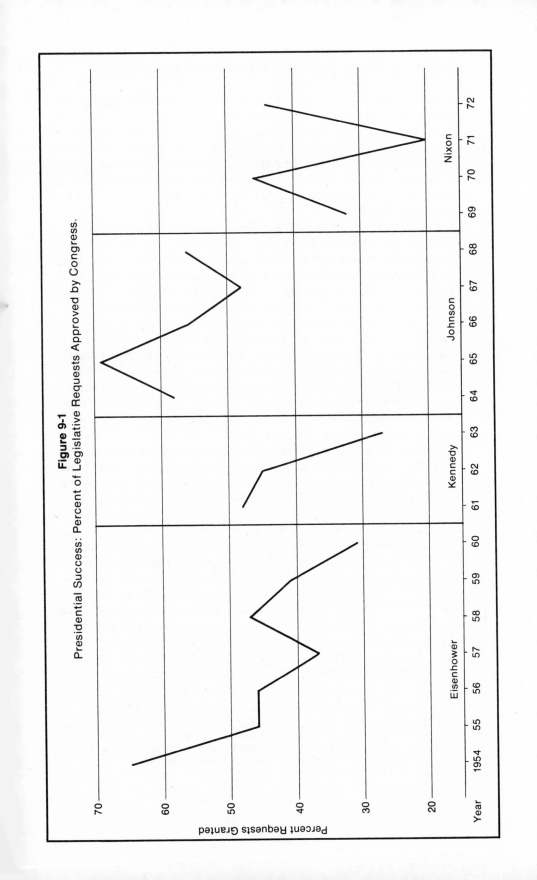

Figure 9-1

Presidential Success: Percent of Legislative Requests Approved by Congress.

which a president was able to get more than 50 percent of his proposals enacted were in 1954, when Eisenhower still had a Congress controlled by his party to work with, and the years that Lyndon Johnson was president (1964 through 1968). Eisenhower, Kennedy, and Johnson all suffered declines in their ability to get what they wanted as their terms wore on. Nixon did not have any notable success with the Democratic Congress he has faced; 1971 represents the least success of any president since 1954.

Presidential impact on congressional policy behavior can also be analyzed in terms of congressional voting—that is, levels of support for the president and shifts in favor of the president's proposals. There is, for example, considerable evidence that many members of Congress will support the foreign policy initiatives of the president if they share the same party label even though they might well oppose those same initiatives if the president belonged to the other party. Thus, for example, a fair number of southern Democrats inclined to be skeptical of such programs as foreign aid under Republican presidents will support such programs under Democratic presidents. Likewise, a substantial number of midwestern Republicans inclined to oppose programs as foreign aid under Democratic presidents will support such programs under Republican presidents.* On the other hand, the president does not seem to have this same kind of pull on domestic issues.†

Figures 9–2 and 9–3 summarize the success of presidents since 1954 in getting support from their own party members in the House and Senate and in getting support from the opposition party. Several generalizations can be made. First, members of the president's party in both houses, no matter which party it is, appear to be increasingly skeptical of presidential initiatives. Second, with the exception of Kennedy, who evoked an unusually partisan reaction from Republicans, all presidents have had about the same amount of support from the opposition party. No opposition party is absolutely adamant in its opposition. Even in the Kennedy years the average Republican supported the president about 40 percent of the time in roll call voting. This suggests that any president is going to have some measure of success almost regardless of the partisan composition of Congress, largely because virtually any president supports a number of routine and noncontroversial matters that always win congressional backing.

---

* See Aage R. Clausen, *How Congressmen Decide* (New York: St. Martin's, 1973); and Mark Kesselman, "Presidential Leadership in Congress on Foreign Policy," *Midwest Journal of Political Science* 5 (1961): 284–289, and "Presidential Leadership in Congress on Foreign Policy: A Replication of A Hypothesis," *Midwest Journal of Political Science* 9 (1965): 401–406.
† Clausen, *How Congressmen Decide:* chapter 8.

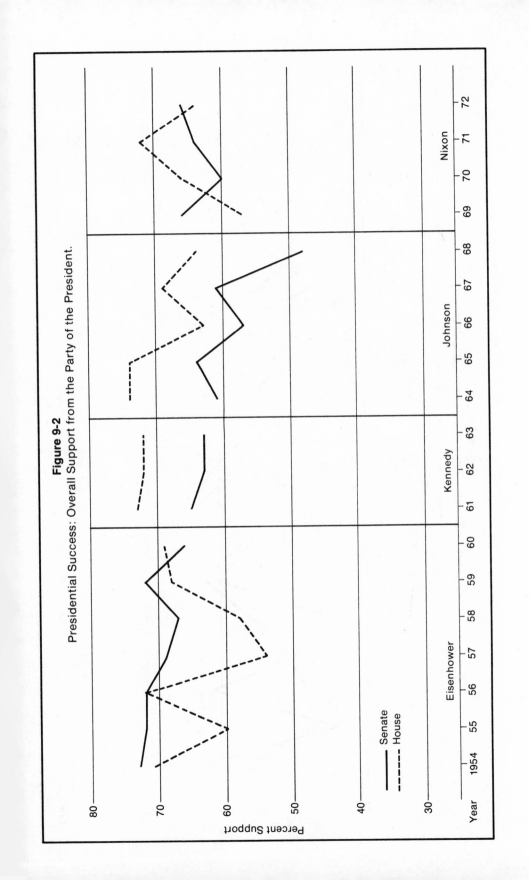

Figure 9-2
Presidential Success: Overall Support from the Party of the President.

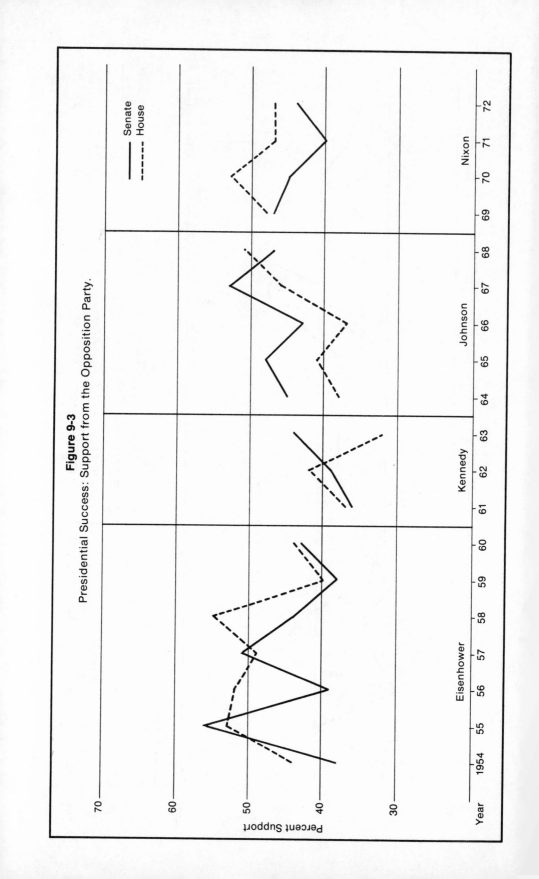

Figure 9-3

Presidential Success: Support from the Opposition Party.

The impact of the president is not limited to empirical measures of success and support, however. One important substantive impact is his contribution to the content of legislation. Primarily he sets the bulk of the legislative agenda for Congress with his various annual and special messages. Thus, even before specific actions are taken, the president, in effect, decides what is and is not most important for Congress to consider.

The agenda-setting power, however, does not necessarily diminish the important substantive contributions Congress can make to legislation. Congress and its leaders can still be creative in approving, amending, and criticizing the proposals of even a very active president. And limited initiation, even though difficult, is not impossible. A recent empirical study of the relative substantive inputs of president and Congress to a broad range of legislation concluded that the congressional contribution was very large.*

In general, much writing about Congress and the president suggests that the president has steadily been gaining influence over public policy at the expense of Congress. And the literature also often suggests that there is some fixed sum of power or influence that must inevitably be divided between Congress and president. It may be argued, therefore, that more aggressive presidents necessarily diminish the legislative power of Congress.

Neither of these generalizations paints an accurate picture of reality. The president has certainly become a more visible policy-maker in this century. But Congress has in many ways also become more important simultaneously, simply because the range of matters with which the federal government deals has increased both in scope and in importance. And the "seesaw" image of relative influence seems simply to be false. Experience in this century suggests that active, influential legislative leaders in Congress can co-exist successfully with an active, influential legislative leader in the White House. Legislative creativity may be present simultaneously within both the White House and the Capitol.

It should also be noted that some of the least active and effective congressional leaders in this century appeared on the scene when some of the least active and effective presidents were in office, suggesting that congressional leaders do not become "strong" only when there is a "weak" President but rather that legislative weakness in the White House may breed legislative weakness in Congress.

Finally, it should be reiterated that a great deal of public policy is

---

* Ronald C. Moe and Steven C. Teel, "Congress as Policy-Maker: A Necessary Reappraisal," *Political Science Quarterly* 85 (1970): 443–470.

not subject to much presidential influence or even to much congressional influence above the committee or subcommittee level. Subgovernments continue to make policy in many areas in much the same way regardless of the overall stance of the president or the congressional leaders.

10

CONGRESS AND
THE BUREAUCRACY

A MONG MODERN NATIONS A LARGE AND, HOPEFULLY, EFFICIENT
bureaucracy is usually an important feature of the central government. The United States is no exception. There are over two and a
half million employees of the federal government directing programs
costing over $300 billion a year and affecting the lives of all citizens
in many ways. Just as citizens have had to accommodate to the reality
of such a bureaucracy so has Congress. The basic congressional response to the fact of a large, expert bureaucracy administering hun-
dreds of programs has been to seek influence by cooperating with the
bureaucracy most of the time and challenging it only now and then.
Congress might well be overwhelmed in a situation of perpetual conflict. Conflict occurs, but cooperation is a more common characteristic. In the recesses of the thousands of relationships between the congressional members and their staff and the bureaucrats a great deal of
American public policy that actually impinges on citizens is decided.

CONGRESS, THE BUREAUCRACY,
AND SUBGOVERNMENTS

At several points in earlier chapters the phenomenon of "subgovernments" or "whirlpools" has been noted. Most of the interaction between
Congress and the bureaucracy represents the ongoing activities of sub-

251

governments. The basic institutional units in typical interaction are standing subcommittees (occasionally a full committee) from the House and Senate and various administrative units below the departmental level in the executive branch such as bureaus, agencies, services, and administrations. Much of the detailed business of the government is carried on between these units, sometimes with the participation of interest group representatives. Larger units (for example, the entire House or Senate, the White House, or the office of a departmental secretary) get involved in details much less frequently. In general, only highly visible and politically sensitive issues are likely to receive attention from the larger units; relatively less visible matters are often handled completely by a bureau speaking for the entire executive branch and a subcommittee speaking for the entire House and Senate. Individual members of the House and Senate and their staff members also get involved with the bureaucracy, usually because of a pending "case" involving a constituent.

A classic case of a subgovernment is provided by Douglass Cater:

> . . . consider the tight little subgovernment which rules the nation's sugar economy. Since the early 1930's, this agricultural commodity has been subjected to a cartel arrangement sponsored by the government. By specific prescription, the sugar market is divided to the last spoonful. . . .
>
> Political power within the sugar subgovernment is largely vested in the chairman of the House Agricultural Committee who works out the schedule of quotas. It is shared by a veteran civil servant, the Director of the Sugar Division in the U.S. Department of Agriculture, who provides the necessary "expert" advice for such a complex marketing arrangement. Further advice is provided by Washington representatives of the . . . producers.*

Richard Neustadt adds the necessary caveat that this system of subgovernments does not cover areas in which there are "jurisdictional entanglements" and "mingled programs" involving several agencies in the bureaucracy. In these areas congressional participation may be much more sporadic.†

The occasions for contact between Congress and the bureaucracy are many. The principal formal point of contact involves subcommittee or committee appropriations hearings that are, in most cases, held an-

---

* Douglass Cater, *Power in Washington* (New York: Random House, 1964): 17–18.

† Richard E. Neustadt, "Politicians and Bureaucrats," in David B. Truman (ed.), *The Congress and America's Future* (Englewood Cliffs, N.J.: Prentice-Hall, 1965): 108.

nually for given agencies and programs. These hearings are taken very seriously both in Congress and in the bureaucracy. Considerable preparation for them goes on in both institutions. Authorization hearings for executive programs are usually less frequent than appropriations hearings, but they are also regarded by participants as very important. In addition to the hearings there are also numerous year-round contacts in the form of lunches, phone calls, and personal visits between personnel from the agencies and members and staff members in the House and Senate.

One relatively recent development affecting contact between Congress and the bureaucracy has been the proliferation of formal liaison units throughout the executive branch.* A few agencies had legislative liaison units in the 1920s and 1930s. But the White House and most of the executive departments did not begin developing formal liaison apparatus until after World War II. White House liaison became a "big-time" operation during the Eisenhower presidency. Every department had a formal liaison staff early in the Kennedy administration. By fiscal 1963 the ten departments then in existence employed 500 liaison employees, almost half of them in the Defense Department. No department employed fewer than 13. The independent agencies (those not in a departmental hierarchy) employed an additional 233 liaison employees.† White House and departmental liaison officials typically work with the leaders of their party in Congress to achieve overall goals on the floor. Their intervention at the committee or subcommittee level is far less frequent. Liaison at the agency or bureau level has also grown. Some departments, such as HEW, have formal liaison units for each of their principal administrative subdivisions. Sub-departmental units in other departments may not have a formal liaison staff but some of their officials will, in fact, spend time engaged in liaison activities.

RESOURCES FOR INTERACTION

Members of Congress and the bureaucracy each possess resources the other values. When relations are going well and smoothly a continuous trading of these resources goes on. When disagreements arise withholding or punitive use of resources can occur. Typically, the advantages of smooth relations far outweigh any advantages to be gained in conflict and so the incentives to strive for smooth relations are great.

---

* On this topic in general see Abraham Holtzman, *Legislative Liaison* (New York: Rand McNally, 1970).

† G. Russell Pipe, "Congressional Liaison: The Executive Branch Consolidates Its Relations with Congress," *Public Administration Review* 26 (1966): 17.

Congressional Resources *

In most instances it is Congress that determines whether a program will live or die. A few small programs can be established by executive order of the president if there is vague statutory authority from some time in the past. But most programs require explicit congressional authorization and virtually all programs—certainly those of any size or permanence—require congressional action in terms of appropriations. Not only can Congress say either yes or no to a program at the time of its establishment, it also holds the power of life or death in the most elemental terms throughout the existence of any program. Inertia is powerful, of course; once a program is established it is not lightly terminated by Congress. But the power to terminate, either by refusal to renew authorization or the refusal to appropriate funds, is firmly lodged in Congress and nowhere else.

The allocation of money to all federal agencies, usually through the appropriations process but also through the creation of trust funds and methods of funding other than appropriations, is controlled by Congress. This is undoubtedly the single most important resource Congress has in its dealings with the bureaucracy.

Congress can also, both by statute and by informal means, help shape the content of programs administered by the bureaucracy. Specific actions can be prohibited; others can be encouraged. In recent years Congress has been aggressive in seeking new ways of assuring itself of this continued power even in the face of a vast proliferation of executive agencies and personnel.† Two means have been particularly effective—the requirement in many cases that programs be authorized annually (virtually all programs also receive annual appropriations) and the requirement for a number of programs that formal committee agreement be solicited and received before specific actions can be taken by the bureaucracy (this is the so-called "legislative veto" or "committee clearance."). The requirement for annual authorizations means that some agencies and programs are subject to four separate congressional reviews each year—those by the relevant House and Senate authorizing committees and those by the relevant House and Senate appropriations subcommittees.

The legislative veto can take several forms. Statutory provisions in an increasing number of fields may contain one of the following requirements:

---

* For a detailed review of congressional resources see chapter 12 of William J. Keefe and Morris S. Ogul, *The American Legislative Process* (Englewood Cliffs, N.J.: Prentice-Hall, 1973, 3rd ed.).

† Neustadt, "Politicians and Bureaucrats," 105–106.

1. That an agency report propose administrative actions in advance to a committee.
2. That an agency "come into agreement" with a committee before a given action is undertaken.
3. That an executive proposal lie before Congress for a fixed period of time before it can be implemented. If Congress, or part of it, (the provisions can vary) disapproves of the specific proposal then the executive is prevented from going forward with its plans. A variation of this requirement does not specifically provide for explicit congressional disapproval, but rather assumes that if Congress does not like a particular executive proposal positive action will be taken to circumvent it rather than vetoing it. This technique is used, for example, in relation to the closing of military facilities.
4. That Congress or some part of it (provisions vary) must give positive approval before the executive can proceed with a planned action.

Congress often approves what the executive proposes, but it is also capable of exercising its power of denial. For example, between 1946 and 1968 Congress rejected twenty-two plans offered by four different presidents for reorganizing parts of the executive branch. One example of the results of its negative actions was that Congress thus preserved the status quo in its relationships with a number of regulatory commissions that handle distributive matters particularly salient to members of Congress.

In addition to these techniques for shaping content, Congress can, of course, simply write specific statutory details in authorization or even appropriations legislation. Such language is theoretically forbidden in appropriations bills, but the practice occurs nonetheless. Informal continuing contact between members of the House and Senate and their staff members and bureaucrats also affords numerous opportunities for substantive congressional input in shaping programs.

Congress also has power over the structure of the bureaucracy. Not only do the House and Senate have veto power over reorganization plans offered by the president, they can also write specific organizational provisions into statutes. Thus they have considerable control over where in the bureaucracy a given program or agency is lodged. It was congressional pressure and activity, for example, that kept the bureaucratic responsibility for air and water pollution in motion for a decade. The responsibility was located in at least four different bureaus for short periods.

In this case Congress was trying to instill some aggressiveness into the bureaucracy in the area of abatement enforcement. Congress can also have considerable impact on the internal structure of individual bureaus or agencies. Personnel within the executive branch, both at an aggregate and an individual level, are subject to congressional influence. At the aggregate level, Congress provides the money for salaries. Congress also often sets limits on the number of slots open for an agency's top-level executives such as assistant secretaries and "super-grade" civil servants.

At the individual level Congress will sometimes specify the status of a specific job. For example, when the Department of Housing and Urban Development was created Congress stipulated that one of the five assistant secretary positions allocated to the Department be filled by the Federal Housing Commissioner. This signalled congressional devotion to the FHA program because it routinely provided visible benefits for middle class citizens eager to own homes and also accustomed to voting and warned the new HUD secretary that he should not try to downgrade it.

Also at the individual level, members of Congress support specific persons for specific open jobs in the bureaucracy. They concentrate their attention on top jobs, not on postmasterships and relatively unimportant jobs.*

The Senate has to ratify a number of presidential appointments. The Constitution, in Article II, section 2, speaks of the "Advice and Consent" of the Senate as necessary for a number of positions—both those specified in the Constitution and those later established by law with a ratification provision. How much "advice" the President seeks varies, but the "consent" in the form of a majority vote is necessary. Between 1947 and 1970 only 14 presidential nominations (out of over 134,000) were rejected outright, but over 2400 were withdrawn and over 24,000 remained unconfirmed. Many of these appointments are of military officers. The most important offices requiring Senate ratification include cabinet and sub-cabinet secretaryships, ambassadorships, and federal judicial officials, including Supreme Court justices, district and appeals court judges, and U.S. marshals and attorneys. High officials who serve on an interim basis before confirmation must proceed very cautiously in making decisions. Rejection of an important nominee is embarrassing to the administration and may also frustrate the achievement of some policy goals.

Finally, Congress has the power to investigate the activities of bureaus, both through normal authorization and appropriation hearings and also through specific hearings on individual programs or even individual changes in personnel. For example, a subcommittee of the

---

* Ibid., p. 105.

Senate Commerce Committee held hearings to investigate the firing of a Civil Aeronautics Administration official during the Eisenhower years. Just as important, Congress can also deliberately refrain from conducting a thorough probe of the activities of an agency.

Bureaucratic Resources

The projects and activities that a bureau administers are important to members, either because of their views regarding the importance and utility of particular programs or because they perceive that their constituents' interests are affected by a bureau's activities.

The decisions that bureaus make about the physical locations of their projects and activities are important to senators and representatives, who are generally anxious to increase the number of federal projects and activities in their respective districts and states. Occasionally, they may want to make sure that a controversial project or activity, such as a Job Corps camp, is *not* located in their constituency.

Bureaus are responsible for the handling of individual "cases"—that is, instances in which some person or persons disentangle themselves from the aggregate mass of bureau clients and beneficiaries to demand special, personalized attention. These cases are constituents of some representatives and senators and are, therefore, potentially important to him or her.

Bureaus possess vast amounts of program information that is useful to members of the House and Senate in many ways. This information can be used by a member to increase his knowledge about programs, aid in his decision-making, and improve his performance as a committee member. An adroit use of information can increase a member's intellectual reputation and therefore enhance his status with fellow members. The member's reputation for knowledgeability and responsibility among his constituents is improved if he commands information well.

Departmental legislative liaison personnel help the bureaucracy in the use of these resources but they are not a substitute for direct contact between the bureaus and committees. Neither do they get involved in the appropriations process, perhaps the single most important area of congressional-executive interaction. The best study of legislative liaison in the executive branch concludes that liaison personnel are important because they help congressmen meet their own perceived self-interest and needs. Specifically, liaison personnel can provide access to the secretary of a department for a congressman who needs it; they can help provide individual members with a substantive point of view about programs; they provide "collaborators" for congressmen who are legislative activists; and they can help congressmen meet constituent needs.*

THE JOINT SHAPING OF PUBLIC POLICY: INITIATION AND SUPPORT

Much public policy is jointly shaped by interaction between the bureaucracy and members of Congress. Even if one branch dominates the development of legislation in a given area there are still many occasions for intimate interaction as that area is administered. And, in many cases, the basic statutes themselves are jointly developed. For most fields, there are three areas where shared policy development is possible: 1) in the development of substantive legislation; 2) in the development of appropriations legislation; and 3) in the development of projects, rules, regulations, procedures, and the other details of day-to-day administration. Many of the conditions for shared influence vary in each of these fields. In general, however, the partisan situation cuts across all three areas: the chances of relatively smooth relations and shared influence between Congress and the bureaucracy are enhanced if the majority of both houses and the White House are controlled by the same party; the chances are diminished if there is split control.

Authorizing Legislation

One of the classic questions in the scanty literature on bureaucratic-congressional relations is: who initiates? For some reason the answer to this question has been viewed as highly significant, although the significance is usually never analyzed except in terms of either applauding or bemoaning the supposed demise of Congress. Also, much of this literature seems to assume that it is only in the initiation of authorizing legislation that Congress can have a significant impact on the shape of national policy.

The "who initiates" question is important only if the answer indicates that over time one branch or the other is effectively shut out of any role in shaping authorizing legislation. The best evidence seems to indicate that regardless of the source of initiation, the other branch—whether it be Congress responding to bureaucratic initiative or the bureaucracy responding to congressional initiative—ordinarily makes some important changes.

While there are no general studies focusing specifically on Congress

---

* Holtzman, *Legislative Liaison:* 51–53. See chapters 7 and 8 for a lengthy discussion of the strategies and tactics used by liaison officers.

and the bureaucracy, two overall assessments of the relative influence of Congress and the president have been made in recent years.* The president and the bureaucracy are, of course, distinct from each other but in these two studies the distinction is somewhat blurred. They are, however, the best available relevant studies.

The first of these was published in 1946 by Lawrence Chamberlain, a study of ninety major laws in ten different categories from 1890 to 1940. Using impressionistic standards, Chamberlain attributed the legislative initiative to Congress in about 40 percent of the cases, to the president in about 20 percent of the cases, and to both jointly in about 30 percent of the cases. In about 10 percent of the cases the initiative was credited to interest groups.†

In 1970 Ronald Moe and Steven Teel published a study which used the same impressionistic standards for the period from 1940 to 1967, with several changes: the substantive categories were altered to fit the changed concerns of both the Congress and the executive branch, and greater attention was given both to congressional activity prior to the formal introduction of a bill and to congressional modification of executive proposals as ways in which genuine influence could be wielded. This study reached basically the same conclusion: that Congress was still extremely important in the development of authorizing legislation. The authors summarized their findings: "Our conclusion challenges the conventional wisdom that the president has come to enjoy an increasingly preponderant role in national policy-making. . . . The evidence suggests that Congress continues to be an active innovator and very much in the legislative business." °

Instances of joint collaboration between parts of Congress and parts of the bureaucracy on specific authorization bills are legion. A few illustrations will suffice.

In the housing field in recent years much of the bill drafting was done jointly by staff members from the General Counsel's office in the Department of Housing and Urban Development and its predecessor, the Housing and Home Finance Agency, who collaborated with the staff director of the Housing Subcommittee of the House Committee on Banking and Currency.‡

In the consumer protection area the same kind of relationship be-

---

* Lawrence H. Chamberlain, *The President, Congress and Legislation* (New York: Columbia University Press, 1946); and Ronald C. Moe and Steven C. Teel, "Congress as Policy-Maker: A Necessary Reappraisal," *Political Science Quarterly* 85 (1970): 443–470.

† Chamberlain, *The President, Congress and Legislation.*

° Moe and Teel, "Congress as Policy-Maker: A Necessary Reappraisal," 467–468.

‡ Harold Wolman, *Politics of Federal Housing* (New York: Dodd, Mead, 1971): 107.

tween bureaucrats and congressional staff members developed. "There has been a great deal of staff contact between Senator Nelson's subcommittee investigating prescription drugs and the Food and Drug Administration. The Commerce Committee staff worked with the Federal Power Commission on gas pipeline safety. There has been a whole range of these ad hoc contacts . . ." * In this field the ad hoc contacts also tend to vanish once the issue is off the congressional agenda. This is probably because consumer protection is a relatively new field and there are jurisdictional instabilities in both the executive and legislative branches. In other fields, where jurisdictions are clearer and more well established, contacts are also likely to be more permanent.

In the air pollution field, even though Congress has taken the initiative, there has been informal cooperation from the executive branch staff. This cooperation has come despite formal bureaucratic positions that often ran counter to congressional initiatives. For example, in 1962 legislative and technical experts from the Public Health Service and the General Counsel's office in the Department of Health, Education, and Welfare worked with a representative of the United States Conference of Mayors (an interest group representing roughly the 100 largest cities in the country), and a few senators and representatives and their staffs to produce draft legislation even though the Public Health Service formally was opposed to some of the provisions they were drafting.†

Appropriations

Both agencies and subcommittees approach the matter of appropriations in such a way that general patterns of behavior can be discerned and described.° Executive officials, above all, seek to reduce uncertainty in the process. They want to know as early as they can how much money they have to spend and they want to be able to predict how much they will have in the future so they can plan ahead. Typically, officials seek to reduce uncertainty by seeking the confidence of the appropriations subcommittee members to whom they are responsible. In seeking confidence they are especially careful in preparing for the hearings of their subcommittees so that they appear to be "on top" of their job. They also are assiduous in maintaining personal contacts outside of the formal hearings.

---

* Mark V. Nadel, *The Politics of Consumer Protection* (Indianapolis: Bobbs-Merrill, 1971): 115.

† Ripley, "Congress and Clean Air: The Issue of Enforcement," 244, 250, 251.

° The following paragraphs summarize the meticulous work of Richard F. Fenno, Jr., *The Power of the Purse* (Boston: Little, Brown, 1966), especially parts of chapters 6, 7, and 11.

The members of the appropriations subcommittees, especially in the House, start with the view that all budgets can be cut. Their basic suspicion of bureaus and bureaucrats is overcome when they gain a level of confidence in particular individuals. They are particularly rigorous in investigating proposed increases, proposed new programs, and programs with little client support. Well-established programs with a satisfied and politically potent clientele do not receive such rigorous scrutiny. Thus the foreign aid agency budget and the Office of Economic Opportunity budget regularly get cut heavily whereas the Soil Conservation Service or the Federal Bureau of Investigation get about what they ask for. The members are eager to keep the relationship strictly between themselves and responsible bureau officials. For that reason they bar departmental liaison officials from participation and limit the number of witnesses outside the government. In 1963, for example, government witnesses at House appropriations hearings outnumbered non-government witnesses by two to one; in only two subcommittees of twelve was the number of outside witnesses greater than the number of government witnesses.* The Senate Appropriations Committee differs from the House Appropriations Committee principally because its deliberations always follow those of the House chronologically and senators are used to serving as an appeals court in which the executive officials who feel that the House was too severe can make their case.

Not all subcommittees and agencies interact as described above.† Ira Sharkansky has shown how both the agency and the committee can behave otherwise in examining the interaction between one House appropriations subcommittee and four of the agencies for which it is responsible over a period of a dozen years. He summarizes the behavior of the subcommittee as follows:

> Evidently, the legislators vary their oversight activity among agencies. They devote more than the average amount of supervisory and control efforts to the agencies that spend the most money, whose requests have increased the most rapidly, and whose behavior toward the subcommittee has deviated most frequently from subcommittee desires. In a sense, they allocate their time and staff assistance to agencies most "in need" of supervision and control.°

---

* Ibid., 342.

† See Ira Sharkansky, "Four Agencies and an Appropriations Subcommittee: A Comparative Study of Budget Strategies," *Midwest Journal of Political Science* 9 (1965): 254–281, and "An Appropriations Subcommittee and Its Client Agencies: A Comparative Study of Supervision and Control," *American Political Science Review* 59 (1965): 622–628.

° Sharkansky, "An Appropriations Subcommittee and Its Client Agencies," 628.

Writing from the perspective of the agencies, Sharkansky concluded that agencies vary in the level of assertiveness with which they approach appropriations subcommittees; that those agencies with greater public and administration support are more assertive; and that administrators are not totally guided to their levels of assertiveness by suubcommittee attitudes and behavior, which usually appear fuzzy anyway.*

Day-to-Day Administration

Congressional influence on the bureaucracy does not end once authorization and appropriations statutes have been passed. Interaction continues on a daily basis as agencies administer their programs. Some examples can provide the flavor of the interaction. The following discussion of the Office of Education is illustrative:

> Perhaps more important than formal amendments, however, congressional influence on administrative behavior is manifest in the nature of questions put to officials in hearings; in subcommittee requests for information; in press statements and in public speeches attacking or questioning existing practices within an agency; in letters or telephone calls to the Commissioner or to the Secretary of HEW. Agencies live by congressional favor, and congressional power is variable. For this reason, the views, opinions, and attitudes of key legislators (especially committee and subcommittee chairmen and their immediate staffs) are powerful influences on administrative behavior. Francis Keppel (the Commissioner of Education) spent agonizing months trying to fill top level vacancies because Congressman Adam Clayton Powell insisted upon a number of Negro appointees. A great deal of time of top officials is taken up in the laborious and often harrowing processes of meeting both the legitimate and illegitimate calls of Congress for program review.†

When the subgovernment phenomenon is prevalent there is likely to be intimate congressional involvement in administration. Theodore Lowi describes the situation in the agricultural field, where he identifies ten different "self-governing systems" dealing with different sets of programs:

> Each of the ten systems has become a powerful political instrumentality. The self-governing local units become one important force in a system that administers a program and maintains the autonomy of that program against political forces emanating from

---

* Sharkansky, "Four Agencies and an Appropriations Subcommittee," 279–280.
† Stephen K. Bailey and Edith K. Mosher, *ESEA: The Office of Education Administers a Law* (Syracuse: Syracuse University Press, 1968): 185.

other agricultural programs, from antagonistic farm and nonfarm interests, from Congress, from the Secretary of Agriculture, and from the President. To many a farmer, the local outpost of one or another of these systems *is* the government.

The politics within each system is built upon a triangular trading pattern involving the central agency, a Congressional committee or sub-committee, and the local district farmer committees (usually federated in some national or regional organization).*

Several empirical studies lead to some general statements about when a congressional committee is more or less likely to pursue its oversight of an agency's daily activities vigorously.† Oversight is promoted by the existence of autonomous subcommittees; ample committee staffs; perceptions of partisan advantage on the part of the majority party members; and perceptions that service to constituents can be enhanced by such activity. Oversight is also most likely on the part of committees that are highly prestigious and oriented toward a relatively large amount of legislative output. Oversight is most vigorously pursued when a committee is considering major revisions in policy. Thus, for example, congressional oversight in the housing field has been heavy for several decades because most of the above conditions were met. Oversight over enforcement of civil rights laws has been made more sporadic because a number of the above conditions have not been met.

Vigorous oversight is discouraged if there are close, mutually rewarding contacts between members and agency officials that might be disrupted by such activity. Aggressive oversight is also to be avoided if it seems to members that a great deal of negative reaction from interest groups, important to them and part of an existing subgovernment, is likely.

CONFLICT OVER PUBLIC POLICY

Much of the time, most members of Congress have strong incentives to get along with the various parts of the federal bureaucracy. Thus in most policy areas congressional-bureaucratic relations proceed relatively smoothly and inconspicuously.

But conflict does occur. When congressmen—particularly members of relevant committees and subcommittees—perceive their interests to

---

* Theodore J. Lowi, "How the Farmers Get What They Want," in Theodore J. Lowi and Randall B. Ripley (eds.), *Legislative Politics U.S.A.* (Boston: Little, Brown, 1973, 3rd ed.).

† See John F. Bibby, "Committee Characteristics and Legislative Oversight of Administration," *Midwest Journal of Political Science* 10 (1966): 78–97; and Seymour Scher, "Conditions for Legislative Control," *Journal of Politics* 25 (1963): 526–551.

be threatened they will react by seeking to bring agency policy into line with their preferences. The motivation for the conflict may be programmatic or political, but the effect is the same: Congress and the executive branch engage in conflict over substantive policy statements and actions. Either side may prevail in these conflicts. The bureaucracy has considerable resources with which to pursue its point of view. But in cases where congressional feeling is intense Congress usually prevails, at least in symbolic ways that mollify the protesting members.

In a conflict situation those congressmen (again usually organized in committees or subcommittees) who are involved use all of the resources available to them in order to prevail. A number of examples illustrate how conflicts can be resolved.

The harshest punishment Congress can administer in settling a conflict is to kill an existing program. Congress administered that fatal stroke to the Area Redevelopment Administration in 1963, even though it had only been created in 1961. The principal reason for this action was that a number of members had become convinced that, despite clear provisions in the law, the ARA was encouraging industries to relocate in redevelopment areas. In the eyes of those congressmen and their constituents from districts losing such industries the ARA was engaging in "piracy." * After being assured by the administration that such abuses would not occur in the future, Congress re-established the ARA program in 1965 under a different name—the Economic Development Administration.

Congress can demand and obtain major programmatic concessions in exchange for extending the life of a program. For example, in dealing with a small juvenile delinquency program during the Kennedy administration, Edith Green, chairman of the House subcommittee with jurisdiction over the program extracted the following concessions to put the program more in line with her vision of it in return for extending the program in 1963: †

1. The extension was changed from three years to two years and was, by informal agreement, considered the terminal extension.

---

* See Randall B. Ripley, *The Politics of Economic and Human Resource Development* (Indianapolis: Bobbs-Merrill, 1972): chapter 2, and the literature cited therein.

† John E. Moore, "Controlling Delinquency: Executive, Congressional and Juvenile, 1961–1964," in Cleaveland and associates, *Congress and Urban Problems:* 166–67. Interestingly, one thing that had offended Green was that the program sought to put a project in her home district before the local officials had submitted what she considered to be a good plan. She refused to play politics with the program, even though it meant losing some federal money at home.

2. Funds were authorized for only one year, which meant that annual justification of the program before Congress would be necessary.

3. New projects would not be comprehensive in scope but rather would be limited demonstration projects. The director of the Office of Juvenile Delinquency provided a written statement for Green to read into the record to make this agreement explicit.

4. A special amendment was added to the bill requiring, in effect, that a project be started in the District of Columbia.

Congress can redefine the jurisdictional authority of a regulatory agency so that it no longer has the power to make decisions in a particular area. This was the case when the Federal Trade Commission first sought to move against cigarette advertising. An irate Congress simply removed the FTC's jurisdiction that would have allowed it to accomplish what it wanted to do. It was not until several years later that a weakened version of the original FTC position was allowed to be implemented.*

Congress can determine what standards a program will be allowed or required to use in evaluating its operation. When the Army Corps of Engineers wanted to implement new, more accurate cost-benefit standards for determining which water projects it should undertake, Congress passed an amendment to the Transportation Act of 1966 prohibiting the implementation of more rigid standards and preserving the standards that would maximize the number of Corps projects throughout the country, despite the dubious economic validity of some of them.†

Congress can reverse an organizational edict issued by an agency if it feels pressure to do so. In 1968 HEW sought to decentralize programs authorized under the Elementary and Secondary Education Act of 1965. This decentralization would have spread responsibility for the programs to HEW field establishments and would have diminished the power of the Office of Education officials in Washington. The move was opposed by "the education lobby." Wilbur Cohen, Secretary of HEW at the time, told how the chairman of the relevant Senate appropriations subcommittee reversed the HEW decision:

> When we went up to Senate Appropriations, the committee reduced the Office of Education's budget by about $2.4 million. So I paid a visit to Sen. (Lister) Hill (D.-Ala.), and I said, 'What goes?' And

---

* See Lee A. Fritschler, *Smoking and Politics* (New York: Appleton-Century-Crofts, 1969).

† Robert Haveman and Paula Stephan, "The Domestic Program Congress Won't Cut," in Raymond E. Wolfinger (ed.), *Readings on Congress* (Englewood Cliffs, N.J.: Prentice-Hall, 1971): 367–370.

he replied, 'The National Education Association doesn't want that program decentralized.' I said, 'If I rescind that order, will you give me that money back?' And he said, 'Yeah.' So I rescinded that order and I doubt whether to this day it's been reissued.*

Congress can use the threat of investigative hearings to influence the policy decisions of an agency. Only the threat of negative publicity from hearings in both the House and Senate seems to have moved the food and Drug Administration to refuse certification in 1969 for a drug called Panalba manufactured by a major pharmaceutical company. Until the impact of that threat was considered, the FDA seemed disposed to go along with the company and the representative from the company's district.†

CONGRESSIONAL-BUREAUCRATIC RELATIONS:
A SUMMARY ASSESSMENT

The analysis in this chapter may to some extent suggest that conflict is unimportant in the policy-making process of the national government. This is clearly not the case. But there is a great amount of cooperation between Congress and the bureaucracy and it is in good measure based on mutual self-interest. There is nothing insidious about this cooperation; most prolonged human relationships are characterized by the desire for relative harmony and calm. Harmony and calm may produce either beneficial or useless public policy. However, the same may be said for conflict.

Occasional conflict at least has the merit of raising questions about the status quo in any given policy area. The resolution of the conflict may ultimately result in little movement away from that status quo, but at least its content is examined. And, occasionally, substantial departures from the status quo follow major conflict. Thus, for example, a number of the policy innovations of the mid-1960s (the New Frontier and Great Society measures such as basic federal aid to elementary and secondary education, medical care for the aged, and several poverty programs) came after extended periods of conflict over similar or related proposals for the preceding years.

A superficial consideration of congressional-bureaucratic relations tends to suggest that Congress dominates the bureaucracy. This is not the case. Congressional influence is substantial but in many areas the powerful members choose not to exercise it. In addition, even in those cases in which a few members or subcommittees do seek to exercise their influence they may win some skirmishes or battles only to lose

---

* *National Journal* (December 16, 1972): 1932–1933.

† Nadel, *The Politics of Consumer Protection*: 77–78.

the war of overall policy direction. This can happen when the president and presidency lend the full weight of their support to a particular part of the bureaucracy under attack. This kind of support by the presidency occurs infrequently, but when it is used it is often effective because the weapons are very powerful: the impounding of large amounts of money that Congress has appropriated for specific purposes, the withholding of vital information from Congress under the claim of "executive privilege," and the taking of initiatives while Congress is out of session.

At root, the predominance of incentives for both bureaucrats and members of Congress to maintain good relations with each other so that the trading of valued resources is not disrupted also loads the legislative process in favor of the status quo. Habits and patterns of personal interaction and thought about public policy develop and become firmly entrenched. Participants hesitate to stray very far from policies that are known to command widespread support, regardless of their true value, their shortcomings, or the nature of their impact on American society. Disruptive forces such as visionary or aggressive presidents or major party upheavals can and do alter this situation, but they are the exception and not the rule. Not all policy change is minute or slow-moving, but most of it is. This situation may result in either "good" or "bad" policy; it certainly results in familiar policy.

PART IV

An
Assessment
of Congressional
Policy
Impact

11

CONGRESS
AND POLICY

As Congress works with questions of public policy it must deal with a variety of constraints. Some of these constraints are not likely to change. There is little Congress can do to alter the conditions discussed in the first chapter—members elected from fixed constituencies in the context of a weak national party system, the existence of a powerful president and large bureaucracy, and a demanding and complicated workload.

But these conditions do not absolutely determine the policy role that Congress will play. There are aspects of the congressional environment, both internal and external, that are subject to planned modification. Two are particularly important: 1) the internal distribution of influence in the House and Senate; and 2) the essential character of relations with the executive branch.

The Impact of the Internal Distribution
of Influence

Congress strives to achieve two objectives: a responsiveness to national problems, and the maintenance of a central role in policy-making. The way influence is distributed in the House and Senate has a profound effect on the degree to which these goals can be met. Ideally, the internal distribution of influence should promote the following conditions, all of which are important to a strong congressional policy-making role: ready access for members to the most important points in the legislative process, efficient procedures that allow a relatively steady stream of output, and a moderately high degree of institutional stability.

These conditions in turn affect a set of values that influence congressional responsiveness to public needs; thoroughness, representativeness, and responsibility. *Thoroughness* is present in congressional actions if the major aspects of a problem are identified and appraised and the major alternative solutions to the problem are also identified and appraised. *Representativeness* is present if the main contending interests are heard and weighed during the decision-making process. *Responsibility* is present if the agents who have the most influence in making decisions are readily visible. Where responsibility is lacking, arbitrary action is more likely to be invisible and undetected.

The distribution of influence in the House and Senate involves a variety of traditions and units within the institution: party leaders, committees, committee chairmen, prevailing norms, and socialization patterns. It is the members of Congress as individuals that finally determine how Congress will operate. The distribution of influence is not the result of any single individual's efforts; it is, however, affected by the behavior and decisions of a variety of individuals. For example, a committee chairman who takes an aggressive role in running his committee or party leaders who work diligently to achieve party unity on roll call voting help shape broader and longer lasting patterns of influence distribution.

The distribution of influence in the House and Senate is subject to varying degrees of centralization. In a centralized distribution control is exercised by influential and aggressive central party leaders and committee chairmen who are loyal to those leaders and who have considerable authority in their respective committees and use that authority to pursue outcomes desired by the leaders. Individual senators and representatives are oriented toward their party and possess only limited personal influence.

In a decentralized distribution party leaders are at most only moderately aggressive and influential, while standing committee chairmen and subcommittee chairmen are largely independent from party leaders and tend to be relatively influential in their own committees in pursuit of outcomes defined with little concern for what the party leaders want. Individual members, especially the more senior ones, are also influential within the specific committees and subcommittees on which they sit.

A classic case of centralized distribution existed in the period during the first few years of Woodrow Wilson's presidency (1913 and 1914). The majority leaders in both houses—Oscar W. Underwood in the House and John W. Kern in the Senate—guided their respective caucuses in making sure that the most important bills emerging from the standing committees had their approval and the support of the majority of Democrats. Committee chairmen worked closely with these leaders in shaping details of bills so that they would be true to the general policy positions taken by the leaders and by the caucuses. Individual members had their major policy impact through their participation in the party caucus, through loyal support of the positions that emerged from the caucus, and through bills that came from the standing committees that were in accord with caucus directions.

In many ways a very strong pattern of decentralization was dominant in both houses during much of the 1940s and 1950s (with the partial exception of the two Republican-controlled Congresses in 1947–48 and 1953–54). Despite the presence of Sam Rayburn as Speaker of the House during the entire period and Lyndon Johnson as majority leader of the Senate during the latter part of the period only some committee chairmen were consistently concerned with the policy preferences of those energetic and resourceful leaders. In a way Rayburn and Johnson seemed so resourceful because they had to exercise considerable wile to have any substantive impact on the products that emerged from the standing committees. And, regularly, conservative-dominated committees ignored their preferences and produced legislation unacceptable to the leaders but—given the number of Republicans and conservative southern Democrats in Congress at the time—which often passed both in committee and on the floor.

A high degree of decentralization is probably the "natural" state of Congress in that the structure and norms of both houses seem to emphasize independent action on the part of individual members that often gets translated into support for "strong" committees and "weak" leaders. However, there is nothing inevitable about the dominance of decentralization. Some members argue that there is more genuine independence in working with aggressive central party leaders than in working more immediately under both the thumb and gaze of domineering committee or subcommittee chairmen. There is constant ferment in Congress about the proper ratio of powers that should be allocated to and exercised by party leaders, caucuses, and standing committees. Judging by the last sixty years it seems safest to predict that the forces favoring increased centralization will lose more than they will win; but it is not accurate to say that that has been a uniform outcome during the sixty years or that it will be a uniform outcome in the future.

Different values are served by differing distributions of influence. *Thoroughness* of consideration seems to be most likely at the decentralized end of the spectrum and least likely at the centralized end. As decentralization increases, more members of the House and Senate increase both their substantive expertise and their degree of specialization. This means that virtually all members of the Senate and most members of the House have the potential of becoming expert on some legislative matter. They are aided by a relatively large number of knowledgeable and independently important staff members. There is more chance that thorough examination will take place under such conditions than when the committees are merely doing the bidding of the party leaders, without independent contributions from individual members or staff members.

Representativeness of the greatest number of interests is also most likely to occur in a situation of decentralization of influence and least likely to occur in a situation in which influence is centralized. With influence highly fragmented many interests have a chance to ally themselves with a key subcommittee or individual senator or representative or staff member, and thus become effectively represented. In a highly centralized situation the interests that are close to the party leaders are represented, but competing interests may not be.

If *representativeness* is considered in a second sense, however—that of weighing competing interests—it may be facilitated more by a centralized distribution of influence than by a decentralized distribution. Since political parties have to agree to compromises between interests in order to attract broad electoral support, the centralized situation may lead to a weighing of competing interests before matters reach the Senate and House floors. Similarly, since an important subcommittee chairman does not necessarily have to weigh competing interests and because his judgment, in the form of a bill, usually passes on the floor, only one interest may dominate a specific, relatively small area of public policy. Perhaps, in the matter of representativeness, when both number of interests and the weighing of competing interests are considered responsiveness to national problems is best promoted by a situation in which the standing committees dominate their subcommittees, thus preventing the subcommittees from becoming autonomous satrapies.

Responsibility is most likely in a highly centralized situation and least likely in a highly decentralized one. In the former situation the party leader or leaders, along with the president, can be held responsible for what the Senate and House do legislatively. These leaders may be arbitrary, but the arbitrariness is highly visible. When decentralization is the norm, however, it is often impossible to assign responsibility in any meaningful sense.

In short, no single distribution of influence maximizes all of the values of *thoroughness, representativeness* in both senses, and *responsibility* simultaneously. High decentralization seems most like to provide thorough consideration and action. High centralization seems most likely to provide responsible consideration and action. And some midpoint between the two extremes seems most likely to provide representative consideration and action.

THE IMPACT OF THE CHARACTER OF RELATIONS WITH THE EXECUTIVE

The way Congress shapes its relations with the executive determines in large part not only how effective it will be in day-to-day duties, but also its effectiveness in policy-making in general and its responsiveness to broad public needs. A variety of factors help determine the level of cooperation between Congress and the president. These include: the party label of the president and majority parties in the House and the Senate; how leadership is defined by the president and congressional leaders; personal styles of the people in both institutions; the skill with which resources are used; and the willingness to compromise.

Relations with the Executive and Performance of Basic Congressional Functions

Alternative Institutional Goals for Congress. Congress is, of course, composed of a large and diverse group of individuals, and most of the time these individuals, alone and in groups, differ in their goals for Congress. It is possible, however, for a sizeable majority of the members to articulate and pursue (with varying degrees of consciousness) broad institutional goals. Pursuit of these broad goals enables Congress to have specific kinds of impact on the substance of public policy.

Three alternative goals seem particularly relevant in affecting the substance of public policy. The first is to *maximize support for the substantive program of the president.* The second is to *maximize the in-*

dependent influence of Congress on positive policy actions by the government. The third is *to maximize ability of Congress to limit governmental innovation and to restrain the increase in governmental activity.*

Among the most articulate advocates of these three goals are James MacGregor Burns, who has written in support of maximum congressional support for the program of the president,* Theodore J. Lowi, who would like to see Congress exert its independent influence,† and James Burnham, who has argued that Congress should take the lead in curtailing governmental activity.°

Most public debate on the proper role of Congress focuses on the conflict between the Burns position and the Burnham position, and the seeming radical contradiction between them. Little public attention has thus far been given the Lowi or "independent influence" position.

The Burns and Burnham positions do, to be sure, conflict. They are, as stated by their proponents, wedded to differing ideologies—the Burns position to a liberal ideology and the Burnham position to a conservative ideology. In an important sense both Burns and Burnham would make Congress dependent on adherence to rather rigid ideological considerations rather than promoting flexibility and adaptability in the institution. This dependent position for Congress would vary with changes in presidents and changes in the status quo within the bureaucracy. When Burns initially stated his position, for example, his ideal was congressional subservience to a strong, liberal Democrat as president. He would be unlikely to espouse similar subservience to Richard Nixon but would instead insist on continuing single-minded pursuit of outcomes in line with his own liberal ideology. When Burnham initially stated his position he could probably think comfortably of Congress working well with many of the bureaus and their programs in the executive branch because many of them were quite limited and conservative in their goals. Those that appeared too aggressive, large, or threatening to his conservative vision of government should be challenged by Congress until they too had adopted the proper perspective. During a period of relatively expansionist, liberal bureaucracy—such as that during the 1964–66 era—Burnham would no doubt favor a more assertive Congress seeking to impose its ideological vision on the executive branch.

---

* James MacGregor Burns, *Congress on Trial* (New York: Harper, 1949) and *The Deadlock of Democracy* (Englewood Cliffs, N.J.: Prentice-Hall, 1963).
† Theodore J. Lowi, "Congressional Reform: A New Time, Place and Manner," in Lowi and Ripley (eds.), *Legislative Politics U.S.A.* (Boston: Little, Brown, 1973, 3rd ed.).
° James Burnham, *Congress and the American Tradition* (Chicago: Regnery, 1959).

Congressional Performance of Functions to Attain Different Goals.
The way in which Congress performs its functions of lawmaking, oversight of administration, education of the public, and representation will
help determine which goal or goals are in fact being sought. If, as is
often the case, Congress consciously chooses no single goal and no
single mode of performing its functions then bits and pieces of all
three goals will in fact be pursued simultaneously.

To achieve maximum *support for the program of the president,*
Congress should perform its lawmaking functioning by enacting whatever legislative proposals the president submits or supports. It should
perform its oversight function very generally, if at all, in the cases of
agencies and programs that appear to have presidential approval. If,
for example, the president seems satisfied with the activities of the
Department of Defense, then the uncritical stance of a Mendel Rivers
or of an F. Edward Hebert (recent chairmen of the House Armed
Services Committee) is quite appropriate. The president may, however,
be concerned about the activities of some of the agencies and programs
theoretically under his control and might welcome careful congressional
scrutiny to help him influence matters that otherwise might be independent of any real checks. In these cases the president can make
clear to various congressional committees those programs and agencies
that he wants overseen and Congress can assist him in this way.

Congress should perform its public education function by propa-
gandizing in favor of presidential proposals before enactment and on
behalf of presidential performance after enactment. It should perform
its representation function by concentrating on narrow activities (casework for individuals and corporations and division of federal "good-
ies") in order to avoid conflict with the executive branch on broader
questions—except in those few cases in which the president might view
such conflict as beneficial to his program.

To achieve maximum *independent influence on positive policy positions,* Congress should perform its lawmaking function by including
explicit standards for administering new programs in all legislation it
enacts. Congress can demand that the executive branch include such
standards in draft legislation, it can add such standards amending bills
coming from the executive branch, and it can include them in bills
initiated in Congress. Placing a termination date on all legislation
would also help propel Congress toward the goal of maximum independent influence.

Congress should perform its oversight function by examining the
role of specific federal agencies and programs in meeting or not meeting broad national needs. This form of oversight can uncover new

areas and problems in which legislation is needed. Oversight to meet the goal of maximizing independent congressional impact should insist on rigorous adherence by executive branch agencies to the standards of performance included in the statutes authorizing the programs administered by those agencies. This form of oversight should also insist that agencies develop their own rigorous standards for evaluating performance and relative degrees of success or failure. Congressional committee members and staff members could themselves help in the development of such standards.

Congress should perform its public education function by selecting specific substantive areas in which efforts to stimulate public attention and support should be concentrated. Congress has little impact as a collectivity when it tries to educate the public on every side of every issue simultaneously. But if there is some genuine consensus, either bipartisan or at least on the part of the majority party in Congress, on which issues need special and constant attention, then Congress—through its most visible members—can educate at least the attentive part of the public.

Finally, Congress should perform its representation function by concentrating considerable attention on questions of national concern such as the total federal responsibility in relation to racial equality or environmental quality. For maximum impact such activity should be limited to only a few subject areas. If virtually every issue is claimed to involve matters of profound principle and the national good, the impact of the claim becomes diluted. Naturally, Congress would also continue the narrower kinds of representation (casework for individuals and corporations and division of federal largesse) and these are perfectly proper activities as long as they do not conflict with a focus on a limited number of broad-based proposals and questions reflecting the central problems of American society.

To achieve *limited governmental innovation and to restrain the increase in governmental activity,* Congress should perform its lawmaking function very sparingly, restricting the number of new laws enacted. Those that are enacted should contain "legislative veto" provisions guaranteeing continued tight congressional control. Similar provisions should be added to existing legislation. It should perform its oversight function by constantly involving itself in the details of the administration of all programs. Representative Edith Green's proprietary attitude toward some juvenile delinquency and education programs would become the model for congressional behavior (see chapter 10). Given the seniority system there are always new proprietors in training when established ones leave Congress. Relationships with key bureaucrats and interest group representatives for purposes of maintaining the status quo in a wide range of programs should be cultivated and maintained.

Congress should perform its public education function by warning about asserted dangers of big government such as invasion of privacy or too much spending. Simultaneously, selective public education efforts should be undertaken to support existing specific programs (for example, coalitions might emerge to stress the benefits of existing cotton price supports, the Department of Defense relations with the aerospace industry or with specific companies within it, and the Appalachian development program). Finally, Congress should perform its *representation* function by concentrating exclusively on casework and the division of federal benefits.

Relations with the Executive and Congressional Involvement in Policy-making

In chapter 1 four models of congressional involvement in policy-making were presented: executive dominance, joint program development, congressional dominance, and stalemate. It is instructive to review the congressional record in major policy areas over the last few decades in terms of these models for in all these areas Congress has at times shown its capacity for developing substantive impact, although the impact varies between areas.

Congressional Involvement in Economic Policy. Congress is heavily involved in policy and program decisions affecting the domestic economy, the usual model being that of joint program development, whether the specific programs concern appropriations, taxation, or management of the public debt.*

Despite its important role in individual programs it is virtually impossible for Congress to develop and implement an overall economic policy of its own. Almost inevitably this task must fall to the president and his top advisers, who set general economic goals and strategies in the annual budget message and economic report and monitor performance in light of those goals on a continual basis.

Congress also contributes to the more general debate through the work of two joint committees: the Joint Economic Committee and

---

* See Ralph K. Huitt, "Congressional Organization and Operations in the Field of Money and Credit," in Commission on Money and Credit, *Fiscal and Debt Management Policies* (Englewood Cliffs, N.J.: Prentice-Hall, 1963): 399–495; and Harvey C. Mansfield, "The Congress and Economic Policy," in David B. Truman (ed.), *The Congress and America's Future* (Englewood Cliffs, N.J.: Prentice-Hall, 1965): 121–149.

the Joint Committee on Internal Revenue Taxation. But these committees cannot perform a consolidating function in lieu of presidential activity. As one student of this policy area has concluded:

> The experience of the Joint Economic Committee testifies that it is possible to organize a unit in Congress that can open up national perspectives on the economy and draw on the most advanced techniques of economic analysis to make prescriptions. But it is not conceivable that the JEC could acquire the power to enact them; it is a teacher, not a governor.

> The experience of the Joint Committee on Internal Revenue Taxation testifies that it is possible to organize a unit in Congress sufficiently powerful to control the use of the taxing power. But it is not conceivable that the taxing committees, in doing so, will apply the prescriptions, or even adopt the perspectives of the JEC.*

A specific example of an economic policy issue that moved from a stalemate model to joint program development model is provided by what became the Area Redevelopment Act.† In the 1950s Senator Paul Douglas, an Illinois Democrat, began to build a coalition in favor of giving special federal aid to economically depressed areas of the country. Gradually that coalition became a majority in Congress, and Douglas' bill passed. President Eisenhower, however, vetoed the bill containing the program and Congress did not override the veto (stalemate). When a Democrat became president the new administration and the congressional supporters reached agreement on details and the bill passed (joint development). After the administrators of the original program had committed some fatal blunders a new liaison effort between congressional supporters and the executive branch produced a revised program and a renamed agency (joint development).

Congressional Involvement in Poverty and Human Resource Development Policy.° In recent years the government has become increasingly involved in efforts to alleviate the effects of poverty, involvement which has taken many specific forms. Some of the programs have been generated in a fashion much like the model of executive dominance. This was true of the development and passage of the Economic Opportun-

---

* Mansfield, "The Congress and Economic Policy," 148.

† See Ripley, *The Politics of Economic and Human Resource Development:* chapter 2: Roger Davidson, *Coalition-Building for Depressed Area Bills: 1955–1965,* Inter-University Case Program no. 103 (Indianapolis: Bobbs-Merrill, 1966); and Sar A. Levitan, *Federal Aid to Depressed Areas* (Baltimore: Johns Hopkins, 1964).

° See Ripley, *Politics of Economic and Human Resource Development,* and Sar A. Levitan, *The Great Society's Poor Law* (Baltimore: Johns Hopkins, 1969).

ity Act of 1964 as well as the Model Cities program. Other parts of the specific programs, however, were generated in accord with a joint policy development model. The Appalachia program of 1964 is an example of such development. It also involved state and local officials as initiators.

But even in programs like EOA and Model Cities, in which the immediate initiative clearly came from the executive branch, there had been a prior history of at least sporadic (and unsuccessful) congressional initiative. For very different reasons, for example, both liberal and conservative critics of urban renewal had laid some of the groundwork for the Model Cities program. Likewise, Democrats in the 1950s had taken a variety of initiatives—for a Youth Conservation Corps, for example—that were absorbed by the executive branch in its fashioning of the Economic Opportunity Act.

Congressional Involvement in Urban Problems. Congressional involvement has been critical to the successful establishment of programs in many urban problem areas, including air and water pollution control, juvenile delinquency, food stamps, aid to airports and to mass transit. The conclusion of a number of case studies of congressional impact in these areas was that in all except juvenile delinquency "Congress provided the leadership, the continuity, the persistence in formulating new policies and programs and guiding them through the political thicket of the legislative process to final decision." * Individuals from interest groups and the executive branch assisted in some of these initiatives but in other cases the executive branch was characterized by division and uncertainty. In a few cases the executive branch actively opposed the initiatives coming from Congress.

It should be underlined that the period covered included both the last half of the Eisenhower administration and the first term of Kennedy and Johnson. Thus the pattern that is found in this area cannot be attributed to the political differences between Eisenhower and a Democratic Congress. Congress often had to push the Democratic administration as well as the Republican administration.

In assessing the case studies in these areas only juvenile delinquency comes close to fitting the model of executive dominance. There was also an abortive effort to establish an Urban Affairs Department in 1961 and 1962 that fits the stalemate model. Food stamps, aid to airports and to mass transit best fit the model of joint program development. Air and water pollution fit rather closely the model of congressional dominance.

---

* Frederic N. Cleaveland and associates, *Congress and Urban Problems:* 355.

Congressional Involvement in Educational Policy. Between World War II and the present, Congress has enacted a great number of education laws. There is a popular misconception that, until the major educational legislation of the Johnson administration in the mid-1960s, which was impressive in both scope and magnitude, all federal aid to education proposals had been stalemated. This is true of general aid to elementary and secondary education but is untrue in other fields. In the pre-1965 period, for example, the federal government provided aid to higher education through various "G.I. bills" for ex-servicemen, subsidies for college dorms, and the National Defense Education Act. Elementary and secondary education also received aid from the NDEA as well as from an extensive program of aid to school districts that were considered to be "federally impacted" because the proximity of large federal installations increased the school age population. These various measures emerged in large part on the basis of the joint program development model. The major Johnson accomplishments—particularly the Elementary and Secondary Education Act of 1965—were also developed jointly.*

Congressional Involvement in Foreign Policy. One of the most common generalizations in both scholarly and popular literature on Congress is that the executive branch, especially the president, has completely overshadowed Congress in foreign policy matters and that Congress holds that the president takes all major initiatives in foreign affairs without any opposition.† Like most generalizations, this one fails to portray a complicated relationship very accurately.

In many ways the model of executive dominance may well have described a period from roughly 1955 to roughly 1965.° Before the mid-1950s Congress was heavily involved in the post-World War II foreign policy initiatives of the United States: the United Nations, the

---

* See Eugene Eidenberg and Roy D. Morey, *An Act of Congress* (New York: Norton, 1969).

† For statements of this position see Aaron Wildavsky, "The Two Presidencies," in Wildavsky (ed.), *The Presidency* (Boston: Little, Brown, 1969): 230–243; and James A. Robinson, *Congress and Foreign Policy-Making* (Homewood, Illinois: Dorsey, 1967, revised ed.).

° For material supporting this thesis that congressional impotence in foreign affairs was mainly limited to one identifiable period of time in the late 1950s and early 1960s see Ronald C. Moe and Steven C. Teel, "Congress as Policy-Maker: A Necessary Reappraisal," in Moe (ed.), *Congress and the President* (New York: Goodyear, 1971); John F. Manley, "The Rise of Congress in Foreign Policy-Making," *Annals of the American Academy of Political and Social Science* 337 (1971): 60–70; and Holbert N. Carroll, *The House of Representatives and Foreign Affairs* (Boston: Little, Brown, 1966).

Marshall Plan and other foreign aid, and NATO. Members of the House and Senate were involved in the early planning of these initiatives and consideration of them by Congress was comprehensive. In recent years Congress has again become more assertive—particularly in reaction to Vietnam and the power of the president to wage an undeclared war—but also on other questions, such as foreign aid. For approximately ten years Congress did not raise major objections to the expansion of presidential influence. Congress was willing to pass resolutions that gave the president virtually a unilateral right to use American troops almost anywhere in the world if he deemed such action to be wise and in the national interest. The last resolution of this sort was the now-repealed Gulf of Tonkin Resolution passed in 1964. Even in this period of congressional passivity, however, Congress had major influence in the creation of the Development Loan Fund in 1957 and the International Development Association in 1958.* These were new facets of the foreign aid program stressing loans and grants to underdeveloped nations for economic purposes only.

It is true that presidential influence on roll call voting in Congress is stronger in the area of "international involvement" than in any other. In fact, in four other areas: government management, social welfare, agricultural assistance, and civil liberties, his influence on roll call voting is virtually absent.†

On the matter of initiative and influence in foreign policy, one of the studies concluding that the president predominates, was able to find a number of cases in which congressional influence was predominant and a few cases in which the initiative was congressional (six of twenty-two cases were found to have been initiated by Congress).° An even stronger position is taken in another study, based on a survey of a large number of cases. In many areas congressional participation was noted to be vigorous, although not dominant. This was true as regards the role of the Senate in treaty-making (the Japanese Peace Treaty of 1952, the North Atlantic Treaty, and the United Nations Charter are cited as examples) and the role of the House Appropriations Committee in a number of foreign policy areas. In addition, Congress was found to dominate "many areas of foreign policy which in themselves appear to be peripheral. Collectively, however, they constitute a major portion of U.S. foreign policy. For example, Congress is generally credited with dominant influence over decisions on economic aid

---

* See David A. Baldwin, "Congressional Initiative in Foreign Policy," *Journal of Politics* 28 (1966): 754–773.

† For an analysis of these patterns of presidential influence on voting on the five dimensions see Aage R. Clausen, *How Congressmen Decide* (New York: St. Martin's, 1973), especially chapter 8.

° Robinson, *Congress and Foreign Policy-Making:* 65.

policy, military assistance, agricultural surplus disposal, and the locations of facilities, to name only a few. In addition, immigration and
tariff policies are generally considered part of foreign policy and there
is considerable evidence to indicate that Congress remains a major
actor in these fields." *

A balanced conclusion about the relative positions of the president
and Congress in foreign policy-making must recognize that the participants have different capabilities that enable each to perform some
things better than the other. The president has some natural advantages
that allow him to dominate certain aspects of foreign policy. For example, his greater degree of mobility and his superior information
sources are assets in diplomacy. Imagine, for instance, the likelihood
of the multi-headed Congress arranging and successfully executing a
re-opening of ties with China, an accomplishment that President Nixon
and his foreign advisor, Henry Kissinger, managed with apparent ease
in 1972. The enormous press coverage inherent in such foreign policy
coups as the China thaw lends a great deal of support to the misconception of the president's ability to dominate all foreign affairs.

Foreign policy spectaculars such as the resumption of contact with
China are rare events. Much policy-making in foreign affairs is without
glamor and may receive little or no press coverage, which results in low
public visibility, but it is no less important to the total foreign policy
picture. And it is generally in these less visible areas that congressional involvement is likely to be high. For example, work on the details
of trade policy, foreign aid, and immigration policy, though slow and
tedious, is important to shaping overall U.S. policy toward much of the
world. And Congress has considerable influence in these fields.

In conclusion, there is no single model of congressional-executive
relations that applies to the foreign policy area. On some occasions
executive dominance emerges, but more often the pattern is one of
joint development. This is particularly evident if the 1955 to 1965
period is viewed as an aberrant period, rather than as "normal."

Congressional Involvement in Defense Policy. Congress is often written off entirely in the defense field. But closer analysis reveals some
substantial congressional impact. As in the case of foreign policy a
facile generalization about the total power of the executive is not
accurate.

On the one hand, there is good evidence that particularly in the
late 1950s and early 1960s individual members did not consider the
broad aspects of defense policy when they were called on to make

---

* Moe and Teel, "Congress as Policy-Maker," 49.

Table 11–1
Average (Mean) Congressional Change in the President's
Defense Budget, 1960–1970.

	Mean Change (%)
Total Department of Defense Budget	2.3
Personnel	1.1
Operations and Maintenance	1.2
Procurement	4.4
Research, Development,Testing and Evaluation	4.5

Source: Adapted from Arnold Kanter, "Congress and the Defense Budget: 1960–1970,"
American Political Science Review *66 (1972): 134.*

decisions about that policy. For example, the Armed Services Committees often were more concerned about "real estate" decisions (the location or closing of military facilities) than about defense policy writ large. Members in general felt technically incompetent to challenge the judgment of military personnel.* And, at the institutional level, it is true that Congress does not usually make major cuts in the overall defense budget proposed by the president.†

But a closer look at defense budgets in the 1960s shows that congressional impact was substantial. The key to understanding the nature of congressional impact is to disaggregate the budget into its component parts.° Although congressional impact on the overall budget figures for the Department of Defense appears to be limited, when the budget is split into four categories ‡—personnel; operations and maintenance; procurement; and research, development, testing, and evaluation—a more precise view of congressional impact is evident. Congress makes only small changes in the areas of personnel and operations and maintenance, and these areas account for over half of the budget. There is considerable congressional activity in the areas of procurement and research, development, testing, and evaluation. Table 11–1 summarizes the average congressional change in the president's budget by category for the eleven years between 1960 and 1970. The distinction between the

* Lewis A. Dexter, "Congressmen and the Making of Military Policy," in Raymond E. Wolfinger (ed.), *Readings on Congress:* 371–387.
† See Douglas M. Fox, "Congress and U.S. Military Service Budgets in the Post-War Period: A Research Note," *Midwest Journal of Political Science* 15 (1971): 382–393.
° What follows is drawn from Arnold Kanter, "Congress and the Defense Budget: 1960–1970," *American Political Science Review* 66 (1972): 129–143.
‡ Construction is not included in the categories.

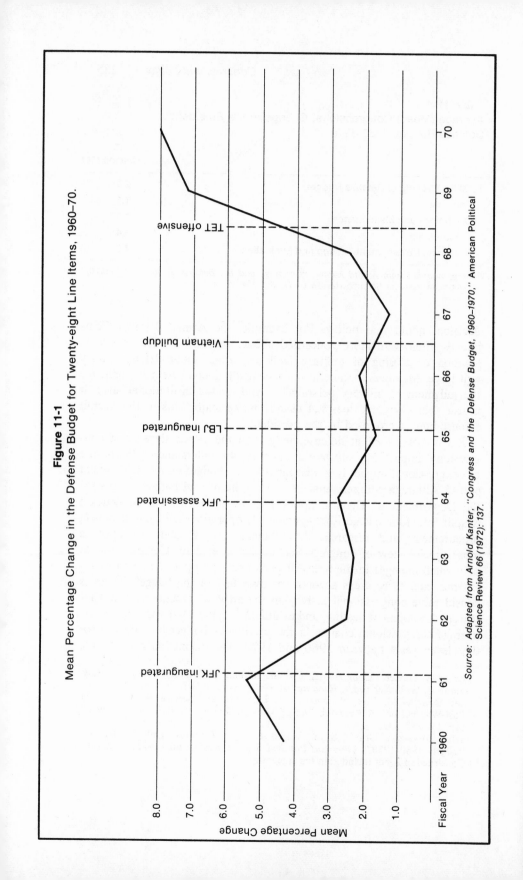

Figure 11-1

Mean Percentage Change in the Defense Budget for Twenty-eight Line Items, 1960–70.

Source: Adapted from Arnold Kanter, "Congress and the Defense Budget, 1960–1970," American Political
Science Review 66 (1972): 137.

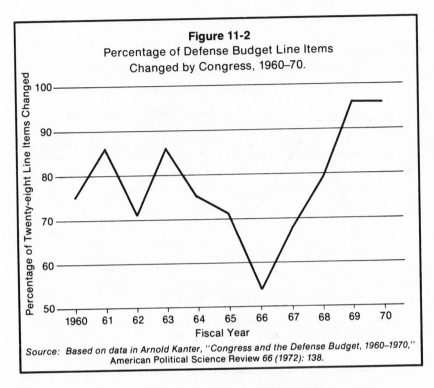

Figure 11-2
Percentage of Defense Budget Line Items
Changed by Congress, 1960–70.

Source: *Based on data in Arnold Kanter, "Congress and the Defense Budget, 1960–1970,"*
American Political Science Review *66 (1972): 138.*

two no-change categories and two substantial change categories becomes clear in this table.

A careful analysis of congressional action on the defense budget also supports the proposition that Congress was relatively acquiescent in the mid-1960s but has become more aggressive in recent years. Figure 11–1 shows the mean percentage change in the defense budget between 1960 and 1970 for twenty-eight specific line items that remained constant in terms of content throughout the period. The increase of congressional changes in the budget after the Tet offensive (an aggressive attack by North Vietnamese and the Viet Cong) in early 1968 is particularly dramatic. Likewise, Congress was much more aggressive in changing specific line items in 1969 and 1970 than it had been earlier. The incidence of no changes was highest in the mid-1960s. Figure 11–2 summarizes the distribution of change/no change outcomes in terms of the percentage of the twenty-eight line items that Congress altered each year.

This discussion of defense budgets in the 1960s does not mean to imply that Congress makes defense policy. In fact, the model of executive dominance applies to the field as a whole. But the example does

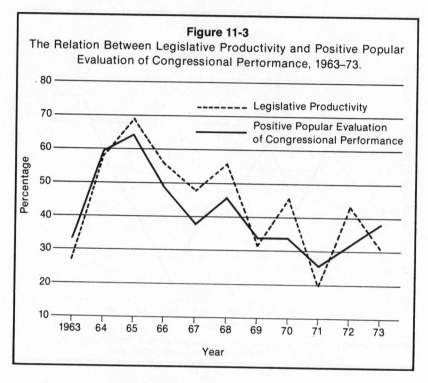

Figure 11-3
The Relation Between Legislative Productivity and Positive Popular Evaluation of Congressional Performance, 1963–73.

suggest that even in a situation of executive dominance there is room for substantial congressional impact.

THE POPULAR STANDING OF CONGRESS

Popular estimates of Congress tend to vary as the productivity of Congress varies. Figure 11–3 makes the relationship between popular estimates of congressional performance and the legislative productivity of Congress dramatically clear. From 1963 through 1971 these two items coincided in variation almost exactly. The line reporting popular evaluation of Congress represents the percentage of the population responding "excellent" or "pretty good" when asked "How would you rate the job which has been done by Congress this past year: excellent, pretty good, only fair, or poor?" by the Harris Poll. The line reporting legislative productivity represents the annual "presidential boxscore" reported by *Congressional Quarterly*. This is simply the percentage of presidential requests enacted into law.

After 1971 the relationship between evaluation and productivity is less clear. The Harris Poll did not ask the question about the popular rating of Congress in 1972. The 1973 figure of 38 percent for the excellent and pretty good categories comes from a poll in February of that year, just before the Watergate scandal began to develop. By January 1974, the excellent and pretty good answers had dropped to 21 percent. Watergate and related matters had lowered the public's view of Congress as well as of most public institutions and officials. Another poll taken in July 1974, however, showed popular evaluation of Congress beginning to rise slightly—now the excellent and pretty good categories contained 29 percent of the respondents. If President Ford helps restore confidence in the government as a whole and if he and Congress are able to arrive at some policy compromises that increase congressional output then the positive evaluation should again begin to rise. If stalemate on policy matters returns after the popular relief at ridding the presidency of Richard Nixon, however, then the popular rating of Congress is likely to remain quite unfavorable.

This relationship between popular esteem and productivity suggests a dilemma for Congress: it is perceived in positive terms only when it reacts positively to presidential initiatives. Yet the leaders of Congress take a very understandable and reasonable position when they resist proceeding on an executive dominance model. At minimum it seems likely that joint policy development must be extensively used as a model. An aggressive group of members of Congress (particularly party leaders and committee chairmen) are not likely to acquiesce to executive dominance; likewise, an aggressive president and bureaucratic officials are not likely to acquiesce to a wide use of the congressional dominance model. The stalemate model, of course, is the most counterproductive of all in terms of popular reaction to Congress. Much of what transpired in 1963 and 1969–71 could fairly be called stalemate; these years also represent the low points of congressional popularity in the last decade.

Congress has not been alone in its decline in the estimation of the general public. All institutions of government (and, in fact, the leading institutions and professions in society) have also dwindled in public esteem. Political cynicism in general grew during the 1960s. For example, in 1964 76 percent of the population felt they could trust the government always or most of the time. Only 22 percent felt they could trust the government only some of the time. In 1968 these figures had changed to 59 percent with high trust in the government and 35 percent with low trust. By 1972 only 52 percent fell in the high trust category, but 45 percent fell in the low trust category. Similar patterns of response over the same time period can be observed in answers to questions about the waste of tax money, for whose benefit the government is run, whether government employees know their jobs, and whether politicians are crooked.* The revelations following the Watergate break-in have done little to inspire confidence in public officials. Political cynicism and mistrust continued to grow in the 1970s.

In the long run, the most important implication of the public's estimation of Congress may be in terms of the kinds of individuals who are attracted to a career in Congress. The very best individuals might not be much interested in seeking membership in a body that is, over a long time period, held in low esteem. Year-to-year fluctuations are not so dangerous from this standpoint but long periods of low public evaluation of congressional performance are.

CONGRESSIONAL EFFICACY: A CONCLUDING WORD

Congress is generally responsive to positions articulated by large masses of people, effective interest groups, an aggressive president, and skilled bureaucrats.† But the nature and timing of congressional response is never fully determined by the extra-congressional forces and pressures. In some policy areas outside pressures may be weak or conflicting or absent some of the time, thus increasing the room for congressional maneuver and initiation. Congress faces constraints, but they are far from absolute or overwhelming.

The overall efficacy of Congress is best gauged by its ability to respond to national problems in the short run. Both scholarly and popular literature abound with prescriptions of how Congress can increase its short-run responsiveness and thus its potency. These prescriptions include: 1) eliminating seniority for selecting committee chairmen; 2) disclosing personal financial worth and holdings of members; 3) strengthening conflict of interest laws; 4) setting a retirement age for members; 5) increasing staff; 6) installing computers; and so on. Many of these suggestions make sense in their own right. Certainly it is important to promote ethical behavior with regard to finances and conflicts of interest. It is also important to increase the availability of information to Congress—at least part of it from sources other than interest groups or the executive branch—by such measures as increasing staff and using computers to facilitate the flow and accessibility of information. The impact of a change in the seniority system or an age limit on service is much less clear. However, it should be stressed that

---

* These data come from studies conducted by the Survey Research Center. I am grateful to my former colleague Arthur H. Miller for providing me with a summary of the relevant data.

† See chapters 7–10 in this volume and Alan Rosenthal, "The Effectiveness of Congress," in Gerald M. Pomper and others, *The Performance of American Government* (New York: Free Press, 1972): 139–149.

no such changes—either singly or in any combination—constitute a magic formula for insuring congressional responsiveness and potency.

It is here argued that "reform" in the classic sense—such as the prescriptions enumerated above—may be useful but is probably not central to congressional performance. What is central involves the will of the members of the House and Senate. The machinery of Congress is not inherently deficient. The links with the public are not deficient. The electoral system is not deficient. The ties with the other organs of government are not deficient. What may be deficient is resolve on the part of a sufficient number of members to make the machinery, the ties to other publics and agencies, and the "system" work. It can work when that resolve is present. But the willingness to experiment consciously with internal structures and arrangements and the willingness to take stands that might at least temporarily be unpopular with a mass public, an elite public, or other officials are critical in determining potency. In that general sense this book ends on a "reformist" note: a hope that members of the House and Senate will not relax with set patterns of thinking and doing but will instead seek new patterns, even within the confines of existing congressional institutions. The institutions allow for both stagnation and innovation; the critical question is how the people responsible for making the institutions function behave.

SELECTED BIBLIOGRAPHY

The amount of writing on Congress is vast. The following bibliography is selective and omits a great deal of good literature. It is intended as a guide for readers who want to explore further the topics treated in this volume. A number of items are included not cited in the footnotes. The bibliography is generally organized along the lines of the book itself, with a few variations. Some of the articles and books cited are useful for several purposes. The annotations attempt to indicate these additional uses.

I. GENERAL

This section includes items that could not be conveniently categorized under other topics. It does not include textbooks or general books of selected readings published previously. Several items on "reform" are included.

American Political Science Association, "Toward a More Responsible Two-Party System," *American Political Science Review* 44 (1950), supplement. A classic statement of the case for reform inside Congress in order to enhance "party responsibility." Written by a committee chaired by E. E. Schattschneider.

Bibby, John F. and Roger H. Davidson, *On Capitol Hill* (Hinsdale, Ill.: Dryden, 1972, 2nd ed.). Original case studies of campaigns, workdays of members, party leadership, a committee, and legislative action.

Bolling, Richard, *House Out of Order* (New York: Dutton, 1965). A reformist analysis of the House by an important liberal Democrat from Missouri.

Burnham, James, *Congress and the American Tradition* (Chicago: Regnery, 1959). A conservative view of the proper role of Congress: i.e., to stop executive expansion of governmental activities.

Burns, James MacGregor, *The Deadlock of Democracy* (Englewood Cliffs, N.J.: Prentice-Hall, 1963). A liberal attack on Congress for being unresponsive to national needs, especially as interpreted by the president.

Cater, Douglass, *Power in Washington* (New York: Random House, 1964). Primarily a study of "subgovernments" in action.

Clapp, Charles L., *The Congressman* (Washington: Brookings, 1963). A report and commentary on interviews with and discussions by about fifty members of the House in 1959. Good material on relations with constituents and interest groups, the impact of party leadership, and the working of committees.

Clark, Joseph S., *Congress—The Sapless Branch* (New York: Harper, 1965, revised ed.). A reformist argument by a former Democratic Senator from Pennsylvania.

Congressional Quarterly. Publications of this Washington-based organization are indispensable for the student of the post-World War II Congress. Especially useful are the weekly reports it has issued since 1945, the yearly almanacs, its *Guide to the Congress of the United States* (1971), and *Congress and the Nation* (volume 1 covers politics and policy from 1945 through 1964; volume 2 covers 1965 through 1968; volume 3 covers 1969 through 1972).

Davidson, Roger H., David M. Kovenock, and Michael K. O'Leary, *Congress in Crisis: Politics and Congressional Reform* (Belmont, Calif.: Wadsworth, 1966). A study of how members feel about specific reform proposals.

de Grazia, Alfred (ed.), *Congress: The First Branch of Government* (Garden City, N.Y.: Doubleday Anchor Books, 1967). Twelve original essays on topics such as oversight, decision-making, liaison, information systems, and congressional handling of the budget.

Dexter, Lewis A., *The Sociology and Politics of Congress* (Chicago: Rand McNally, 1969). A collection of essays by one of the most original students of Congress. Especially useful on elections and relations with constituents and interest groups.

House Republican Task Force on Congressional Reform and Minority Staffing, *We Propose: A Modern Congress* (New York: McGraw-Hill, 1966). The views of a number of House Republicans on needed reforms.

Huitt, Ralph K. and Robert L. Peabody, *Congress: Two Decades of Analysis* (New York: Harper & Row, 1969). Part I of this book is a long and very useful essay by Peabody summarizing and evaluating the literature on Congress. Part II is a collection of articles by Huitt, one of the pioneers of modern congressional research. These articles include his classic studies of Lyndon Johnson as a Senate Majority Leader and William Proxmire as a maverick senator.

Miller, Clem, *Member of the House* (New York: Scribner's, 1962). Insightful letters from a California representative to his constituents. Good material on House procedure, the workload of a representative, the impact of party in the House, and relations with interest groups.

National Journal. This Washington-based publication comes out weekly and is focused on policy developments. Excellent material on executive-congressional relations.

Saloma, John S. III, *Congress and the New Politics* (Boston: Little, Brown, 1969). An analysis of congressional capabilities and performance. Useful material on workload, relations with constituents, and relations with the executive branch.

Tacheron, Donald G. and Morris K. Udall, *The Job of the Congressman* (Indianapolis: Bobbs-Merrill, 1966). Intended as a manual for new representatives. Also contains much basic information useful to the student of the House.

II. CONGRESSIONAL DEVELOPMENT

This section includes contemporary writing about congressional development and a few of the best of older items such as memoirs and biographies.

Alexander, DeAlva S., *History and Procedure of the House of Representatives* (Boston: Houghton Mifflin, 1916). Still an important work on the House.

Blaine, James G., *Twenty Years of Congress,* 2 vols., (Norwich, Conn.: Henry Bill Publishing Co., 1884–86). Memoirs of the period between 1860 and 1880 by an important Speaker of the House.

Chiu, Chang-wei, *The Speaker of the House of Representatives Since 1896* (New York: Columbia University Press, 1928). A standard work on the Speakership during a period of transition.

Clark, Champ, *My Quarter Century of American Politics,* 2 vols., (New York: Harper, 1920). Insightful memoirs of a long-time member who was a Speaker of the House.

Dunn, Arthur W., *From Harrison to Harding,* 2 vols., (New York: Putnam's, 1922). Memoirs of a journalist that contain much valuable material on Congress and congressional-executive relations during the period.

Farrand, Max, *The Framing of the Constitution of the United States* (New Haven: Yale University Press, 1913). Indispensable source for understanding the original vision of the role of Congress (and the alternative visions that were rejected).

Follett, Mary P., *The Speaker of the House of Representatives* (New York: Longmans, Green and Co., 1896). An excellent treatment of the speakership in the nineteenth century.

Galloway, George B., *History of the United States House of Representatives* (New York: Crowell, 1962). An "official" history of the House; brief, but useful. Also available as House Document No. 246, Eighty-seventh Congress, First Session (1962).

Gwinn, William R., *Uncle Joe Cannon, Archfoe of Insurgency* (New York: Bookman Associates, 1957). A useful biography of Speaker Cannon.

Hamilton, Alexander, John Jay, and James Madison, *The Federalist* (New York: Random House, n.d.). Contains a number of papers explaining the founders' notion of how Congress would function in the total political system.

Haynes, George H., *The Senate of the United States,* 2 vols., (Boston: Houghton Mifflin, 1938). A standard history of the Senate.

Huntington, Samuel P., "Congressional Responses to the Twentieth Century," in David B. Truman (ed.), *The Congress and America's Future* (Englewood Cliffs, N.J.: Prentice-Hall, 1973, 2nd ed.). A reformist analysis of House development.

MacNeil, Neil, *Forge of Democracy: The House of Representatives* (New York: McKay, 1963). Summarizes much of the anecdotal material on the House. Contains a good bibliography.

Patterson, James T., *Congressional Conservatism and the New Deal* (Lexington: University of Kentucky Press, 1968). A study of executive-legislative relations and internal congressional politics from 1933 to 1939. Explores the rise of the "conservative coalition" of Republicans and southern Democrats.

Polsby, Nelson W., "Institutionalization in the U.S. House of Representatives," *American Political Science Review* 62 (1968): 144–168. Explores and documents the growing stability of the House in the twentieth century.

Price, H. Douglas, "The Congressional Career—Then and Now," in Nelson W. Polsby (ed.), *Congressional Behavior* (New York: Random House, 1971). Contrasts the instability of nineteenth century congressional membership with the stability of twentieth century membership.

Rothman, David J., *Politics and Power in the United States Senate, 1869–1901* (Cambridge: Harvard University Press, 1966). An excellent account of the evolution of the Senate from chaos to party government.

Stephenson, Nathaniel W., *Nelson W. Aldrich: A Leader in American Politics* (New York: Scribner's, 1930). Fine biography of the most important Republican leader in the Senate in the late nineteenth and early twentieth centuries.

Wilson, Woodrow, *Congressional Government* (New York: Meridian, 1956). This classic interpretation of Congress was first published in 1885 and still contains many valid observations.

Young, James S., *The Washington Community, 1800–1828* (New York: Columbia University Press, 1966). A fascinating study of the national government in its youth. Rich material on Congress of the period.

III. CONGRESSIONAL DECISION-MAKING

Clausen, Aage R., *How Congressmen Decide* (New York: St. Martin's, 1973). A study of five substantive dimensions of voting in the House and Senate.

Fenno, Richard F., Jr., "The Internal Distribution of Influence: The House," in David B. Truman (ed.), *The Congress and America's Future* (Englewood Cliffs, N.J.: Prentice-Hall, 1973, 2nd ed.). A summary assessment of how things get done in the House.

Froman, Lewis A., Jr., *The Congressional Process* (Boston: Little, Brown, 1967). A discussion of the use and impact of the rules in the House and Senate.

Huitt, Ralph K., "The Internal Distribution of Influence: The Senate," in David B. Truman (ed.), *The Congress and America's Future* (Englewood Cliffs, N.J.: Prentice-Hall, 1973, 2nd ed.). A summary assessment of how things get done in the Senate.

Kingdon, John W., *Congressmen's Voting Decisions* (New York: Harper and Row, 1973). An analysis, based largely on interviews, of how members of the House make up their minds on floor voting.

Matthews, Donald R., *U.S. Senators and Their World* (Chapel Hill: University of North Carolina Press, 1960). An analysis of decision-making in the Senate in the 1940s and 1950s.

Matthews, Donald R. and James A. Stimson, "Decision-Making by U.S. Representatives: A Preliminary Model," in S. Sidney Ulmer (ed.), *Political Decision-Making* (Cincinnati: Van Nostrand Reinhold, 1970). An attempt to quantify the influence of different factors on decision-making by individual members of the House.

Mayhew, David R., *Party Loyalty Among Congressmen* (Cambridge: Harvard University Press, 1966). A roll call study that shows that Democrats support each other's interests better than do Republicans.

Ripley, Randall B., *Power in the Senate* (New York: St. Martin's, 1969). Focused on decision-making in the Senate in the 1960s. Also has some material on Senate history.

Shannon, W. Wayne, *Party, Constituency and Congressional Voting* (Baton Rouge: Louisiana State University Press, 1968). An intensive roll call analysis for the period from 1959 through 1962 in the House. Compares the impact of party to the impact of constituency.

Turner, Julius and Edward V. Schneier, Jr., *Party and Constituency: Pressures on Congress* (Baltimore: The Johns Hopkins Press, 1970, revised ed.). A roll call analysis of the comparative importance of party and constituency for scattered congresses between 1921 and 1967.

IV. COMMITTEES

Fenno, Richard F., Jr., *Congressmen in Committees* (Boston: Little, Brown, 1973). A comparative study of the workings of six House committees.

Fenno, Richard F., Jr., *The Power of the Purse* (Boston: Little, Brown, 1966). A long and valuable study of appropriations politics, focused primarily on the House Appropriations Committee.

Goodwin, George, Jr., *The Little Legislatures* (Amherst: University of Massachusetts Press, 1970). A brief, but thorough treatment of committees.

Hinckley, Barbara, *The Seniority System in Congress* (Bloomington: Indiana University Press, 1971). A thorough analysis of seniority in Congress that concludes that its policy impact is quite limited.

McConachie, Lauros, *Congressional Committees* (New York: Crowell, 1898). A classic work on the development of standing committees.

McGown, Ada C., *The Congressional Conference Committee* (New York: Columbia University Press, 1927). An early and still useful treatment of conference committees.

Manley, John F., *The Politics of Finance* (Boston: Little, Brown, 1970). A perceptive study of the House Ways and Means Committee.

Masters, Nicholas A., "Committee Assignments in the House of Representatives," *American Political Science Review*, 55 (1961): 345–357. Still the best description of this process.

Robinson, James A., *The House Rules Committee* (Indianapolis: Bobbs-Merrill, 1963). An examination of the functions and internal politics of this important committee.

Select Committee on Committees, U.S. House of Representatives, *Hearings on Committee Organization in the House*, Ninety-third Congress, first session (1973). These hearings explore the entire internal structure of influence in the House. The Committee has also issued a series of working papers by scholars focusing on many aspects of House behavior.

Steiner, Gilbert Y., *The Congressional Conference Committee* (Urbana: University of Illinois Press, 1951). Analyzes conference committee behavior in the 1930s and 1940s.

Vogler, David J., *The Third House* (Evanston: Northwestern University Press, 1971). Analyzes conference committee behavior in the 1950s and 1960s.

V. Party Leadership

Bolling, Richard, *Power in the House* (New York: Dutton, 1968). A history of party leadership in the House with proposals for reform in the direction of responsible party government. Written by a representative from Missouri since 1949.

Brown, George R., *The Leadership of Congress* (Indianapolis: Bobbs-Merrill, 1922). A very perceptive account of party leadership in the first two decades of the twentieth century.

Evans, Rowland and Robert Novak, *Lyndon B. Johnson: The Exercise of Power* (New York: New American Library, 1966). Contains a long and perceptive account of Johnson as Democratic floor leader in the Senate.

Hasbrouck, Paul D., *Party Government in the House of Representatives* (New York: Macmillan, 1927). A first-rate study of the development of party leadership in the House.

Jones, Charles O., *The Minority Party in Congress* (Boston: Little, Brown, 1970). A perceptive analysis of the role of the minority party in Congress with special attention to party leadership.

Jones, Charles O., *Party and Policy-Making: The House Republican Policy Committee.* (New Brunswick: Rutgers University Press, 1964). A detailed analysis of the operations and importance of this party committee from 1959 to 1964.

Peabody, Robert L., "Party Leadership Change in the United States House of Representatives," in Peabody and Nelson W. Polsby (eds.), *New Perspectives on the House of Representatives* (Chicago: Rand McNally, 1969, 2nd ed.) A summary of the process of change in recent years.

Ripley, Randall B., *Majority Party Leadership in Congress* (Boston: Little, Brown, 1969). An analysis of party leadership and leader-president relations based on data from ten Congresses in the twentieth century.

Ripley, Randall B., *Party Leaders in the House of Representatives* (Washington: Brookings, 1967). An analysis that includes some attention to historical development and a focus on leadership in the early 1960s.

Stewart, John G., "Two Strategies of Leadership: Johnson and Mansfield," in Nelson W. Polsby (ed.), *Congressional Behavior* (New York: Random House, 1971). A comparison of the contrasting styles of these two Senate Democratic leaders.

VI. State Delegations, the Democratic Study Group, and Congressional Staff

Butler, Warren H., "Administering Congress: The Role of the Staff," *Public Administration Review* 26 (1966): 3–12. A brief description of the place of congressional staff.

Clausen, Aage R., "State Party Influence on Congressional Party Decisions," *Midwest Journal of Political Science* 16 (1972): 77–101. A roll call analysis that shows the strong influence of state party delegations.

Deckard, Barbara, "State Party Delegations in the U.S. House of Representatives—A Comparative Study of Group Cohesion," *Journal of Politics* 34 (1972): 199–222. An analysis based on interviews.

Ferber, Mark F., "The Formation of the Democratic Study Group," in Nelson W. Polsby (ed.), *Congressional Behavior* (New York: Random House, 1971). An examination of the conditions that led to the creation of the DSG and its early functioning.

Fiellin, Alan, "The Functions of Informal Groups in Legislative Institutions," *Journal of Politics* 24 (1962): 72–91. A study of the New York Democrats in the House.

Kofmehl, Kenneth, *Professional Staffs on Congress* (West Lafayette: Purdue University Press, 1962). A description of congressional staffing that omits only personal staffs for members of the House.

Manley, John F., "Congressional Staff and Public Policy-Making: The Joint Committee on Internal Revenue Taxation," *Journal of Politics* 30 (1968): 1046–1067. An excellent case study of the policy impact of one committee staff.

Patterson, Samuel C., "The Professional Staffs of Congressional Committees," *Administrative Science Quarterly* 15 (1970): 22–37. A concise, but thorough discussion of committee staffs.

Truman, David B., "The State Delegation and the Structure of Voting in the United States House of Representatives," *American Political Science Review* 50 (1956): 1023–1045. An early roll call study that seeks to isolate the impact of state delegations.

VII. Congressional Elections

Cummings, Milton C., Jr., *Congressmen and the Electorate* (New York: Free Press, 1966). A study of the relationship between voting for president and voting for House members.

Fishel, Jeff, *Party and Opposition* (New York: McKay, 1973). A study of all the challengers for House seats in the 1964 election and of the subsequent six years in the careers of those who won.

Hacker, Andrew, *Congressional Districting* (Washington: Brookings, 1964, revised ed.). A brief, but thorough treatment of the subject.

Jones, Charles O., *Every Second Year* (Washington: Brookings, 1967). A study of the effect of the two-year term for House members and of the consequences of various alternative proposals.

Jones, Charles O., "The Role of the Campaign in Congressional Politics," in M. Kent Jennings and L. Harmon Zeigler (eds.), *The Electoral Process* (Englewood Cliffs, N.J.: Prentice-Hall, 1966). A useful overview of the limited importance of campaigns in influencing congressional behavior.

Leuthold, David A., *Electioneering in a Democracy* (New York: Wiley, 1968). A detailed study of the 1962 congressional campaigns in the San Francisco Bay area.

Price, H. Douglas, "The Electoral Arena," in David B. Truman (ed.), *The Congress and America's Future* (Englewood Cliffs, N.J.: Prentice-Hall, 1973, 2nd ed.). An examination of changing electoral patterns and practices in the twentieth century.

VIII. RELATIONS WITH CONSTITUENTS AND INTEREST GROUPS

Bauer, Raymond A., Ithiel de Sola Pool, and Lewis A. Dexter, *American Business and Public Policy* (New York: Atherton, 1963). A case study of a decade of reciprocal trade legislation that concludes that interest groups and constituents had only limited influence.

Davidson, Roger H., *The Role of the Congressman* (New York: Pegasus, 1969). An analysis of the distribution of self-perceived roles, including those relating to representation of constituents and attitudes toward interest groups.

Dexter, Lewis A., *How Organizations Are Represented in Washington* (Indianapolis: Bobbs-Merrill, 1969). A rich source for understanding the subtleties of relations between lobbyists and Congress.

Froman, Lewis A., Jr., *Congressmen and Their Constituencies* (Chicago: Rand McNally, 1963). A study based on election statistics and roll call votes.

Milbrath, Lester W., *The Washington Lobbyists* (Chicago: Rand McNally, 1963). A general study of Washington lobbyists that contains much material on their relations with Congress.

IX. RELATIONS WITH THE PRESIDENT, PRESIDENCY, AND BUREAUCRACY

Chamberlain, Lawrence H., *The President, Congress and Legislation* (New York: Columbia University Press, 1946). Short studies of major legislation passed by Congress for over half a century. Assessments are made of the relative influence of Congress and the executive branch.

Cleaveland, Frederic N. and associates, *Congress and Urban Problems* (Washington: Brookings, 1969). Seven case studies from the 1950s and

1960s offer considerable material on executive-legislative relations in urban policy-making.

Holtzman, Abraham, *Legislative Liaison* (Chicago: Rand McNally, 1970). A study of White House and departmental liaison efforts. Especially strong on the Kennedy presidency.

Moe, Ronald C. and Steven C. Teel, "Congress as Policy-Maker: A Necessary Reappraisal," *Political Science Quarterly* 85 (1970): 443–470. An updating of Chamberlain's work that reaches the same conclusion: Congress is an influential partner in the policy process and is not subservient to the president and bureaucracy.

Neustadt, Richard E., "Politicians and Bureaucrats," in David B. Truman (ed.), *The Congress and American's Future* (Englewood Cliffs, N.J.: Prentice-Hall, 1973, 2nd ed.). An examination of the tripartite relationship between members of Congress, the president, and bureaucrats. Argues that the former two have common interests different from those of the bureaucrats.

Neustadt, Richard E., "Presidency and Legislation: The Growth of Central Clearance," *American Political Science Review* 48 (1954): 641–671. A discussion of growing control by the Executive Office of the President over legislative proposals coming from the bureaucracy.

Neustadt, Richard E., "Presidency and Legislation: Planning the President's Program," *American Political Science Review* 49 (1955): 980–1021. A discussion of the evolution of the "program of the president."

Pipe, G. Russell, "Congressional Liaison: The Executive Branch Consolidates Its Relations with Congress," *Public Administration Review* 26 (1966): 14–24. A description of the size and scope of departmental liaison efforts.

Ripley, Randall B., *Kennedy and Congress* (Morristown, N.J.: General Learning Press, 1972). A case study of congressional-presidential relations in 1961–1963.

Robinson, James A., *Congress and Foreign Policy Making* (Homewood, Ill.: Dorsey, 1967, revised ed.). An intensive study, based in part on interviews, of executive-legislative relations in the area of foreign policy.

Wildavsky, Aaron, *The Politics of the Budgetary Process* (Boston: Little, Brown, 1964). A general treatment of budgeting that contains rich material on relations between bureaus and appropriations subcommittees.

X. CONGRESS AND POLICY

In addition to the following items, Congress itself occasionally issues a number of self-reflective materials on its policy role. In recent years members have been particularly concerned about the institution's role in the budgetary process. Relevant materials have, for example, been issued in recent years by the Ad Hoc Subcommittee on Impoundment of Funds of the Senate Committee on Government Operations; the Committee on Government Operations of the Senate; the Joint Committee on Congressional Operations; the Joint Study Committee on Budget Control; and the Subcommittee on Separation of Powers of the Senate Committee on the Judiciary.

Bailey, Stephen K., *Congress Makes a Law* (New York: Vintage, 1964). A classic case study of the passage of the Employment Act of 1946.

Carroll, Holbert N., "The Congress and National Security Policy," in David B. Truman (ed.) *The Congress and America's Future* (Englewood Cliffs, N.J.: Prentice-Hall, 1973, 2nd ed.). Updates Carroll's earlier work on the House and treats the growing aggressiveness of both houses in this area.

Carroll, Holbert, N., *The House of Representatives and Foreign Affairs* (Boston: Little, Brown, 1966, revised ed.). A careful evaluation of the growing role of the House in foreign policy.

Dahl, Robert A., *Congress and Foreign Policy* (New York: Harcourt, Brace, 1950). A thoughtful early study of the foreign policy role of Congress.

Eidenberg, Eugene and Roy D. Morey, *An Act of Congress* (New York: Norton, 1969). A case study of the passage of the Elementary and Secondary Education Act of 1965.

Huitt, Ralph K., "Congressional Organization and Operations in the Field of Money and Credit," in Commission on Money and Credit, *Fiscal and Debt Management Policies* (Englewood Cliffs, N.J.: Prentice-Hall, 1963). A perceptive study of congressional influence in this field in the 1950s and early 1960s.

Jewell, Malcolm, *Senatorial Politics and Foreign Policy* (Lexington: University of Kentucky Press, 1962). A detailed study of Senate activity in the foreign policy area.

Kanter, Arnold, "Congress and the Defense Budget: 1960–1970," *American Political Science Review* 66 (1972): 129–143. A study that goes behind the facile generation that Congress has little impact on defense policy to show that Congress does have important impact on defense budgets.

Kolodziej, Edward A., *The Uncommon Defense and Congress, 1945–1963* (Columbus: The Ohio State University Press, 1966). A detailed study of the congressional role in defense policy.

Mansfield, Harvey C., "The Congress and Economic Policy," in David B. Truman (ed.), *The Congress and America's Future* (Englewood Cliffs, N.J.: Prentice-Hall, 1973, 2nd ed.). A summary of congressional involvement in economic policy.

Morgan, Donald G., *Congress and the Constitution* (Cambridge: Harvard University Press, 1966). Includes ten case studies of congressional action on matters involving constitutional questions from 1818 through 1964. Urges that Congress not rely on the Supreme Court for constitutional wisdom.

Munger, Frank J. and Richard F. Fenno, Jr., *National Politics and Federal Aid to Education* (Syracuse: Syracuse University Press, 1962). A careful analysis of the congressional role in federal aid to education legislation—both successful and unsuccessful.

Rosenthal, Alan, "The Effectiveness of Congress," in Gerald M. Pomper and others, *The Performance of American Government* (New York: Free Press, 1972). A positive summary evaluation of the policy-making capability and performance of Congress.

Sundquist, James L., *Politics and Policy* (Washington: Brookings, 1968). A detailed study of domestic policy-making and the interaction between Congress and the executive branch from 1953 through 1966. Argues that most of the successful Democratic initiatives of the 1960s were developed in Congress in the 1950s during the Eisenhower administration.

INDEX